Program construction

Also in this series

1 An Introduction to Logical Design of Digital Circuits
   C. M. Reeves 1972
2 Information Representation and Manipulation in a Computer
   E. S. Page and L. B. Wilson, Second Edition 1978
3 Computer Simulation of Continuous Systems
   R. J. Ord-Smith and J. Stephenson 1975
4 Macro Processors
   A. J. Cole, Second Edition 1981
5 An Introduction to the Uses of Computers
   Murray Laver 1976
6 Computing Systems Hardware
   M. Wells 1976
7 An Introduction to the Study of Programming Languages
   D. W. Barron 1977
8 ALGOL 68 – A first and second course
   A. D. McGettrick 1978
9 An Introduction to Computational Combinatorics
   E. S. Page and L. B. Wilson 1979
10 Computers and Social Change
   Murray Laver 1980
11 The Definition of Programming Languages
   A. D. McGettrick 1980
12 Programming via Pascal
   J. S. Rohl and H. J. Barrett 1980
13 Program Verification using Ada
   A. D. McGettrick 1982
14 Simulation Techniques for Discrete Event Systems
   I. Mitrani 1982
15 Information Representation and Manipulation using Pascal
   E. S. Page and L. B. Wilson 1983
16 Writing Pascal Programs
   J. S. Rohl 1983
17 An Introduction to APL
   S. Pommier 1983
18 Computer Mathematics
   D. J. Cooke and H. E. Bez 1984
19 Recursion via Pascal
   J. S. Rohl 1984
20 Text Processing
   A. Colin Day 1984
21 Introduction to Computer Systems
   Brian Molinari 1985

22 Cambridge Computer Science Texts

Program construction

R. G. Stone and D. J. Cooke

Department of Computer Studies, Loughborough University of Technology

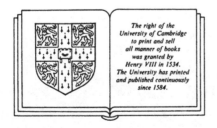

The right of the
University of Cambridge
to print and sell
all manner of books
was granted by
Henry VIII in 1534.
The University has printed
and published continuously
since 1584.

Cambridge University Press

Cambridge

New York   Port Chester

Melbourne   Sydney

CAMBRIDGE UNIVERSITY PRESS
Cambridge, New York, Melbourne, Madrid, Cape Town, Singapore, São Paulo

Cambridge University Press
The Edinburgh Building, Cambridge CB2 2RU, UK

Published in the United States of America by Cambridge University Press, New York

www.cambridge.org
Information on this title: www.cambridge.org/9780521268233

© Cambridge University Press 1987

First published 1987
Reprinted 1988, 1990

A catalogue record for this publication is available from the British Library

Library of Congress Cataloguing in Publication data
Stone, R. G, 1950–
 Program construction.
 (Cambridge computer science texts; 22)
 Bibliography: p.
 Includes index.
 1. Electronic digital computers – Programming.
I. Cooke, D. J. (Derek John), 1947–
II. Title. III. Series.
QA76.6S767 1987 005.1 86-12954

ISBN-13 978-0-521-26823-3 hardback
ISBN-10 0-521-26823-0 hardback

ISBN-13 978-0-521-31883-9 paperback
ISBN-10 0-521-31883-1 paperback

Transferred to digital printing 2006

Contents

Preface   ix

1 A modern approach to computing   1

1.1 An appraisal of the current situation   1
1.2 A way ahead   6

2 Specifications I   11

2.1 The nature of a specification   11
2.2 Pre and post conditions   13
2.3 Type constraints   13
2.4 Sequences of operations   16
2.5 More on types   18
2.5.1 *Primitive and constructed data types*   18
2.5.2 *Pairs*   18
2.5.3 *Triples*   21
2.5.4 *Tuples*   22
2.5.5 *Lists*   24
2.5.6 *Sets*   28
2.6 The characteristics of a specification   31
2.7 Refinement and transformation of specifications   32
2.8 States in specifications   32
2.9 States vs. Input/Output   37
2.10 Conclusion   37

3 Diagrams   39

3.1 Diagrams used in the program development process   39
3.2 An algebra of diagrams   46
3.3 Other diagramming systems   50
3.4 Graphs, networks and trees   55

4 Specifications II   61

4.1 Concise notation   61
4.2 Transformation and proof in specifications   63
4.3 What comes next?   70

5 PDL   72

5.1 Imperative and declarative languages   72
5.2 Why·a PDL?   75
5.3 The PDL stage   76
5.4 The description of a PDL   78
5.4.1 *Function definition*   78
5.4.2 *Statement*   79
5.4.3 *Statements*   79
5.4.4 *Type*   80
5.4.5 *Variable*   81
5.4.6 *Expressions*   81
5.5 PDL data types – list and record   82
5.6 Representing specification data types in PDL   83
5.7 Examples   85
5.8 Other PDL issues   86
5.9 PDL summary   87

6 Code generation   88

6.1 Templates   88
6.2 Templates for Pascal   89
6.2.1 *Templates for control structures in Pascal*   90
6.2.2 *Templates for data structures in Pascal*   95
6.3 Templates for FORTRAN   99
6.3.1 *Templates for control structures in FORTRAN*   100
6.3.2 *Templates for data structures in FORTRAN*   106
6.4 Templates for COBOL   115
6.4.1 *Templates for control structures in COBOL*   115
6.4.2 *Templates for data structures in COBOL*   121
6.5 Templates for a minicomputer assembly language   126
6.5.1 *Templates for control structures*   129
6.5.2 *Templates for data structures*   139
6.6 Templates for a microprocessor assembly language   143
6.6.1 *Templates for control structures*   144
6.6.2 *Templates for data structures*   151

7 Verification   155

7.1 The implication operator   156
7.2 Control-flow diagrams and data-flow specification diagrams   166
7.3 Sequencing and alternation   171
7.4 Repetition   183
7.4.1 *Simple recursion*   184
7.4.2 *Quantifiers and induction*   195
7.4.3 *Iteration*   201
7.5 Conclusion   215

8 Examination of templates and target code 217

8.1 Assignment statements 218
8.2 Control statements 219
8.3 Parameter passing 224
8.4 Summary 226

9 Abstract data types 227

9.1 ADT example – a siding 228
9.2 ADT example – an In_Tray 233
9.3 ADT example – LR Lookup store 236
9.4 ADT example – a binary tree 237
9.4.1 *Recursive implementation of tree operations in PDL* 240
9.4.2 *Non-recursive implementation of tree operations* 242
9.5 On preserving ADT discipline 254
9.5.1 *What is ADT discipline?* 254
9.5.2 *Data Type Encapsulation* 258

10 The mathematical basis of abstract data types 262

10.1 Booleans 262
10.2 Lists 269
10.3 Some numeric types 271
10.4 Sets 282
10.5 Equations versus conditions 285

11 Utilisation of existing programs 289

11.1 Testing for good structure 290
11.2 Restructuring of unstructured programs 302
11.3 Analysis of programs 309

12 A small scale study – topological sorting 326

12.1 Problem formulation 326
12.2 Transformations 331
12.3 Towards PDL 333
12.4 Data structure considerations 336
12.5 PDL 340

Appendices

A Glossary of symbols 342
B Syntax of standard specifications 344
C The description of a PDL 348
D Transformations that remove recursion 353

References 365

Index 367

Preface

This text promotes the disciplined construction of procedural programs from formal specifications. As such it can be used in conjunction with any of the more conventional programming texts which teach a mixture of 'coding' in a specific language and *ad hoc* algorithm design.

The awareness of the need for a more methodical approach to program construction is epitomised by the use of phrases such as 'software engineering', 'mathematical theory of programming', and 'science of programming'. The hitherto all-too-familiar practices of 'designing' a program 'as you write it' and 'patching' wrong programs being more appropriate to a cottage industry rather than a key activity in the current technological revolution.

The cost of producing hardware is decreasing while the production of software (programs) is becoming more expensive by the day. The complexity and importance of programs is also growing phenomenally, so much so that the high cost of producing them can only be justified when they are reliable and do what they are supposed to do – when they are correct.

No methodology can exist by which we can produce a program to perform an arbitrary task. Consequently that is **not** the aim of the book. What we **shall** do is to show how, by using a Program Design Language and templates for your chosen target language, you can develop programs from certain forms of specification.

Although programming is essentially a practical activity, the degree of formality adopted throughout the development process means that sufficient information is available to enable correctness proofs to be investigated if and when required. Moreover, the structured programming forms used throughout the text are all supported by verification rules derived from their total correctness proofs – the notion of correctness never being far from our thoughts.

The material presented has grown out of courses presented to first year Computer Science undergraduates, to 'conversion' M.Sc. students and in

x   *Preface*

industrial short courses in software engineering, and as such has been under development since 1980.

During the evolution of the teaching material included herein we have been influenced by many sources. Of particular note is the work of Cliff Jones (now at Manchester University but previously at Oxford PRG and various IBM research establishments), on Specification; and the work of John Darlington (now at Imperial College, London and previously at Edinburgh University), on Program Transformations. At a more tangible level we wish to record our thanks to Terry Butland of UKAEE Winfrith and Morry van Ments of Loughborough's Centre for Extension Studies for their help in organising our industrial courses, to our colleagues, Mike Woodward and Dave Gittins, who helped modify earlier drafts of the text. to Jacqui Bonsor, Carole Hill and Deborah Harrison who produced the bulk of the typescript and to Ernest Kirkwood of Cambridge University Press for his encouragement and patience.

R. G. Stone
D. J. Cooke
Loughborough, 1985

1
A modern approach to computing

1.1   An appraisal of the current situation.
Is anything the matter?

In the early days of computing the machines were not very powerful, there were not many of them and few people had high expectations of them. All that has changed. Computers seem to have become an essential part of everyday society and large numbers of people are employed in supporting existing computer systems and creating new ones.

Although the use of computers is widespread the public image of computers and the computing profession is in need of improvement. Everyone has their own story to tell of the time when their enquiry was rejected with the excuse that 'it's not possible since we installed the computer system'. There have been some well-publicised disasters with new computing systems.

Yes, something is the matter!

What is wrong with computing today?

Is it the machines? Well they are cheaper, smaller, faster and more reliable than they used to be. No, they do not seem to be the problem.

Is it the programs then? Software today is more expensive, more complex, but no more reliable than it used to be.

Why should this be? Is it the fault of the programmer teams? Are they not as clever as they used to be? No, they have been asked to do the impossible. It is like asking a child who has built toy houses out of Lego bricks to design and build tower blocks for people to live in. Using another analogy, it is like asking people who have discovered how to cross streams by stepping-stones and planks of wood to build a suspension bridge over an estuary. This is the scale of the increase in complexity that has faced programmers in recent years.

The increase in complexity is graphically illustrated by Figure 1.1.

What is being done?

Well until recently, not a lot. It has taken a long time to obtain widespread acknowledgement within the computing community that a problem exists. Now that this is established progress is being made – albeit slowly.

Fig. 1.1

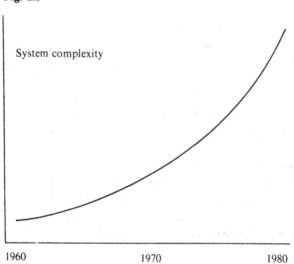

System complexity

1960   1970   1980

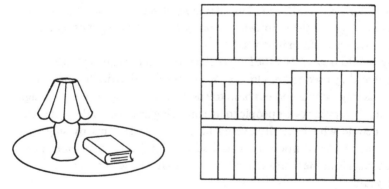

Documentation

There were high hopes that 'Structured Programming' would be the solution. This was only marginally successful but crucially important for creating the idea that training and retraining computer professionals was possible and necessary.

The construction industry

Pursuing the bridge building analogy a little further it is quite clear that real bridges are not built by dumping ballast, concrete, etc., into the middle of the water on day one. In fact a prolonged process of surveying, designing, costing, model building and testing is performed before any construction is begun. This bridge construction process is entirely appropriate for the permanent large scale structures capable of supporting road or rail traffic.

(Of course this is not an appropriate solution for the hiker who simply wants to cross a stream to get to his destination before sunset. He will use only the immediately available materials such as stones, branches, etc., and he will experiment — e.g. to see if it will hold his weight.)

The fault with program construction in comparison to bridge construction is that no equivalent of the detailed drawings of the design of a bridge is in general use. That is not to say that there are no diagrams – there are – but they tend to be used in a 'cavalier' way, not as part of a methodical process.

The world of the artist

Let's move away from the construction industry and consider a possible comparison between program construction and oil painting.

Because it is possible to overpaint any colour with any other using oils, we could say that it does not matter if mistakes are made – they can always be painted over until we get it right.

This is a useful analogy with computing because apart from a small percentage of control programs (notably space shuttle landing programs) the consequences of errors in programs are not disastrous. They are frustrating, cost time and money to put right but are not disastrous, so why bother to get the program right first time?

The snag is that the *ability* to overpaint does not in itself make the person holding the paintbrush into a master artist. In fact the greater the artist the less likely their need to overpaint!

The detection of errors

It is symptomatic of the state of computing that errors are still known as 'bugs', in an attempt to pass off the blame onto some unnamed interfering force that spoils our otherwise perfect programs. (The term 'bug' originates from the days when computers contained large numbers of electromechanical relays into which insects could, and occasionally did, penetrate thus preventing normal operation – those days have passed but the term is still with us!)

Testing, whether performed by the originators of software or specialist teams (or the customer!), may reveal some errors which can be 'corrected'. What then? Who knows if there are as yet undetected errors in the original code or new errors that have been introduced with the 'corrections'?

If you were an astronaut, would you be satisfied with the statement that 'all known bugs in the shuttle landing program have been eliminated'? You would want *proof* that the program would not fail! Alright, but what does that mean? Proofs are available as a tool only in mathematics – we will have to find a way of discussing programs as mathematical objects.

The distribution of effort

There is undeniably a sense of achievement to be had from 'getting a program to run'. People who have the ability to 'fix' problems in programs that have defeated everyone else are highly valued. But in the larger systems currently being built far too large a percentage of project time is being spent on this activity. Much more effort is needed in the early stages to minimise the need for 'testing and debugging'. This means getting the specification right at the beginning and sticking to it.

A powerful argument for getting things right at the beginning is that the cost of correcting errors increases dramatically the later the error is discovered during the production of a system (see Figure 1.2).

What is in a specification?

What does the specification of a bridge achieve? In order to be useful the design must be

  concise　not full scale, no irrelevant detail, but still representing the intended bridge adequately
  consistent plan and elevation agree
  precise　no ambiguities.

These are exactly the requirements for specifications of computer software only the medium for expressing the specification is different.

Flowcharts and other drawings have been tried and found wanting. The English language has been tried and found to be too ambiguous – or if not ambiguous then too verbose. The language that is known to be concise and precise that is currently being encouraged for use in specification is mathematics – which also has the advantage of allowing consistency proofs.

A revolution

The scenario sketched out up to now is that for a revolution in computing. There is a desperate need for formality, the ability to work with mathematical notation, and above all a desire to create high-quality correct software. The skills of coding ingenuity, optimisation and patching are becoming less important in favour of formal specification and systematic implementation with the backing of the rigour and precision of mathematics.

Fig. 1.2

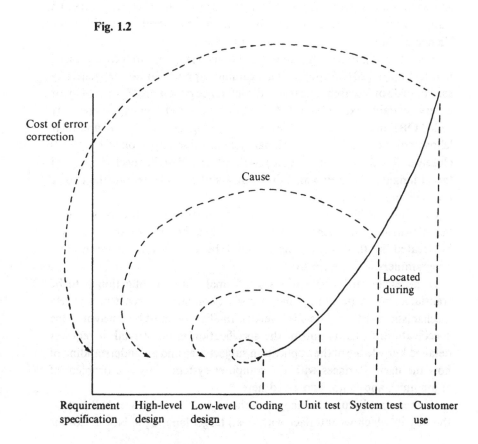

| Requirement specification | High-level design | Low-level design | Coding | Unit test | System test | Customer use |

1.2   A way ahead

So, there is a problem. Much Computer Science research over recent years has been directed at alleviating this 'software crisis' and the methods presented here incorporate some of the more tangible results to emanate from this research. We shall present a **practical** methodology for constructing procedural programs from formal specifications, in such a way that the individual steps can be justified (**mathematically** if necessary).

This book is not a course on algorithm design – such a course requires more detailed study relative to the specific problem domain, such as sorting, numerical analysis, file processing, etc., all proper subjects in their own right. Nor is it a book on 'writing programs in X' (name your own X!!) although coding in some specific language is necessary of course.

Our intention is that you should be able to take a specification, written in a particular Specification Language, and, using a Program Design Language (PDL), extract a program plan which is subsequently encoded in an executable Target Language. Currently, specification languages are in a state of flux. We have chosen to base our presentation on VDM – the Vienna Definition Method, named after the IBM Vienna Laboratories where it was originated – which is the only such language to have appeared in a text book [20]. (Other systems gaining support but not yet generally seen outside of research journals and conference papers are 'Z' – see [17] for a very readable example of a Z specification – and languages variously called OBJ and CLEAR, etc., developed by Goguen and Birstall and their fellow workers [16]. The equational systems presented in our Chapter 10 closely follow the style of CLEAR.) At the other end of the spectrum, typical target languages are Pascal, FORTRAN and assemblers, but the choice here is almost limitless.

Once into PDL the remainder of the construction process is largely 'handle-turning' and hence may be automated; the earlier part cannot yet be treated in this way – there would be no need for conventional programmers if this were so.

Of necessity our specifications are formal – if a specification is to be translated into a program which causes a computer to react in a purely mechanistic way then the same level of formalisation must be inherent in the specification. Construction of the specification is non-trivial, it requires detailed knowledge of the application subject area and an understanding of how the user interfaces with the computer system. This is a problem of ergonomics and is not addressed here.

For reasons discussed at length in the body of the text, we shall restrict the way in which we interface with (real) target languages. Not to do this would necessitate extensive knowledge of the semantics of the particular language and its implementation. The approach adopted gives ample scope for object code optimisers to make the code more efficient; efficiency being a much lower priority than the correctness of the program as delivered by us.

The entire methodology is based firmly on formal specifications and the reader will be better equipped to appreciate how they are to be used after they have been introduced in Chapter 2. Nevertheless, in the hope of whetting the appetite we now attempt a brief overview of our *modus operandi*, our plan. In keeping with our philosophy of using diagrams as a legitimate aid to 'sorting things out' we shall use a diagram here.

Fig. 1.3

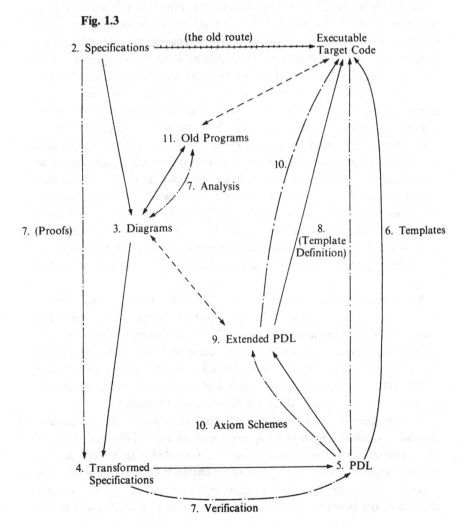

In this diagram the numbers refer to our chapters, the solid lines ($-\rightarrow$) relate to the practical stages in developing code to satisfy a specification, the chained lines ($-\cdot\cdot-\cdot\cdot\rightarrow$) indicate where formal justification can be provided to ensure validity of these methods, and dashed lines ($----\rightarrow$) show other logical connections. The remaining arrow ($\dashv\!\dashv\!\!\rightarrow$) is only for completeness and indicates the old, insecure, link between the problem and an answer (not necessarily a solution!). Notice that it does not have an associated 'proof' arrow although one can be found by going via 4, 5 and 6 (or 4, 5 and 9). To take this logical route is to admit the possibility of a stepwise practical approach, *voila*!

As already noted, Chapter 2 sees the introduction of specifications. It is in the users interest to ensure that what is specified is exactly what he wants specified. This is where **logic programming languages** come into their own, programs in such languages being of similar structure to specifications. However implementations of such languages are too inefficient for the majority of 'final' systems. At their current stage of development logic programming languages are probably most suitable for prototyping (checking out specifications) and as such lie outside the scope of the text.

Diagrams can be used to represent the flow of data through a specification as well as control flow through conventional (procedural) programs. The disciplined use of diagrams is the subject addressed by Chapter 3 and this leads naturally to the specifications in Chapter 4 which presents a glimpse of how we may transform specifications. Ultimately we wish to move from a logical form to a functional one from which we can extract a procedural program. This aim – which is attainable for those tasks which are soluble by computer, although there are theoretical limitations – is a considerable challenge.

As an intermediate goal we introduce PDL in Chapter 5 and then, in Chapter 6, consider how to realise PDL in more familiar languages. Our Program Design Language is similar to Pascal and Algol 68, but is neither. It has simple semantics, which are discussed in Chapter 8, and can be extended by the addition of Abstract Data Types (ADTs) to create a higher level PDL in which the data types are oriented more to particular application areas. These ADTs are introduced in Chapter 9.

Formal questions relating to PDL and its possible extensions are discussed at some length in Chapters 7 and 10. Essentially these look at the requirements of correctness theorems. Knowledge that a correctness theorem **can** be proved for a given specification/program combination is enough, we don't need to prove it again. However, if such a proof is known then so is the program and we need not rewrite it; if any aspect of the problem is new then we ought to consider how to formally verify that our 'solution' **is** a solution. Details of such proofs can often be omitted or checked by an automated theorem prover but the program constructor will still be required to know **how** the specification, the program and the proof inter-relate.

Chapter 11 tackles the question of how to cope with large, existing, important programs; how to rationalise their existence. In a perfect world such potentially 'dodgy' programs would either not exist or could instantly be ejected and replaced by verified software. This is not so, and hence we have Chapter 11.

Finally, Chapter 12 includes a small case study. This is complete except for full formal proofs. Such proofs would probably double the size of this book.

In teaching courses based on this material, notation and terminology has always been a problem. In an undergraduate context, when timescales are much larger and a proper computer-oriented mathematics course is run in tandem, little difficulty is experienced by the student. In the case of industrial short courses or post-graduate 'conversion' courses time itself (or should we say, lack of it) is the main problem. What is required is a facility to treat topics in an abstract mathematical fashion. Mathematics here does not imply such topics as traditional calculus, which is totally irrelevant, but exposure to almost any kind of algebra would be beneficial. At Loughborough we use our own local text [8] and the Alvey directorate has funded the production of short-course material [36] aimed specifically as a pre-requisite for formal software engineering courses. But the use and availability of such material is outside of our dictate. Within the confines of this book we shall attempt to ease the introduction of notation by using two forms. For instance we may initially write IS_EQUAL_TO and later, when the reader is used to 'saying the words' and is getting tired of writing so much, replace it by '$=$'. Consistent with using simple arithmetic examples from the beginning, we shall however presume that the reader can do simple 'sums' and is familiar with the symbols, $+$, $-$, $*$ (for multiplication), $\div$, $<$, $\leqslant$, $=$, etc. The only other symbol not properly introduced in the text is '$\Box$' which is used to indicate the end of a proof; but this is only used in Chapters 7 and 10.

Our assumptions about computers and the readers' knowledge of computers are minimal. As viewed through programming languages they are devices for storing symbolic data, performing simple arithmetic and logical operations – one at a time – under the control of a list of commands, with the added facility that we can jump about within this list.

Before concluding this introduction we must say something about testing. We are concerned with correct programs, testing cannot in any practical sense be used to guarantee that a program is correct – in lucky cases it can show that a program is incorrect. The problem is one of size. Consider the addition of two 32 bit integers taking one millionth of a second. This is a simple operation. To test it properly we need to check it for all possible values (half of which would be wrong!). For the computer to generate all the figures for us to examine would take

$$2^{2*32} * 10^{-6} \text{ seconds} \cong 5.9 * 10^5 \text{ years (over half a million years!)}$$

It would take much longer to print these values, and since the machine could not store all the values it would have to wait during the calculations so the time required would be much longer. And then you (or your great-great...grand children) have to check them. Now try a more complicated problem than adding two numbers! – 'nough said?

To summarise, we expand the ideas presented in [29] and link them to formal specifications.

The book is **not** about algorithm design,

it is **not** about a specific programming language,

it does **not** incorporate real time programming (per se) and

it is **not** a collection of programming recipes.

The book **does** present a framework for solving programming problems,

it **does** allow us to defer decisions regarding data structures and

it **does** highlight key issues and vagaries within a problem, and brings them to a head.

In total, just as someone who knows the English language may not be able to write a (good) novel, it takes more than a knowledge of the words in a programming language to be a (good) programmer. It needs discipline, and an analytical mind. If you're still with us – read on.

2
Specifications I

2.1 The nature of a specification

The task of solving a problem using a computer can be reduced to the outline

> given THIS,
>
> produce THAT

or expanding, a little,

> given some DATA,
>
> produce some RESULTS
>
> which are the proper results for that data.

The results are either the 'proper' results for that data, or they are not. A specification can be viewed as a test that has been devised to check for 'proper' results. It does not need to show HOW the results are to be obtained although it may. Thus the task of solving a problem using a computer may be regarded in general as

> given d,
>
> produce r
>
> such that $S(d,r)$ is True

where $S(d,r)$ is a test (or predicate) which, given the data d and the results r produced from it, delivers the answer True or False, i.e. the results are acceptable (or not) for that data.

Example

> Let d be *169*,
>
> let r be *13*
>
> and suppose $S1(d,r)$ IS_DEFINED_TO_BE $d = r*r$.

(As is conventional in computing we are using '*' to mean multiply. IS_DEFINED_TO_BE is an example of our use of a word or a phrase where a mathematical symbol would have been more concise. However we do not want unfamiliarity with symbols to prevent easy reading at this stage so we obtain clarity at the expense of brevity. The words in the phrases are always joined by underline and should be regarded as a single unit. In later chapters we will introduce the more concise notation.)

Notice that the relation $d = r*r$ is not a recipe for computing results using data – indeed it may look more like a recipe for computing data from results! It is in fact a **test** which is applied to data and results.

If the case $(d,r) = (169,13)$ is investigated, then

　　$S1(d,r)$ is $S1(169,13)$ and

　　$S1(169,13)$ is $169 = 13*13$, which is True.

So *13* is acceptable output when *169* is the input.

There is another number which satisfies *S1* given input *169* and that is -13.

　　$S1(169,-13)$ is $169 = (-13)*(-13)$, which is again True.

This means that the operation which finds *r* given *d* can apparently give either *13* or -13 as the correct output for input *169*. If this is not the behaviour that was required then we will have to make the test (or predicate) *S1* more restrictive.

A new predicate *S2* is required which is more strict (or restrictive) than *S1*. It seems natural to write

　　$S2(d,r)$ IS_DEFINED_TO_BE $S1(d,r)$ AND...

The restrictions on the result *r*, given data *d*, are all those of *S1* together with some more which are as yet unspecified.

If, given $d = 169$, we wish to accept *13* as a value for *r* but reject -13, the extra restriction could be

　　r is positive

meaning *r* is greater than or equal to zero, written $r \geqslant 0$ giving

　　$S2(d,r)$ IS_DEFINED_TO_BE $d = r*r$ AND $r \geqslant 0$

Alternatively, if the other result is required, the restriction could be

　　r is negative or zero

meaning *r* is less than zero or equal to zero, written

　　$r \leqslant 0$

Predicates could have alternative restrictions joined by OR although it is more usual for these to be introduced by *if ... then ... else* – see Chapter 4.

2.2   Pre and post conditions

What sort of result do we expect from *S2* if the data *d* is -169? An *r* is to be found such that

$$-169 = r*r \text{ AND } r \geq 0$$

But no such *r* can be found!

It is not sensible to supply data $d = -169$ and expect results *r* satisfying *S2*. A need has therefore been established for a test (or predicate) which indicates whether it is sensible to proceed with the search for a particular result. This predicate is called a **pre-condition**. In this case

pre--*S2*(*d*) IS_DEFINED_TO_BE $d \geq 0$

Now that pre-conditions have been introduced it will be convenient to call all the previous predicates **post-conditions**, written post-*S*(*d,r*).

The pre- and post- conditions for *S2* are thus

pre--*S2*(*d*)   IS_DEFINED_TO_BE $d \geq 0$

post-*S2*(*d,r*) IS_DEFINED_TO_BE $d = r*r \text{ AND } r \geq 0$

Notice that the pre-condition only refers to the data, while the post-condition refers to both the data and the results.

Now that *S2*(*d,r*) has been renamed post-*S2*(*d,r*), we can think of *S2*(*d,r*) as **being the operation** which, given a value *d* which satisfies pre-*S2*(*d*), will produce a value *r* such that (*d,r*) satisfies post-*S2*(*d,r*).

2.3   Type constraints

It might be supposed that we have completed the description of the operation *S2*(*d,r*) having stated the conditions under which it is reasonable to ask for a result and by choosing only one result when the data is reasonable.

However the world is not composed solely of numbers. What if the data were 'Mr. Smith'? Is it true that

'Mr. Smith' ≥ 0

There has been a tacit assumption so far that the data and results were to be numbers.

In order to make this previously tacit assumption clear, we introduce the concept of the type of an operation. Consider the diagram of the operation *S2* taking data *d* and producing results *r*

A left-to-right arrow (cf. diagram) is used in writing down the type of an operation. In this case it is

> type: *Number → Number*

The description of an operation can now be given in four parts:

> the *name* of the operation,
>
> the *type* of the operation,
>
> the *pre-condition* for the operation, and
>
> the *post-condition* for the operation.

It is this description which is called the **specification** of the operation. Although the specifications given so far contain all that is needed to understand the operations specified it is very useful to give the operations meaningful names. So the operation *S2*, discussed above, is now renamed *POS_SQUARE_ROOT* and has the specification:

> *POS_SQUARE_ROOT*
>
> type: *Number → Number*
>
> pre--*POS_SQUARE_ROOT(d)* IS_DEFINED_TO_BE
>
> > $d \geqslant 0$
>
> post-*POS_SQUARE_ROOT(d,r)* IS_DEFINED_TO_BE
>
> > $d = r * r$ &
> >
> > $r \geqslant 0$

Instead of the last two lines the following could have been written

> $d = r * r$ AND $r \geqslant 0$

It is a matter of style to put each separate clause on a separate line. The '&' symbol is used for brevity but is only used at the end of lines.

The type line may seem to be unnecessary. It could be argued that the information could be included in the pre- and post- conditions.

> pre--*POS_SQUARE_ROOT(d)* IS_DEFINED_TO_BE
>
> > d is_a_Number   &
> >
> > $d \geqslant 0$
>
> post-*POS_SQUARE_ROOT(d, r)* IS_DEFINED_TO_BE
>
> > r is_a_Number   &
> >
> > $d = r * r$ &
> >
> > $r \geqslant 0$

Indeed the pre-condition itself may seem unnecessary. One might argue that the information could be included in a post-condition such as:

post-*POS_SQUARE_ROOT(d,r)* IS_DEFINED_TO_BE

$$(d \; is\_a\_Number \; \& $$
$$d \geqslant 0 \qquad \& $$
$$r \; is\_a\_Number \; \& $$
$$d = r*r \qquad \& $$
$$r \geqslant 0)$$

OR

$$(d \; is\_a\_Number \; \& $$
$$d < 0 \qquad \& $$
$$r = 'Error: \; data \; is \; negative')$$

OR

$$(d \; is\_not\_a\_Number \quad \& $$
$$r = 'Error: \; data \; is \; not \; a \; number')$$

It is obvious that the conditions become longer and harder to read if the type or the pre-condition or both are not included explicitly. This alone could be enough to argue for their retention.

Notice also that the result *r* is sometimes a number and sometimes an 'error message'. Following a use of the *POS_SQUARE_ROOT* operation, it would be necessary to test the result *r* to find out if it was in number or message form! We would have exchanged a pre-condition for a test after the operation and we would not have gained anything.

Another reason for keeping pre-conditions is that it seems sensible to separate the **calculation** aspect of the operation from the decision whether to proceed to the calculation. The most important reason in practise is the ease with which operations may be combined into larger operations. This is discussed in the next section.

(Note: There is yet another problem to do with evaluating expressions like

$$d \; is\_a\_Number \; \text{AND} \; d \geqslant 0$$

to a truth value (True or False) when *d* is not a Number. Using notation that will be properly introduced later we could avoid the problem by writing either

if   *d is_a_Number*

then $d \geqslant 0$

else   False

or

$$Pos\_Num = \{x: x\ IS\_IN\ Number\ \text{AND}\ x \geqslant 0\} \quad \&$$
$$d\ IS\_IN\ Pos\_Num$$

This issue is taken further in Chapter 7 but since we are retaining the type line we do not need to worry about it yet.)

2.4   Sequences of operations

Consider the simple case where the output of one operation provides the input to another operation. This is called operation **sequencing**.

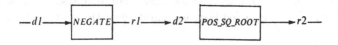

$$r1 = d2$$

It is clear that, although it is not possible to deduce anything about the input $d1$ to the first *POS_SQ_ROOT* operation, the input $d2$ to the second *POS_SQ_ROOT* operation is .the same as the output $r1$ of the first *POS_SQ_ROOT* operation. Now $r1$ must satisfy the type constraint and the post-condition of *POS_SQ_ROOT* so

$$r1\ is\_a\_Number \quad \&$$
$$d1 = r1 * r1 \quad \&$$
$$r1 \geqslant 0$$

Since $d2 = r1$ it is possible to conclude directly that

$$d2\ is\_a\_Number \quad \&$$
$$d2 \geqslant 0$$

Thus $d2$ is bound to satisfy the type constraints and the pre-condition for the second *POS_SQUARE_ROOT* operation. So the second *POS_SQUARE_ROOT* operation cannot 'fail'. It would be unsatisfactory to find the operation *POS_SQ_ROOT* painstakingly going about these tests when they were unnecessary.

Consider the sequence below

$$-d1 \longrightarrow \boxed{NEGATE} - r1 \longrightarrow d2 - \boxed{POS\_SQ\_ROOT} \longrightarrow r2-$$

If *NEGATE* had type

type: *Number* $\rightarrow$ *Number*

then the type constraint on the input to *POS_SQ_ROOT* is bound to be satisfied, but the pre-condition may not be. Thus *POS_SQ_ROOT* should make its pre-condition test explicitly in this case. In the sequence below

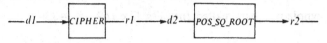

if the operation *CIPHER* was to shift each letter in the input message one place along the alphabet

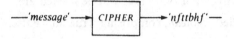

it is clear that the two operations *CIPHER* and *POS_SQ_ROOT* can never be sequenced successfully because the output type of one is incompatible with the input type of the other. Pictorially, the use of types gives a rough fit

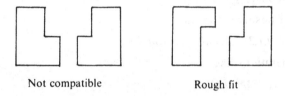

Not compatible   Rough fit

Pre-conditions give a finer fit

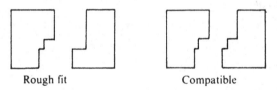

Rough fit   Compatible

Another way of viewing type information and pre-conditions is that they indicate abnormal exit tests. If any of the tests fail the present operation fails and terminates abnormally. If it is part of a sequence of operations, then the whole sequence fails and terminates abnormally. (In computer jargon it 'aborts'.)

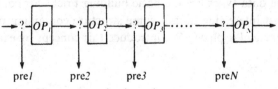

Abnormal termination exits

2.5   More on types

2.5.1   Primitive and constructed data types

So far the input and output of our specified operations have been simple numbers. It is usual in computing to distinguish between

whole numbers, called *Integers*, like *169, 13,* -13

and

a larger set of numbers, called *Reals*, which includes *16.9, 0.13,* $-1.3, 13.0, \pi, \sqrt{2}$, etc.

The other basic or primitive data types that will be needed are

truth values, called *Boolean*, comprising True and False,

and

characters, called *Char*, like 'a', 'b', '1', ':', etc.

We will also have use for the set of natural numbers

$NaturalNo = \{1,2,3,\ldots\}$

and for the set of positive integers

$PosInt = \{0,1,2,\ldots\} = \{0\} \cup NaturalNo$

Thus familiar operations like

SIN, COS, TAN, LOG

have type

Real $\rightarrow$ *Real*

while

ODD

the test for odd numbers, has type

Integer $\rightarrow$ *Boolean*

and

IS_LETTER

a test to decide whether a character is a letter, has type

Char $\rightarrow$ *Boolean*

The primitive data types are the basic building bricks for constructed data types. Most interesting data is some structure containing primitive data types in particular places. We introduce this concept by example.

2.5.2   Pairs

Suppose that we wish to develop an operation to answer the

following question: How far is the point (x,y) from the origin (of a rectangular cartesian coordinate system)?

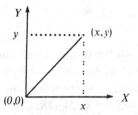

Using Pythagoras' theorem the 'answer' is $POS\_SQ\_ROOT(x^2 + y^2)$.

A 'map' of the calculations involved is shown below. A pair of real numbers *rp* (real pair) is provided as data and a result *dist* is calculated.

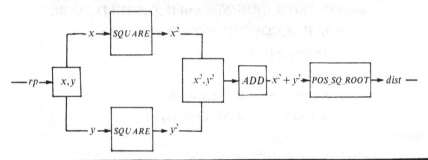

We propose *DIST_FROM_ORIGIN* as the name for this operation. The type of input data to *DIST_FROM_ORIGIN* is a pair of real numbers in a particular order – the *x*-coordinate followed by the *y*-coordinate. To avoid confusion with other uses of parentheses, the form

$\langle x,y \rangle$

is used instead of (x,y).

The specification has need to refer to the whole pair *rp* and to the components *x*, *y* hence the presence of the structural operation *HAS_COMPONENTS* (and later the 'inverse' operation *ARE_COMPONENTS_OF*). Here is the specification of *DIST_FROM_ORIGIN*.

DIST_FROM_ORIGIN

type: *Real*-Pair → *Real*

pre--*DIST_FROM_ORIGIN*(rp) IS_DEFINED_TO_BE

   True

post-*DIST_FROM_ORIGIN*(rp,dist) IS_DEFINED_TO_BE

   rp HAS_COMPONENTS $\langle x,y \rangle$ &

   $x*x = x\_sq$ &

$$y*y=y\_sq \quad \&$$
$$x\_sq+y\_sq=sum\_xsq\_ysq \qquad \&$$
$$dist*dist=sum\_xsq\_ysq \qquad \&$$
$$dist \geqslant 0$$

As it is possible to calculate the distance from the origin of **any** point, the real pair *rp* is not restricted in any way and so the pre-condition for *DIST_FROM_ORIGIN* is always True. Once the type constraint on the input has been met (a pair of real numbers) *DIST_FROM_ORIGIN* can always find a result value which will satisfy its post-condition.

If the operation *POS_SQ_ROOT* as described earlier is available then the post-condition for *DIST_FROM_ORIGIN* can be written

post-*DIST_FROM_ORIGIN*(*rp*,*dist*) IS_DEFINED_TO_BE

rp HAS_COMPONENTS $\langle x,y\rangle$ &

$$x*x=x\_sq \quad \&$$
$$y*y=y\_sq \quad \&$$
$$x\_sq+y\_sq=sum\_xsq\_ysq \quad \&$$
$$dist=POS\_SQ\_ROOT(sum\_xsq\_ysq)$$

Note that

$$dist=POS\_SQ\_ROOT(sum\_xsq\_ysq)$$

is really shorthand for

pre--*POS_SQ_ROOT*(*sum_xsq_ysq*) &

post-*POS_SQ_ROOT*(*sum_xsq_ysq*,*dist*)

In general when we write

$$r=OP(d)$$

in a pre-condition or a post-condition it should be taken to mean

pre--*OP*(*d*) &

post-*OP*(*d*,*r*)

If we were to define the operation *SQUARE* in a suitable way, the post-condition could become

post-*DIST_FROM_ORIGIN*(*rp*,*dist*) IS_DEFINED_TO_BE

rp HAS_COMPONENTS $\langle x,y\rangle$ &

$$x\_sq=SQUARE(x) \quad \&$$
$$y\_sq=SQUARE(y) \quad \&$$
$$x\_sq+y\_sq=sum\_xsq\_ysq \quad \&$$
$$dist=POS\_SQ\_ROOT(sum\_xsq\_ysq)$$

The pre-condition for *POS_SQUARE_ROOT* is that the input value should not be negative. Since the input value is the sum of two squares the pre-condition is satisfied. If we were to define the operation *ADD* with type

> *ADD*
>
> type: *Real*-Pair → *Real*

then the post-condition of *DIST_FROM_ORIGIN* could be rewritten again as

> post-*DIST_FROM_ORIGIN*(rp, dist) IS_DEFINED_TO_BE
>
> rp HAS_COMPONENTS $\langle x, y \rangle$ &
>
> $x\_sq = SQUARE(x)$ &
>
> $y\_sq = SQUARE(y)$ &
>
> $\langle x\_sq, y\_sq \rangle$ ARE_COMPONENTS_OF $rp2$ &
>
> $sum\_rp2 = ADD(rp2)$ &
>
> $dist = POS\_SQ\_ROOT(sum\_rp2)$

This version matches the original diagram very well and gives a good indication of how complicated operations can be specified in terms of a number of simpler operations with this notation.

Note that the six expressions joined by '&' in the post-condition do not have to be written in any particular order. They represent 'observations' about the relationship between *dist* and *rp* which all have to be true. They make just as much sense written and read in the reverse order to that presented above.

2.5.3   Triples

We now extend the notion of a Pair data structure to a Triple and then to longer units. The idea is introduced by an example. Suppose the operation *IN_RANGE* is to take a Triple of characters $ct = \langle c\_test, c\_low, c\_high \rangle$ and decide whether the first character is in the range defined by the other two.

> *IN_RANGE*
>
> type: *Char*-Triple → *Boolean*
>
> pre--*IN_RANGE*(ct) IS_DEFINED_TO_BE
>
> ct HAS_COMPONENTS $\langle c\_test, c\_low, c\_high \rangle$ &
>
> $c\_low \leqslant c\_high$
>
> post-*IN_RANGE*(ct, in_range) IS_DEFINED_TO_BE
>
> ct HAS_COMPONENTS $\langle c\_test, c\_low, c\_high \rangle$ &
>
> $(c\_low \leqslant c\_test$ AND $c\_test \leqslant c\_high) = in\_range$

This last line means that on completion of *IN_RANGE*, the output value *in_range* has the same truth value as (is equal to)

$$(c\_low \leqslant c\_test \text{ AND } c\_test \leqslant c\_high)$$

Or put another way

    if $c\_test \geqslant c\_low$ AND $c\_test \leqslant c\_high$

    then   *in_range* = True

    else   *in_range* = False

If there is any confusion here it is because post-*IN_RANGE* is a predicate having a truth value of its own, but is being used to describe an operation which has a *Boolean* result, i.e. has type

    type: ?? → *Boolean*

2.5.4   **Tuples**

The concept of Pairing and Tripling primitive data types needs to be extended in three ways. Firstly it is possible to mix primitive data types in a single structure. Intead of writing

    T-Triple

for some data type *T*, we may now have to write

    T_1-T_2-T_3-Triple

because each of the T_i could be different. Since the number of types involved will be written out explicitly there will no longer be any need to use the words Pair, Triple, etc., and we use the general word **Tuple** instead.

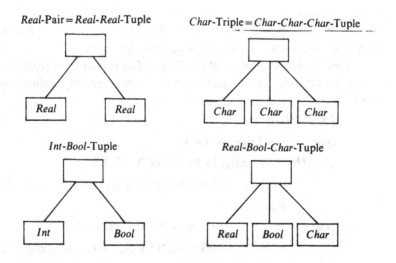

Secondly the structuring must be allowed to be arranged in two or more levels. For example *IN_RANGE* could be redefined to have as input

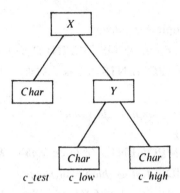

The name *X* in the top box stands for a 2-Tuple, in fact *X* is a *Char-Y*-Tuple where the name *Y* stands for a 2-Tuple. As *Y* is a *Char-Char*-Tuple, we can describe *X* as a *Char-(Char-Char-*Tuple)-Tuple.

This data structuring is so useful and important in defining operations that we introduce the idea of naming a data structure into the notation, e.g.

Name . . .   is defined to be . . .   the structure

Char_range   ::   *Char-Char*-Tuple

In_range_input   ::   *Char-Char_range*-Tuple

We can rewrite *IN_RANGE* completely using this idea.

Char_range   ::   *Char-Char*-Tuple

In_range_input   ::   *Char-Char_range*-Tuple

IN_RANGE_1

type: *In_range_input* → *Boolean*

pre--*IN_RANGE_1(iri)* IS_DEFINED_TO_BE

       iri HAS_COMPONENTS ⟨*c_test,c_range*⟩   &

       c_range HAS_COMPONENTS ⟨*c_low,c_high*⟩   &

       $c\_low \leqslant c\_high$

post-*IN_RANGE_1(iri,in_range)* IS_DEFINED_TO_BE

       iri HAS_COMPONENTS ⟨*c_test,c_range*⟩   &

       c_range HAS_COMPONENTS ⟨*c_low,c_high*⟩   &

       $(c\_low \leqslant c\_test$ AND $c\_test \leqslant c\_high) = in\_range$

The naming of the data structure *In_range_input* may seem a little contrived. A version of *IN_RANGE* avoiding the name is given below for comparison.

> *IN_RANGE_2*
>
> type: Char-*Char_range*-Tuple → *Boolean*
>
> pre--*IN_RANGE_2*(⟨*c_test,c_range*⟩) IS_DEFINED_TO_BE
>
> > *c_range* HAS_COMPONENTS ⟨*c_low,c_high*⟩   &
> >
> > *c_low* ⩽ *c_high*
>
> post-*IN_RANGE_2*(⟨*c_test,c_range*⟩   ,*in_range*)
>
> > IS_DEFINED_TO_BE
> >
> > > *c_range* HAS_COMPONENTS ⟨*c_low,c_high*⟩   &
> > >
> > > (*c_low* ⩽ *c_test* AND *c_test* ⩽ *c_high*) = *in_range*

Finally it is possible to avoid the HAS_COMPONENT lines altogether in the following way

> *IN_RANGE_3*
>
> type: Char-(*Char-Char*-Tuple)-Tuple → *Boolean*
>
> pre--*IN_RANGE_3*(⟨*c_test*, ⟨*c_low,c_high*⟩ ⟩)
> > IS_DEFINED_TO_BE
> >
> > *c_low* ⩽ *c_high*
>
> post-*IN_RANGE_3*(⟨*c_test*, ⟨*c_low,c_high*⟩ ⟩ ,*in_range*)
> > IS_DEFINED_TO_BE
> >
> > (*c_low* ⩽ *c_test* AND *c_test* ⩽ *c_high*) = *in_range*

The third way in which the construction of data types needs to be extended is to allow for arbitrarily long Tuples. The data structures are then called lists and they are described below.

2.5.5   Lists

A **list** is a collection of data objects all of the same type and presented in a definite order. The data objects are called members or elements of the list. The number of members of a list is not predetermined. The ⟨,,,⟩ notation can readily be used for lists, e.g.

> ⟨1,2,3,4⟩   is a list of *Integers*
>
> ⟨1,3,2,4⟩   is a different list of *Integers*
>
> ⟨1,3,2,4,4⟩ is yet another list of *Integers*
>
> ⟨'h', 'e', 'l', 'l', 'o'⟩ is a list of *Chars* representing the word 'hello'

$\langle$'e', '.', 'g', '.'$\rangle$ is a list of *Chars* representing 'e.g.'

$\langle$ $\langle$'0','9'$\rangle$, $\langle$'a','z'$\rangle$, $\langle$'A','Z'$\rangle$ $\rangle$ is a list of *Char_ranges*

$\langle$ $\rangle$ is a list with no members – the **empty list**

We will wish to define operations on lists so we introduce the notation

T-List

to express the type of a list in which the members are all of type *T*. Thus we may begin to define the operation *LENGTH* on a list of *Reals* as follows

LENGTH

type: *Real*-List → *PosInt*

In order to access individual members of a list we use two functions called **head** and **tail**.

head

type: *T*-List → *T*

pre--*head*(ℓ) IS_DEFINED_TO_BE

ℓ IS_NOT_EMPTY

. . .

tail

type: *T*-List → *T*-List

pre--*tail*(ℓ) IS_DEFINED_TO_BE

ℓ IS_NOT_EMPTY

. . .

The function *head* takes a list of any type and returns as result the first member of the list. The function *tail* again takes a list of any type but returns a *list* which is the same as the input list except that the head element is omitted.

$\langle 1,2,3,4 \rangle$

head *tail*

1   $\langle 2,3,4 \rangle$

Since the tail is a non-empty list we can continue

```
⟨1,2,3,4⟩
  /   \
head   tail
 /       \
1        ⟨2,3,4⟩
          /   \
        head   tail
         /       \
        2        ⟨3,4⟩
                  /   \
                head   tail
                 /       \
                3        ⟨4⟩
                          /   \
                        head   tail
                         /       \
                        4        ⟨⟩
```

The process continues until the empty list is reached.

Lists are constructed from their elements as in

$$⟨1,2,3,4⟩$$

or by **concatenation** of existing lists using the operator $\|$. Thus

$$⟨1,2⟩ \| ⟨3,4⟩ = ⟨1,2,3,4⟩$$

and, for any non-empty list ℓ, we have the identity

$$⟨head(\ell)⟩ \| tail(\ell) = \ell$$

As an example of the way in which lists are handled in the specifications of operations, consider the operation *AVERAGE* which is defined below in terms of the operations *SUM* (which *ADD*s up the values of the members of the list) and *LENGTH* (which counts the number of members in the list).

> *AVERAGE*
>
> type: *Real-List* → *Real*
>
> pre--*AVERAGE*($r\ell$) IS_DEFINED_TO_BE
>
> $r\ell$ IS_NOT_EMPTY
>
> post-*AVERAGE*($r\ell$,*average*) IS_DEFINED_TO_BE
>
> $sum = SUM(r\ell)$ &
>
> $length = LENGTH(r\ell)$ &
>
> $average = sum/length$

Some idea of the way that *SUM* and *LENGTH* will be specified can be seen from the following

> $sum(r\ell)$ IS_DEFINED_TO_BE
>
>   if $r\ell$ IS_EMPTY
>
>   then 0
>
>   else $head(r\ell) + sum(tail(r\ell))$

length(rℓ) IS_DEFINED_TO_BE

    if   *rℓ* IS_EMPTY

    then *0*

    else   *1 + length(tail(rℓ))*

The definitions of *SUM* and *LENGTH* contain **recursion** – i.e. their definitions are cyclic. For example the definition of *sum*, acting on a list *rℓ*, involves the use of *sum*, acting on a shorter list, *tail(rℓ)*. The definitions are given below in full.

SUM

type: *Real*-List → *Real*

pre--*SUM(rℓ)* IS_DEFINED_TO_BE

    True

post-*SUM(rℓ,sum)* IS_DEFINED_TO_BE

    if   *rℓ* IS_EMPTY

    then *sum = 0*

    else $rℓ = \langle rℓ\_head \rangle \| rℓ\_tail$ &

            sum_tail = SUM(rℓ_tail) &

            sum = rℓ_head + sum_tail

The 'map' for *SUM* is shown in the diagram. Notice that it is recursive.

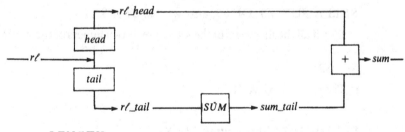

LENGTH

type: *Real*-List → *PosInt*

pre--*LENGTH(rℓ)* IS_DEFINED_TO_BE

    True

post-*LENGTH(rℓ,length)* IS_DEFINED_TO_BE

    if   *rℓ* IS_EMPTY

    then *length = 0*

    else   *rℓ_tail = tail(rℓ)* &

            length_tail = LENGTH(rℓ_tail) &

            length = 1 + length_tail

2.5.6   Sets

If the definite order is removed from the concept of a list, the resulting collection of data objects all of the same type is referred to as a **set**. (Note, mathematicians might argue that lists should be defined in terms of sets not sets in terms of lists as we have here.) The number of members or elements of a set is not predetermined. The $\langle ,,, \rangle$ notation is altered to $\{ ,,, \}$ for sets. Thus

the *set* of elements in the *list* $\langle 1,2,3,4 \rangle$ is $\{1,2,3,4\}$

the *set* of elements in the *list* $\langle 1,3,2,4 \rangle$ is $\{1,2,3,4\}$

the *set* of elements in the *list* $\langle 1,3,2,4,4 \rangle$ is $\{1,2,3,4\}$

the *set* of elements in $\langle 'h','e','l','l','o' \rangle$ is $\{'e','h','l','o'\}$

A set is defined by a membership test, an object is either in the set or it is not. It does not make sense to ask if the object is included twice.

The operations applicable to sets are

IS_IN, IS_A_SUBSET_OF, =,

UNION, INTERSECT, WITHOUT

IS_IN

x IS_IN S, also written $x \in S$,

is True if x is a member of the set S

IS_A_SUBSET_OF

$S1$ IS_A_SUBSET_OF $S2$, also written $S1 \subseteq S2$,

is True if all the members of the set $S1$ are also members of the set $S2$

=

$S1 = S2$

is True if $S1 \subseteq S2$ AND $S2 \subseteq S1$

UNION

$S1$ UNION $S2$, also written $S1 \cup S2$,

is the set containing all the members of $S1$ and $S2$

(with repeats removed)

e.g. $\{1,2,3\}$ UNION $\{3,4,5\} = \{1,2,3,4,5\}$

INTERSECT

$S1$ INTERSECT $S2$, also written $S1 \cap S2$,

is the set containing all the members that $S1$ and $S2$ have in common

e.g $\{1,2,3\}$ INTERSECT $\{3,4,5\} = \{3\}$

WITHOUT

S1 WITHOUT *S2*, also written *S1\S2*,

is the set containing all the members of *S1* which are not members of *S2*

e.g. $\{1,2,3\}$ WITHOUT $\{3,4,5\} = \{1,2\}$

WITHOUT is sometimes called the **set difference** operator.

The **empty set** is written $\emptyset$ and contains no elements.

The types of the set operators are given below. *X* stands for any chosen type.

IS_IN	type:	X-(X-Set)-Tuple $\rightarrow$ *Boolean*
IS_A_SUBSET_OF	type:	(X-Set)-(X-Set)-Tuple $\rightarrow$ *Boolean*
=	type:	(X-Set)-(X-Set)-Tuple $\rightarrow$ *Boolean*
UNION	type:	(X-Set)-(X-Set)-Tuple $\rightarrow X$-Set
INTERSECT	type:	(X-Set)-(X-Set)-Tuple $\rightarrow X$-Set
WITHOUT	type:	(X-Set)-(X-Set)-Tuple $\rightarrow X$-Set

The definition of the operation *AVERAGE* on a *set* of Reals, *rs*, can now be given.

AVERAGE

type: *Real*-Set $\rightarrow$ *Real*

pre--*AVERAGE(rs)* IS_DEFINED_TO_BE

$rs \neq \emptyset$

post-*AVERAGE(rs,average)* IS_DEFINED_TO_BE

$sum = SUM(rs)$ &

$size = SIZE(rs)$ &

$average = sum/size$

where

SUM

type: *Real*-Set $\rightarrow$ *Real*

pre--*SUM(rs)* IS_DEFINED_TO_BE

$rs \neq \emptyset$

post-*SUM(rs,sum)* IS_DEFINED_TO_BE

if $rs = \{lone\_member\}$

then $sum = lone\_member$

else $rs = rs1$ UNION $rs2$ &

$rs1$ INTERSECT $rs2 = \emptyset$ &

$rs1 \neq \emptyset$ &

$rs2 \neq \emptyset$ &

$sum1 = SUM(rs1)$ &

$sum2 = SUM(rs2)$ &

$sum = sum1 + sum2$

Thus the sum of a set $\{1,2,3,4\}$ is expresed as

$$SUM(\{1,2,3,4\}) = SUM(X) + SUM(Y)$$

where X UNION $Y = \{1,2,3,4\}$, X INTERSECT $Y = \emptyset$ and X,Y are not empty. In this case there are 14 choices for X and Y including

$X = \{1\}$ $Y = \{2,3,4\}$

$X = \{1,2\}$ $Y = \{3,4\}$

$X = \{1,2,3\}$ $Y = \{4\}$

Picking the second

$$SUM(\{1,2,3,4\}) = SUM(\{1,2\}) + SUM(\{3,4\})$$

The calculation path will be (diagrammatically)

Other possible paths would be

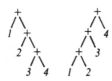

For completeness a specification of the operation *SIZE* is given below

SIZE

type: *Real-Set* → *PosInt*

pre--*SIZE(rs)* IS_DEFINED_TO_BE

    True

post-*SIZE(rs,size)* IS_DEFINED_TO_BE

    if $rs = \emptyset$

    then $size = 0$

else

if	$rs = \{lone\_member\}$	
then	$size = 1$	
else	$rs = rs1$ UNION $rs2$	&
	$rs1$ INTERSECT $rs2 = \varnothing$	&
	$rs1 \neq \varnothing$	&
	$rs2 \neq \varnothing$	&
	$size1 = SIZE(rs1)$	&
	$size2 = SIZE(rs2)$	&
	$size = size1 + size2$	

2.6   The characteristics of a specification

The specification of SUM is written 'precisely' in the sense that the output *sum* is properly defined for all valid input, but the specification is deliberately vague as to the process by which the necessary elementary additions are carried out. This is the goal of all initial specifications.

We argue that the choice of 'calculation path' should be delayed as long as possible. Similarly we argue that nothing should be fixed by the specification of an operation that is not absolutely required. This should give the implementor of the operation the greatest choice and help to keep the specification concise.

What characterises an acceptable specification and what is it trying to achieve? The aim of a specification is to describe an operation

precisely,

clearly, and

concisely.

The specification should be unambiguous and complete, preferably without restricting in any way **how** the operation might proceed computationally. It is a **what** rather than a **how** definition.

It is all too easy to overspecify an operation and conceal or prevent a particular implementation. One of the principal pitfalls is to introduce ordering which is inessential.

In data-structuring this would be to insist on viewing the data as a list when it is not really ordered and a set would be more appropriate. In a calculation this could be forcing a calculation to proceed in a specific order which is not essential.

2.7   Refinement and transformation of specifications

Given a complete unambiguous specification, part or all of it can be transformed until the programmer is confident of his ability to code the operations and data structures into the Program Design Language (PDL) or target language he has decided to use.

The specification of the *AVERAGE* of the members of a real set introduced in the last section requires the set to be partitioned into two subsets. The specification given does not require this to be performed in any particular way. As soon as the decision is taken as to how the set data structure might actually be represented in the eventual program, one particular method of partitioning may be preferable to all others. In particular if a representation using lists is chosen, then partitioning into two subsets with one element in the first subset and all the rest in the other may be the most obvious.

$$\{1,2,3,4\} = \{1\} \text{ UNION } \{2,3,4\}$$

The revised specification (in this case including a particular style of partitioning) would be called a **refinement** of the original specification. A refinement of a specification brings it closer to the final program while still being compatible with the original specification. The refinement may be done in several stages. At each stage a check or even a proof is required that the latest refinement is compatible with the previous one.

Thus the idea of refinement is one of making a definite choice from a range of possibilities. It is also possible to consider more drastic changes to a specification by replacing some or all of it with a different but equivalent specification. This is usually called a **transformation**. For example it may be advantageous to combine two operations into one operation. This is the case with the *SUM* and *LENGTH* operations on lists (or *SUM* and *SIZE* operations on sets) introduced above. The transformation of the separate operations *SUM* and *LENGTH* into a combined operation *SUMLENGTH* is shown in detail in Chapter 4.

2.8   States in specifications

The specification style introduced so far is complete in the **functional** sense that any operation which consumes input and produces output can be specified. However if the notation is to be used in a transformation sense to develop a procedural program it is deficient in that there is no support for 'variables'. Given a **procedural** program environment with integer variable v, it is common to write

$$v := v + 1$$

meaning

> refer to the current value associated with v,
>
> add one to it,
>
> and associate this new value with v in place of the original

The specification

> *INC_1*
>
> type: *Integer → Integer*
>
> pre--*INC_1(i)* IS_DEFINED_TO_BE
>> True
>
> post-*INC_1(i,new_i)* IS_DEFINED_TO_BE
>> $new\_i = i + 1$

does not capture the idea of 'storing the result' in the place from where the input was provided. The crucial idea that is adopted into the specification at this point is the idea of a (background) state. The state is a data structure of definite shape (or type) that is accessible to an operation. The operation may inspect the values stored in the structure and alter them, but cannot alter the shape (or type) of the structure.

The type of the structure is introduced as a separate line in the specification. The pre-condition is augmented so as to show dependence on the initial state as well as the input. The post-condition is changed to refer to

> the initial state,
>
> the input,
>
> the final state, and
>
> the output.

A convenient notation is to use v' (pronounced v dash or v prime) for a value in the final state originating from a value v in the initial state. Thus if the operation does not change a value in the state, the post-condition includes

> $v' = v$

The general form of a specification will now be

> *OP*
>
> states: *S*
>
> type: *D → R*
>
> pre--*OP(s,d)* IS_DEFINED_TO_BE
>> ...

post-*OP(s,d,s',r)* IS_DEFINED_TO_BE

. . .

and a suitable diagram of the operation would be

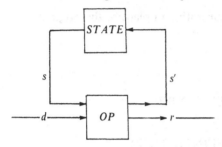

Thus *INC_1* can now be specified as an operation on the state as

INC_1

states: *Integer*

type: →

pre--*INC_1(v,d)* IS_DEFINED_TO_BE

True

post-*INC_1(v,d,v',r)* IS_DEFINED_TO_BE

$v' = v + 1$

There is no input or output so there is no type written on either side of the type arrow (→). The notation *d,r* for input and output is superfluous and could be omitted, giving

pre--*INC_1(v,)* . . .

post-*INC_1(v,,v',)* . . .

The notation is still precise if multiple commas are reduced to one and leading and trailing commas are omitted altogether since the order

initial state, input, final state, output

is fixed and the states and type lines indicate which parts **have** to be present.

The next example shows how the operation *LENGTH* is altered if all the objects are manipulated in the state.

LENGTH

states: (*Real*-List)-(*PosInt*)-Tuple

type: →

pre--*LENGTH(⟨rℓ,count⟩,)* IS_DEFINED_TO_BE

True

post-$LENGTH(\langle r\ell,count\rangle,,\langle r\ell',count'\rangle,)$ IS_DEFINED_TO_BE

     if $r\ell = \langle\rangle$

     then $count' = count$ &

             $r\ell' = r\ell$

     else $r\ell\_tail = tail(r\ell)$ &

             $count1 = count + 1$ &

             pre--$LENGTH(\ \langle r\ell\_tail,count1\rangle,)$ &

             post-$LENGTH(\ \langle r\ell\_tail,count1\rangle,,\langle r\ell',count'\rangle,)$

Within the specification of the operation *LENGTH* there is an abbreviation for the following two lines from the post-condition

     pre--$LENGTH(\ \langle r\ell\_tail,count1\rangle,)$ &

     post-$LENGTH(\ \langle r\ell\_tail,count1\rangle,,\langle r\ell',count'\rangle,)$

Following the style introduced earlier, we substitute

     $\langle r\ell',count'\rangle = LENGTH(\ \langle r\ell\_tail,count1\rangle\ )$

In general, when the operation involves the state, we write

     $(s',r) = OP(s,d)$

to stand for

     pre--$OP(s,d)$ &

     post-$OP(s,d,s',r)$

If the states line is empty, then the abbreviation would read

     $(,r) = OP(,d)$

and if the type line is empty, then the abbreviation would read

     $(s',) = OP(s,)$

It is possible to shorten these further to

     $r = OP(d)$

and

     $s' = OP(s)$

as suggested for the operation *LENGTH* above. Note that the number zero does not occur in the specification of the operation *LENGTH*. The success of this specification depends on establishing an initial state containing

     $\langle original\_real\_list,0\rangle$

e.g.

     $\langle\ \langle 3.2,7.6,1.0,9.8\rangle\ ,\ 0\ \rangle$

and progressing through the stages

$\langle\ \langle 7.6, 1.0, 9.8\rangle\ ,\ 1\ \rangle$

$\langle\ \langle 1.0, 9.8\rangle\ ,\ 2\ \rangle$

$\langle\ \langle 9.8\rangle\ ,\ 3\ \rangle$

$\langle\ \langle\ \rangle\ ,\ 4\ \rangle$

leaving the empty real list and the number 4.

This 'initialisation of variables' is well known in programming both as a necessity and as a frequent source of errors. The initialisation has to be specified and this gives rise to a two level specification of a single operation. A full example of this is given in Chapter 12.

Notice that in the pre-condition it would be nice to write

'count = number of elements removed from the list so far'

but this would require the original list to be available in the state. Note that in this specification the names $r\ell\_tail$ and $count1$ are superfluous and the else part could be rewritten as

else $\langle r\ell', count'\rangle = LENGTH(\langle tail(r\ell), count+1\rangle)$

Having done this it is 'straightforward' to code into a programming language that allows recursion, e.g. the PDL of Chapter 5

$r\ell$: Real*

count : PosInt

function *length*

type: →   --no parameters, no 'result' value

if $r\ell \neq \langle\ \rangle$

then $count \leftarrow count+1$

        $r\ell \leftarrow tail(r\ell)$

        length   --*recursive call, no parameters*

fi

The initialisation and call would be

count ← 0

length

{length of list $r\ell$ has been computed and stored in variable 'count'}

The next step is to use the coding templates given in Chapter 6 to produce the final code. This may require the recursion removal techniques of Appendix D to produce something like

count ← 0

while $r\ell \neq \langle \rangle$

do

      $count \leftarrow count + 1$

      $r\ell \leftarrow tail(r\ell)$

od

2.9   States vs. input/output

Given an apparently free choice between working with the functional style, using only input/output and the procedural style using the state as well, the novice needs to be advised which to choose. One possible answer is to choose separately for each object involved in such a way as to minimise the size of the resulting specification. Given the recent trend in computing towards a functional style, alternative advice would be to avoid the use of the state if possible and only introduce it if a particular programming language or efficiency considerations demand it.

The idea of a state is said to be efficient because store is reused (updated values overwrite the old ones) compared with input/output which requires new space for the output of the operation and the space occupied by the input is of no further use. In the case that the output contains a significant proportion of the input unchanged then time is spent copying from input to output which could be avoided using the 'overwriting' facility of the state.

The main reason for using the functional style and input/output rather than the state is that reasoning (formal proof, rigorous justification) is much easier.

2.10   Conclusion

In summary, an initial specification should be

      functional (rather than procedural with states),

      with carefully chosen data structures,

      concise,

      precise, yet clear, unambiguous and complete.

This first specification can then be manipulated mathematically if required to allow a program to be written in the chosen programming language. The manipulation may mean algebraic simplification and transformation, movement of objects from input/output to state, removal of recursion in favour of iteration, etc.

Exercises 2

1 Complete the specification of the operation *MAXS* which finds the maximum value in a set.

MAXS

states:

type: *Integer*-Set → *Integer*

. . .

2 Complete the specification of the operation *MAXL* which finds the maximum value in a list.

MAXL

states:

type: *Integer*-List → *Integer*

. . .

3 Complete the specification of the operation *ALL_SAME* which is True if all the characters in the list are the same, False otherwise.

ALL_SAME

states: *Char*-List

type: → *Boolean*

. . .

4 Complete the specification of the operation *CONCATS* which accepts a set of lists and produces a list which is the result of concatenating all the lists in the set.

CONCATS

states:

type: (*Item*-List)-Set → *Item*-List

. . .

3

Diagrams

In this chapter many kinds of diagram are discussed. They all show structure in some way. They may broadly be classified into program structure diagrams and data structure diagrams – but note that sometimes programs are data to other programs so the distinction is imprecise.

3.1   Diagrams used in the program development process

This section discusses the use of diagrams in the program development process.

There are many kinds of diagram and everyone has favourites. It is the intention of this chapter to demonstrate the usefulness of a disciplined approach to diagrams and to stress the similarities between kinds of diagrams rather than to advocate one particular diagramming technique above all others.

In computer programming, the main uses for diagrams are:

to show the flow of control in a program (= flowchart)

to show the structure of data (= data structure diagram), and

to show the structure of a programming language (= syntax diagram).

All these diagramming systems show **structure** in some way.

All the systems can be used intuitively and informally to organise initial ideas or they can be used formally as part of a disciplined design process.

In looking for the similarities rather than differences between different diagramming systems, the critical observation is that all systems have a way of showing

sequencing

selection

repetition

The diagram below shows the way these structure forms are drawn in three different diagramming systems.

Sequence

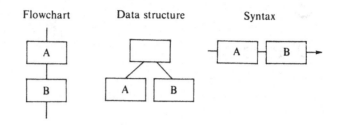

Selection

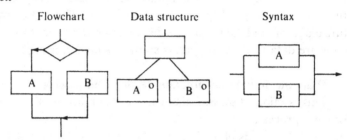

Repetition

Type (i) – the body of the loop may be traversed zero or more times

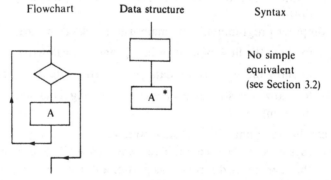

Type (ii) – the body of the loop is traversed at least once

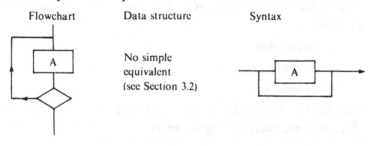

In the flowchart diagram system, type (i) repetition is called a **pre-check loop** and type (ii) repetition is called a **post-check loop**.

The only remaining ingredient needed to make a diagramming system is a rule for combining these structures.

The usual way to express the combining rule is to give an initial minimal diagram and then a replacement rule. That is to say that part of the existing diagram is replaced by one of the allowed structures.

Minimal diagrams

Flowchart   Data structure   Syntax

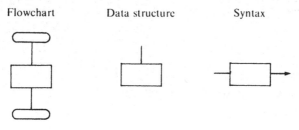

Replacement rule

Replace any occurrence of the shape below with any other allowed structure.

Flowchart   Data structure   Syntax

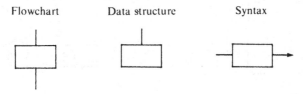

An example of this construction method is given in each diagramming system simultaneously.

Initial diagram

Flowchart   Data structure   Syntax

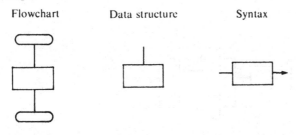

Step 1
Replace with a sequence structure

Flowchart   Data structure   Syntax

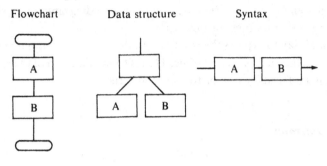

Step 2
Replace second part of sequence with selection

Flowchart   Data structure

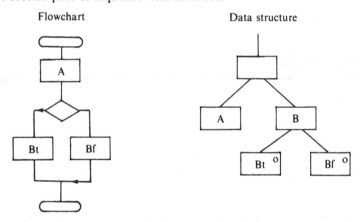

Syntax

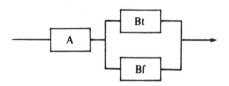

Step 3
Replace right-hand/lower part of selection with a sequence

Flowchart   Data structure

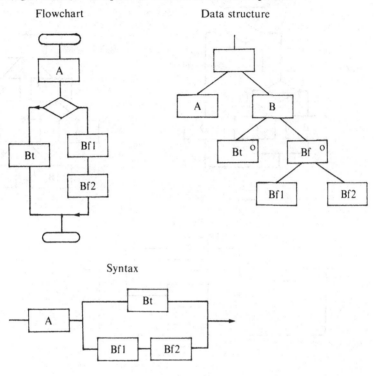

Syntax

This is a highly disciplined use of the diagramming system. In practice, a 'complete' diagram is often drawn first and then it is 'shrunk' back to the minimal diagram. If this process succeeds then the original diagram is acceptable. Thus we may reverse the expansion process just described. Here are three equivalent diagrams in the three notations of some 'mystery' process. We wish to check that the diagrams are properly structured.

Mystery process

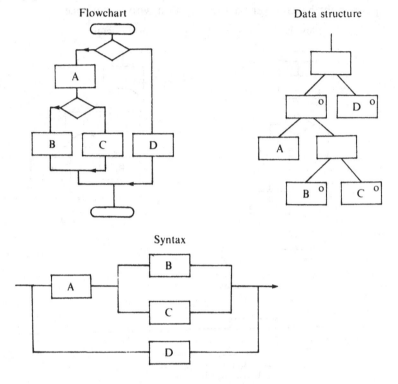

Flowchart   Data structure

Syntax

Step 1

Replace selection by simple process

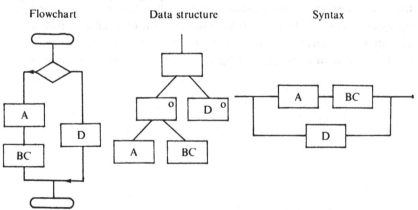

Flowchart   Data structure   Syntax

Step 2
Replace sequence by simple process

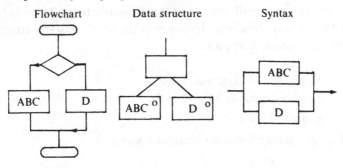

Flowchart   Data structure   Syntax

Step 3
Replace selection by simple process

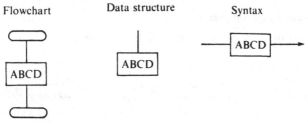

Flowchart   Data structure   Syntax

Since all three diagrams have been successfully reduced to their respective minimal diagrams they were all properly structured originally. Since they were all reduced by the same steps in the same order they must also be equivalent structures.

This process of 'shrinking' is not normally performed by redrawing in this way but by drawing a rectangle round the structure to be simplified. This provides a quick and easy test to perform by hand.

The criterion for a diagram to be acceptable is not that it is pretty. The next example shows this.

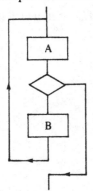

Although this diagram is 'pretty' it is not structured by the rules given above. It is obviously intended to be a repetition of some sort but it is not reducible to one of the allowed structures. This structure, often called a mid-check loop, is a contender for inclusion in the set of allowable structures – but we will exclude it at present.

3.2   An algebra of diagrams

In school algebra 0 (zero) is the identity for addition because

$$x+0=0+x=x$$

and 1 is the identity for multiplication because

$$x*1=1*x=x$$

So we introduce the identity process into the diagrams.

Identity processes on diagrams

Flowchart   Data structure   Syntax

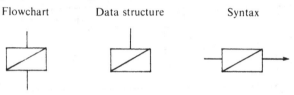

And we have the 'obvious' simplification rules for sequence. For example we have for flowchart diagrams

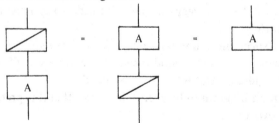

Thus the common flowchart for selection with no *else* part, which is often drawn

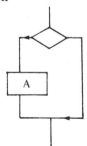

should strictly be drawn as

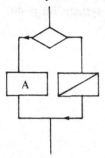

This identity process now allows us to show an equivalent form of the pre-check loop using selection and a post-check loop.

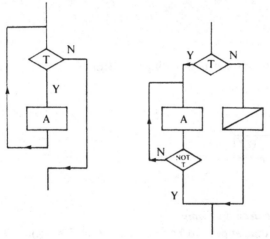

Similarly a post-check loop can be replaced by an equivalent structure using sequencing and a pre-check loop, but this does not need the identity process.

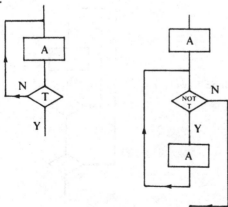

Now finally we can fill the 'missing' forms in the 'repetition' rows of the original table which introduced the diagramming systems on p. 40.

Repetition – missing forms

Repetition type (i) – syntax diagram form

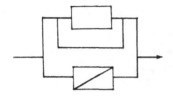

Repetition type (ii) – data structure diagram form

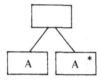

Apparently unstructured diagrams

Not all diagrams that appear to be unstructured at first sight are really unstructured. For example

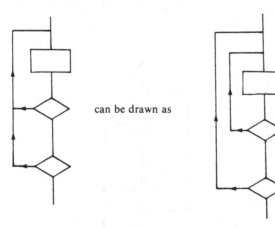

can be drawn as

which is then a repetition type (ii) inside a repetition type (ii). In a similar way

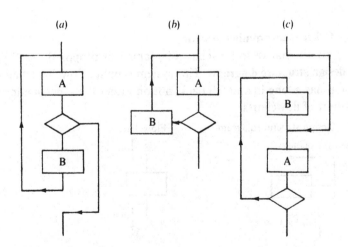

which is a selection inside a selection.

When the diagram really does turn out to be unstructured it is possible (often at the cost of repeating portions of the diagram) to make it structured. The mid-check loop mentioned above can arise in a variety of disguises

One way of producing a structured form of this is to show the process A twice as in

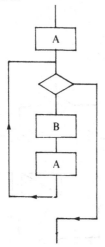

The restructuring of badly structured programs is discussed further in Chapter 11 which presents techniques for handling programs which have not been constructed using any disciplined method.

Sources
Flowcharts in programming are regarded as 'traditional'. The data structure diagrams presented here are those of Jackson [19]. The Syntax Diagrams are those of Wirth [32] p. 118.

3.3   Other diagramming systems
An alternative to flowchart diagrams was proposed in [28] and called **design structure diagrams.** This system is unlike flowchart diagrams because it has a 'one-in and fall back' notion rather than the 'one-in, one-out' notion of flowcharts.

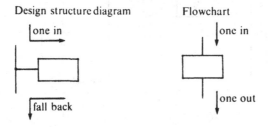

The system is as follows

Initial diagram

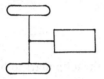

Replacement rule
Replace any occurrence of

with a sequence, selection or repetition form from those given below.

Sequence

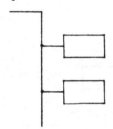

Selection

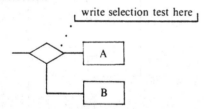

By convention the upper process A is entered when the selection test yields True and the process B when the test yields False.

Repetition
Type (i) – pre-check loop

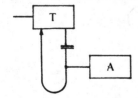

Type (ii) – post-check loop

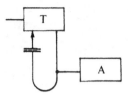

The loop control test T is applied at the place in the loop marked by ═══.

In order to compare the two program structure diagram systems the following flowchart and design structure diagrams have the same structure.

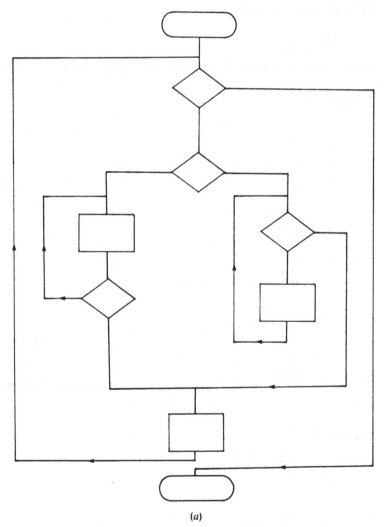

(*a*)

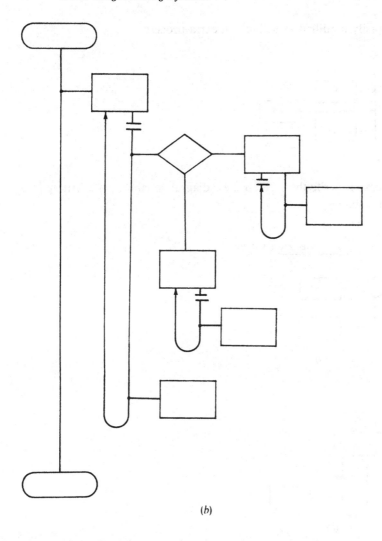

(b)

The advantages claimed for this system over flowcharts are that
(i) The diagrams are easy to extend. For example, the sequence

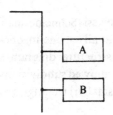

can be easily modified to include an extra process

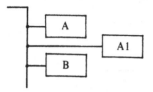

(ii) It is easy to write the 'test' on these diagrams – there is no writing into 'diamond' shapes

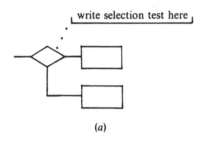

(a)

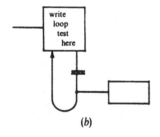

(b)

(iii) It is much easier to ensure that the diagram is structured

Because each process is linked into the diagram at only one place it is much easier to keep to the structuring rules.

Another system worth mentioning is the use of Nassi–Schneiderman Diagrams [26]. There are no flow lines in this system at all (cf. one-in, one-out of flowcharts and in-and-fall-back of design structure diagrams). Starting with an initial (large!) rectangle any one of the allowed subdivisions shown in the diagram below can be made. Any of the (smaller) rectangles so formed may be further subdivided, etc.

Nassi–Schneiderman diagrams

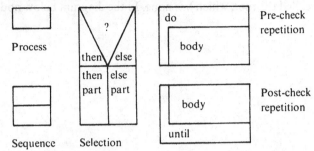

Process

Sequence   Selection

Pre-check
repetition

Post-check
repetition

3.4   Graphs, networks and trees

Certain diagrams from mathematics are commonly used in computing of which the most common are graphs, networks and trees. In the language of this chapter these are specialised data structure diagrams.

A **graph** is a set of labelled **nodes** (drawn as points) connected by **edges** (drawn as lines). If the edges are **directed** (have arrows on them) then the graph is called a **directed graph** or **digraph**. Directed edges are also called **arcs**.

A digraph

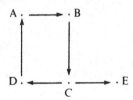

A **cycle** is a path from a node along the directed edges back to the original node. A **network** is a digraph on which there are no cycles.

A network

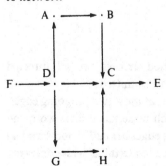

A **tree** is a network on which every node has exactly one incoming edge except one, called the **root**, which has none. In the diagram below node A is the root.

A tree

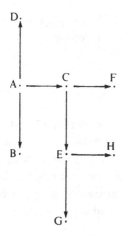

In computing trees are most often drawn downwards from their root, e.g.

A downward growing tree

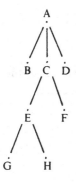

When a tree is drawn like this the implied arrows are all directed downwards and hence can be (and usually are) omitted.

A **binary tree** is a tree in which each node has at most two outgoing edges. A **complete binary tree** is a tree in which each node has either two or no outgoing edges. The nodes with two outgoing edges are called **non-terminal nodes** while those with no outgoing edges are called **terminal nodes** or **leaves**.

A binary tree

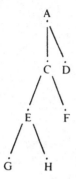

A **list** is a tree in which each non-terminal node has exactly one outgoing edge.

A list

A   B   C   D

Exercises 3

1 Four diagramming systems all capable of displaying sequence, selection and repetition have been compared in this chapter. They were

> Flowcharts
>
> Data Structure Diagrams,
>
> Syntax Diagrams, and
>
> Design Structure Diagrams.

Redraw the following four diagrams in each of the other three diagramming systems.

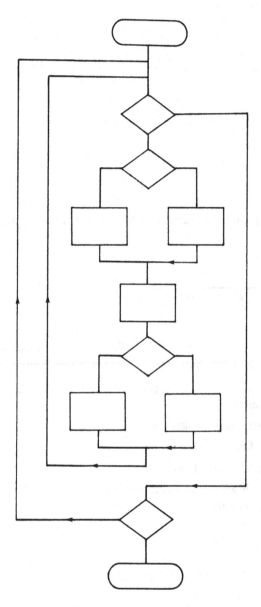

Flowchart for exercise 3.1

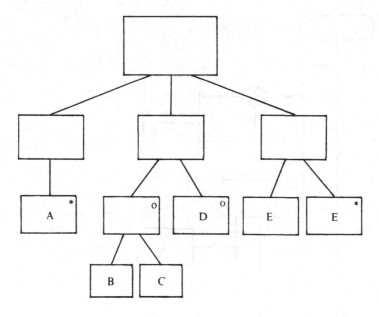

Data Structure Diagram for exercise 3.1

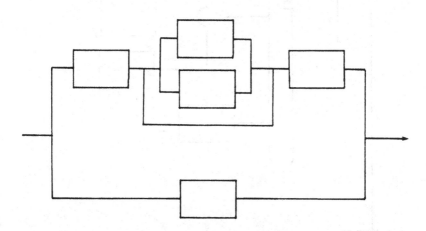

Syntax diagram for exercise 3.1

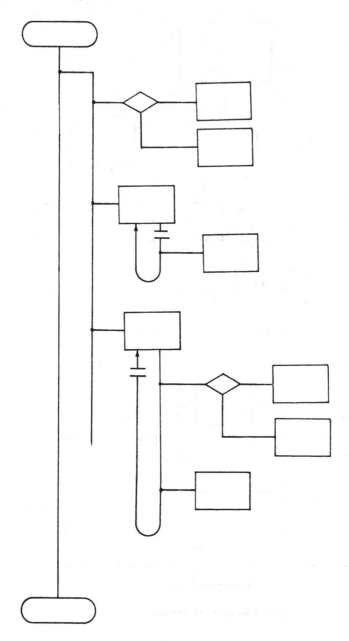

Design Structure Diagram for exercise 3.1

4
Specifications II

In Chapter 2 we investigated one notation in which specifications for programs could be written and suggested that a series of specifications may be produced

$$S_1 \to S_2 \to S_3 \to \ldots \to S_n$$

with each stage being a refinement or a transformation of the previous stage. It was pointed out that a check or proof ought to accompany each stage to show that it was compatible with the previous stage.

In this chapter we will give an example of a significant transformation and the associated proof. However before starting on this we will introduce some alternative notation which is more concise than that used in Chapter 2.

4.1   Concise notation

In Chapter 2 when we were discussing specifications for the first time only essential notation was introduced. Several words were consistently used in places where a mathematical symbol or notation could have been used. This hopefully made the chapter easier to read but certainly made the specifications longer than they needed to be. In the discussion of specifications again in this chapter the concise notation will be used. The full list of new notation with explanations appears below.

Real	is replaced by	$\mathbb{R}$
Integer		$\mathbb{Z}$
Boolean		$\mathbb{B}$
NaturalNo		$\mathbb{N}$
PosInt		$\mathbb{P}$
AND		$\wedge$
OR		$\vee$
NOT		$\neg$
IS_IN		$\in$

IS_A_SUBSET_OF	$\subseteq$
UNION	$\cup$
INTERSECT	$\cap$
WITHOUT	$\backslash$

These are in accordance with standard mathematical practice. The mathematical view of a **tuple** is that it is an element of a set which is a Cartesian product (or cross-product) of two or more sets. The symbol for Cartesian product is $\times$. So we change

$\langle a1,a2\rangle$	IS_IN A-A-Pair
$\langle a1,a2,a3\rangle$	IS_IN A-A-A-Triple
$\langle a,b,c\rangle$	IS_IN A-B-C-Triple
$\langle a,b,\ldots,n\rangle$	IS_IN A-B-$\ldots$-N-Tuple

to

$\langle a1,a2\rangle$	$\in$	$A \times A$
$\langle a1,a2,a3\rangle$	$\in$	$A \times A \times A$
$\langle a,b,c\rangle$	$\in$	$A \times B \times C$
$\langle a,b,\ldots,n\rangle$	$\in$	$A \times B \times \ldots \times N$

The mathematical view of a list of type T (i.e. T-List) is that

if the list is empty then it is a member of $\{\langle\rangle\}$,

if it is of length 1 then it is a member of T,

if it is of length 2 then it is a member of $T \times T$,

if it is of length 3 then it is a member of $T \times T \times T$,

etc.

The infinite union

$$\{\langle\rangle\} \cup (T) \cup (T \times T) \cup (T \times T \times T) \cup \ldots$$

which is sometimes written

$$T^0 \cup T^1 \cup T^2 \cup T^3 \cup \ldots$$

is usually abbreviated to

$$T^*$$

so we use this 'star' notation in place of the word 'List'. Thus

T-List   is replaced by T^*

We also change the notation T-Set as follows.

The mathematical notation for the set of all subsets of a particular set X is

$\mathscr{P}(X)$

which is read as the **powerset** of X.

$\mathscr{P}(X) \triangleq \{ S : S \subseteq X \}$

For example, if $X = \{1,2,3\}$ then

$\mathscr{P}(X) = \{ \varnothing , \{1\}, \{2\}, \{3\}, \{1,2\}, \{2,3\}, \{1,3\}, \{1,2,3\} \}$

This is exactly what was intended by the notation

X-Set

used in Chapter 2. So we have

X-Set   is replaced by $\mathscr{P}(X)$

There are several sorts of equality that appear in specifications. We have used IS_DEFINED_TO_BE, HAS_COMPONENTS, ARE_COMPONENTS_OF as well as the familiar ' = '. For brevity we now substitute symbols for the words.

IS_DEFINED_TO_BE   is replaced by $\triangleq$

HAS_COMPONENTS $=$

ARE_COMPONENTS_OF $=$

This completes the changes of notation to be introduced in this chapter.

4.2   **Transformation and proof in specifications**
Consider the definition of $AVERAGE$ described earlier in terms of lists.

$AVERAGE$

states:

type: $\mathbb{R}^* \to \mathbb{R}$

pre--$AVERAGE(,r\ell) \triangleq$

     $r\ell \neq \langle \rangle$

post-$AVERAGE(,r\ell,,average) \triangleq$

     $sum = SUM(r\ell)$ &

     $length = LENGTH(r\ell)$ &

     $average = sum/length$

(Remember that a shorthand notation is being used here.

     $sum = SUM(r\ell)$

is really a shorthand for $(,sum) = SUM(,r\ell)$ which in turn is shorthand for

pre--$SUM(,r\ell)$ &

post-$SUM(,r\ell,,sum)$

as introduced in Chapter 2.)

This specification could be criticised from a procedural or computational point of view by saying that each element in the list is visited twice, first by *SUM* and then by *LENGTH*. Recall that the definitions of *SUM* and *LENGTH* are at present:

SUM

states:

type: $\mathbb{R}^* \to \mathbb{R}$

pre--$SUM(,r\ell) \triangleq$

> True

post-$SUM(,r\ell,,sum) \triangleq$

> if $r\ell = \langle \rangle$
>
> then $sum = 0$
>
> else $r\ell = \langle r\ell\_head \rangle \| r\ell\_tail$ &
>
> $sum\_tail = SUM(r\ell\_tail)$ &
>
> $sum = r\ell\_head + sum\_tail$

LENGTH

states:

type: $\mathbb{R}^* \to \mathbb{P}$

pre--$LENGTH(,r\ell) \triangleq$

> True

post-$LENGTH(,r\ell,,length) \triangleq$

> if $r\ell = \langle \rangle$
>
> then $length = 0$
>
> else $r\ell = \langle r\ell\_head \rangle \| r\ell\_tail$ &
>
> $length\_tail = LENGTH(r\ell\_tail)$ &
>
> $length = 1 + length\_tail$

Given the intuition that the operations *SUM* and *LENGTH* could somehow be merged to produce *sum* and *length* results simultaneously with only one visit to each element of the list, we transform *AVERAGE* as follows:

> *AVERAGE*
>
> states:
>
> type: $\mathbb{R}^* \to \mathbb{R}$
>
> pre--$AVERAGE(,r\ell) \triangleq$
>
> > True
>
> post-$AVERAGE(,r\ell,,average) \triangleq$
>
> > $\langle sum, length \rangle = SUM\_LENGTH(r\ell)$ &
> >
> > $average = sum/length$

A new operation *SUM_LENGTH* has been introduced which combines the effect of *SUM* and *LENGTH* separately. The result is a pair $\langle sum, length \rangle \in \mathbb{R} \times \mathbb{P}$. The specification of *SUM_LENGTH* is just:

> *SUM_LENGTH*
>
> states:
>
> type: $\mathbb{R}^* \to \mathbb{R} \times \mathbb{P}$
>
> pre--$SUM\_LENGTH(,r\ell) \triangleq$
>
> > True
>
> post-$SUM\_LENGTH(,r\ell,,\langle sum, length \rangle) \triangleq$
>
> > $sum = SUM(r\ell)$ &
> >
> > $length = LENGTH(r\ell)$

So far nothing has been gained. However it is now possible to substitute for *SUM* and *LENGTH* in post-*SUM_LENGTH* and simplify the resulting expression. This will result in a definition of *SUM_LENGTH* which does not rely on the definitions of *SUM* or *LENGTH*. The process of substitution is called **unfolding**. The final step, which will involve reverse substitution, is called **folding**. Thus this transformation is called an **unfold–fold** transformation [6].

Before the unfolding is done it is important to note that the naming of input and output values is of little significance to the logic of the specification (however important it is to the human reader!). Thus the definitions of *SUM, LENGTH* could have been:

> *SUM*
>
> states:
>
> type: $\mathbb{R}^* \to \mathbb{R}$

pre--$SUM(,vv) \triangleq$

  True

post-$SUM(,vv,,ww) \triangleq$

  if $vv = \langle \rangle$

  then $ww = 0$

  else $vv = \langle xx \rangle \| yy$ &

    $zz = SUM(yy)$ &

    $ww = xx + zz$

LENGTH

states:

type: $\mathbb{R}^* \to \mathbb{P}$

pre--$LENGTH(,v) \triangleq$

  True

post-$LENGTH(,v,,w) \triangleq$

  if $v = \langle \rangle$

  then $w = 0$

  else $v = \langle x \rangle \| y$ &

    $z = LENGTH(y)$ &

    $w = 1 + z$

Thus by substituting the post-expressions of these operations into post-*SUM_LENGTH*, we obtain

post-$SUM\_LENGTH(,r\ell,,\langle sum, length \rangle) \triangleq$

  if $r\ell = \langle \rangle$

  then $sum = 0$

  else $r\ell = \langle xx \rangle \| yy$ &

    $zz = SUM(yy)$ &

    $sum = xx + zz$

  &

  if $r\ell = \langle \rangle$

  then $length = 0$

  else $r\ell = \langle x \rangle \| y$ &

    $z = LENGTH(y)$ &

    $length = 1 + z$

Informally this seems to suggest a simplification to

post-$SUM\_LENGTH(,r\ell,,\langle sum,length\rangle) \triangleq$

      if $r\ell = \langle\rangle$

      then $sum = 0$ &&

             $length = 0$

      else $r\ell = \langle xx\rangle \parallel yy$ &&

             $r\ell = \langle x\rangle \parallel y$ &&

             $zz = SUM(yy)$ &&

             $z = LENGTH(y)$ &&

             $sum = xx + zz$ &&

             $length = 1 + z$

Now xx and x must be equal as must yy and y. This gives a simplification of the else part to:

      else $r\ell = \langle xx\rangle \parallel yy$ &&

             $zz = SUM(yy)$ &&

             $z = LENGTH(yy)$ &&

             $sum = xx + zz$ &&

             $length = 1 + z$

And this can be simplified by reverse substitution to:

      else $r\ell = \langle xx\rangle \parallel yy$ &&

             $\langle zz,z\rangle = SUM\_LENGTH(yy)$ &&

             $sum = xx + zz$ &&

             $length = 1 + z$

Thus SUM_LENGTH has been transformed into

    SUM_LENGTH

    states:

    type: $\mathbb{R}^* \rightarrow \mathbb{R} \times \mathbb{P}$

    pre--$SUM\_LENGTH(,r\ell) \triangleq$

        True

    post-$SUM\_LENGTH(,r\ell,,\langle sum,length\rangle) \triangleq$

      if $r\ell = \langle\rangle$

      then $sum = 0$ &&

             $length = 0$

else $r\ell = \langle xx \rangle \| yy$ &

$\langle zz,z \rangle = SUM\_LENGTH(yy)$ &

$sum = xx + zz$ &

$length = 1 + z$

Thus SUM_LENGTH eventually emerges, following a consistent renaming for the human reader, as:

SUM_LENGTH

states:

type: $\mathbb{R}^* \rightarrow \mathbb{R} \times \mathbb{P}$

pre--$SUM\_LENGTH(,r\ell) \triangleq$

True

post-$SUM\_LENGTH(,r\ell,,\langle sum,length \rangle) \triangleq$

if $r\ell = \langle \rangle$

then $sum = 0$ &

$length = 0$

else $r\ell = \langle r\ell\_head \rangle \| r\ell\_tail$ &

$\langle sum\_tail,length\_tail \rangle = SUM\_LENGTH(r\ell\_tail)$ &

$sum = r\ell\_head + sum\_tail$ &

$length = 1 + length\_tail$

This transformed version of SUM_LENGTH can be used with the last given specification of $AVERAGE$ to produce a specification which hints at calculating the sum and length with only one visit to each element of the list.

Although the steps in the above sequence consist only of substitution it cannot yet be guaranteed that the result obtained is entirely equivalent to the original specification. This is because no mention has been made of checking pre-conditions during the substitution. Since the pre-conditions are all 'True', the result stands in this case.

The 'simplification' of the double 'if' version of post-SUM_LENGTH needs further justification. The form of the 'if' is:

if p

then t

else f

or in purely logical terms

$(p \wedge t) \vee (\neg p \wedge f)$

(This does not conflict with the definition given in Chapter 7 – see the exercises for that chapter.)

So taking two 'if' expressions together with the **same** test p

> if p
>
> then $t1$
>
> else $f1$ &
>
> if p
>
> then $t2$
>
> else $f2$

we obtain

$$(p \wedge t1) \vee (\neg p \wedge f1)$$
$$\wedge$$
$$(p \wedge t2) \vee (\neg p \wedge f2)$$

This has the form

$$(A \vee B)$$
$$\wedge$$
$$(C \vee D)$$

which, using the axioms of Boolean algebra as introduced in Chapter 7, expands to

$$(A \wedge (C \vee D)) \vee (B \wedge (C \vee D)) \qquad \text{--axioms 9,5}$$

and further to

$$(A \wedge C) \vee (A \wedge D) \vee (B \wedge C) \vee (B \wedge D) \qquad \text{--axiom 9}$$

By substituting for A, B, C, D, we obtain

$$(p \wedge t1 \wedge p \wedge t2) \vee (p \wedge t1 \wedge \neg p \wedge t2) \vee$$
$$(\neg p \wedge f1 \wedge p \wedge t2) \vee (\neg p \wedge f1 \wedge \neg p \wedge f2)$$

By using rules such as:

$X \wedge = X$	--axiom 12
$X \wedge Y = Y \wedge X$	--axiom 5
$X \wedge \neg X = \text{False}$	--axiom 8
$X \wedge \text{False} = \text{False}$	--axiom 11
$X \vee Y = Y \vee X$	--axiom 1
$X \vee \text{False} = X$	--axiom 3

this simplifies to

$$(p \wedge t1 \wedge t2) \vee (\neg p \wedge f1 \wedge f2)$$

Finally, by rewriting in 'if' form again, we have

> if p
>
> then $t1$ &
>
> $t2$
>
> else $f1$ &
>
> $f2$

which is the form which was used in the simplification of *SUM_LENGTH*.

This completes the proof of the transformation of the specification of *SUM_LENGTH*. One reason for showing this unfold/fold transformation is because it is a particularly useful one in practice. However an equally important reason is to show that transformations of mathematical specifications are **possible**. It is just not possible to manipulate English language specifications and (FORTRAN) programs in this way.

4.3   What comes next?

Once the process of initial specification, refinement and transformation have been mastered, the problem arises:

'When is a specification finished?' and

'What comes next?'

The answer depends on the programmer and the programming language involved. Computer programming languages fall into two main categories **declarative** and **imperative**. The declarative languages are much closer to specification languages than imperative languages but are not yet in common use. The main languages in use are all imperative in style so we need to develop the ability to code into imperative style given a specification. For the languages which are most often used commercially (FORTRAN, COBOL) this task is sufficiently difficult to be broken up into two stages. The extra stage involves the use of a program development language (PDL) which is the subject of the next chapter.

Exercises 4

1 Complete the specification of the operation SQ which squares every element of a list.

> SQ
>
> states:
>
> type: $\mathbb{Z}^* \to \mathbb{Z}^*$
>
> pre--$SQ(,z\ell) \triangleq$ True
>
> post-$SQ(,z\ell,,z\ell\,sq) \triangleq$
>
> $\cdots$

2 Rewrite the specification of the operation SUM given earlier in this chapter so that it finds the sum of an integer list.

> SUM
>
> states:
>
> type: $\mathbb{Z}^* \to \mathbb{Z}$
>
> pre--$SUM(,z\ell) \triangleq$ True
>
> post-$SUM(,z\ell,,sum) \triangleq$
>
> $\cdots$

3 Transform the specification of SUM_SQ below using the unfold–fold technique so that it becomes a simple recursive specification which does not rely on the operations SUM or SQ. (Note: the full list of squares formed by the operation SQ is not required in the final result so it will be necessary to remove the expression relating to it at some stage following the unfold substitution.)

> SUM_SQ
>
> states:
>
> type: $\mathbb{Z}^* \to \mathbb{Z}$
>
> pre--$SUM\_SQ(,z\ell) \triangleq$ True
>
> post-$SUM\_SQ(,z\ell,,ssq) \triangleq$
>
> $\quad z\ell sq = SQ(z\ell)$ &
>
> $\quad ssq = SUM(z\ell sq)$

5

PDL

We have been discussing the specification of programs and the refinement of specifications. These are clearly processes that precede the coding into the final programming language. On the assumption that the final programming language will be imperative rather than declarative, we introduce another stage in the programming methodology before the final coding. This stage will use a PDL –a Program Development Language (or Program Design Language).

In this chapter we compare imperative languages and declarative languages and show why the transition from a declarative specification to final (imperative) code should be performed in two stages (i.e. via PDL). We then introduce one possible PDL but point out that a PDL should be chosen to suit a particular team or project. PDL versions of all the specifications in earlier chapters are shown as examples. Chapter 6 deals with the translation of PDL into various real imperative languages.

5.1   Imperative and declarative languages

The great majority of programs in existence are written in **imperative** style. This is because FORTRAN, COBOL, PL/1, Algol, Pascal, Ada and assembly languages are all imperative languages.

In case this seems to include the whole world of programming languages, let us point out that the alternative to the imperative languages is the use of declarative programming languages which include **functional** languages (e.g. (Pure) Lisp, KRC, Hope, Miranda, FP) and the **logic** languages (e.g. Prolog).

In this context the word imperative is intended to convey the sense of a command or instruction to **do** something straight away. In comparison the word declarative has much less urgency and is only intended to communicate an idea. The declarative languages tend to associate output (as though it already existed) with input while imperative languages work on input only to generate output.

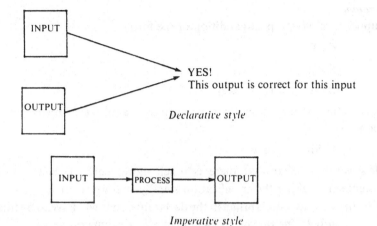

Declarative style

Imperative style

Declarative and Imperative styles

The specification style we have introduced actually has a decidedly declarative flavour. To demonstrate this and to see the potential gap between the declarative and imperative style consider the following examples.

Example 1

If we have a post-condition specification of the form

$$x' = y + 1$$

then the imperative version is

ASSIGN the value $y + 1$ to x

or

$$x \leftarrow y + 1$$

or

$$x := y + 1$$

or however else it may be written. In this case the gap between declarative and imperative is minimal.

Example 2

If we have a post-condition specification of the form

$$y = x' + 1$$

then we can 'make x' the subject of the equation' giving

$$x' = y - 1$$

and the imperative assignment follows quite easily.

Example 3

Suppose we have a post-condition of the form

$$x' \in X \wedge$$

$$x' > y \wedge$$

$$((z \in X \wedge z > y) \Rightarrow x' \leqslant z)$$

This is still a specification of just one value (x') and so the imperative style should still be

ASSIGN ? to x

However it is clear that there is much more required than a simple assignment. Taking the specification step-by-step we see that

    (i) $x' \in X$ as a **declaration** in the declarative style will have to be turned into an **instruction** to **choose** an x in the imperative style.

    (ii) $x' > y$ in the declarative style **announces** a property of x. In the imperative style it becomes a **test** which can be applied to candidates chosen in (i). Candidates can be rejected if they fail the test.

    (iii) $((z \in X \wedge z > y) \Rightarrow x' \leqslant z)$ is in fact a declaration that x' is the smallest of all the elements of X that are greater than y. Imperatively speaking, the smallest of all the candidates which passed the test in (ii) has to be chosen.

Thus an imperative solution to the specified problem could be in three steps as follows

    (i) Make available all the elements x of X

    (ii) Reject all those members of X which are not greater than y

    (iii) Find the smallest of the remainder

In practice, experienced programmers would tend to code the following

    (i) Organise the elements of X into a sequence

$$x[1], x[2], x[3], \ldots, x[n]$$

    (ii) Find the first i such that $x[i] > y$

    (iii) Continue searching through the $x[i]$ to discover any elements that are greater than y but less than the current minimum.

In the PDL (which is to be defined later) this may be expressed as follows

```
i ← 1
while  x[i] ≤ y
do     i ← i + 1
od
   p ← i
```

```
while  i < n
do
       if     x[i] > y
       then
              if     x[i] < x[p]
              then   p ← i
              fi

       fi
od
x ← x[p]
```

(Note: this code takes no account of the possibility that there may be no value x in X that satisfies the specification.)

5.2   Why a PDL?

We have shown that when a declarative specification has to be coded imperatively then some parts may be trivial and some parts much harder. So there is still some program design to be done after the specification is finished. But why use a PDL, why not use the final coding language direct?

This is a difficult question to answer in general. We may have a specification which, although declarative, is still close to the imperative style (like $x' = y + 1$) and we may be able to program in a modern high-level imperative language (like Pascal). In this case the remaining coding task is relatively straightforward. At the opposite extreme we may be faced with a decidedly declarative specification (not simply $x' = y + 1$) and having to code in assembly language. In this case the coding task is sufficiently difficult for a multistage solution not only to be attractive but necessary.

The circumstances under which the task changes from being straightforward and finished in one step to being considered hard and to require two or more steps depends on the individual but the multistage solution is most often required.

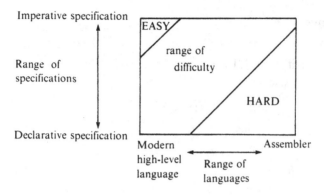

The difficulty of producing final code from a specification

Thus we have argued that PDL is necessary because the difficulty of the problem demands an intermediate stage. But there is another completely different reason for using a PDL.

If a programming team's output is always in one language (FORTRAN, for example) then there is a tendency for team members to think and communicate in that language. So another reason for using a PDL is to combat the stultifying effect of **thinking** in the final coding language. The possibility of choosing a PDL (and including in it more advanced or modern features dreamt of but not available locally) upgrades the thinking language and provides better facilities for solving problems.

5.3   The PDL stage

As soon as we have decided to break the specification to final code into two distinct stages, the question arises as to what is to be done in each stage.

The basic idea of the PDL stage is to capture in full the imperative solution of the problem without being weighed down by the restrictions or lack of expressive power of the intended final computer programming language.

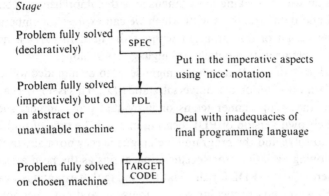

Stage

Problem fully solved (declaratively) — SPEC

Put in the imperative aspects using 'nice' notation

Problem fully solved (imperatively) but on an abstract or unavailable machine — PDL

Deal with inadequacies of final programming language

Problem fully solved on chosen machine — TARGET CODE

A three-stage solution

The sort of restrictions that occur in computer programming languages which interfere with the development of the solution to a problem are:

> given data structure concepts like 'array of' and 'set of', we find that although we can have arrays of sets we cannot have sets of arrays (this is true of Pascal).

> recursion as a control structure may be absent (this is true of FORTRAN).

By lack of expressive power we mean

> cumbersome notation, e.g.

$$pointer\uparrow.element := pointer\uparrow.element + 1$$

which is an inelegant piece of Pascal.

> insufficient variety of control structures and/or data structures, e.g. while . . . do and records missing from FORTRAN.

In the search for our PDL we are looking for an ALGOrithmic Language in the sense meant by the designers of ALGOL. However ALGOL itself is not satisfactory because, while it has adequate control structures, it is badly deficient in data structures.

As far as data structures are concerned we largely ignore at the PDL level the details of implementation. The question of whether a list will finally appear as a sequential file, a vector or a collection of records with pointer fields is secondary to the main task of establishing the algorithm. It is the manipulative notation for creating, initialising, accessing and deleting data structures which is important.

To sum up we are looking for a language with comprehensive control structures and data structures with which we can express the imperative algorithmic design of our program without the need to carry a heavy burden of implementation details or language restrictions.

The PDL description that follows might seem to be intended to be the basis of a formal definition of a universal, static PDL. This is not the case. It is intended that programmer teams or individual programmers should develop their own version of PDL bearing in mind the type of problems they have to solve and the programming language they normally use and even developing variations for specific applications as the need arises.

Thus there is no one PDL for all situations and to that extent it is a vague concept. However any particular version in use is (and must be) precise.

5.4   The description of a PDL

A PDL program consists of a function definition with subsidiary function definitions as required.

5.4.1   Function definition

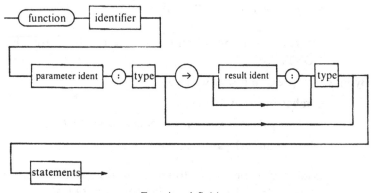

Function definition

Notes

1. This definition apparently restricts all functions to one parameter. Strictly this is true. However several 'parameters' can be assembled into a record and the record passed as a single parameter. The access to each parameter is then a little clumsy leading to a shorthand – see the example involving *dist_from_origin* below.

2. If 'result ident' is omitted it is assumed to be the same as the function identifier.

3. If there is no result, the function is more conveniently called a procedure.

4. Function, parameter and result identifiers are written in lower case.

5.4.2   Statement

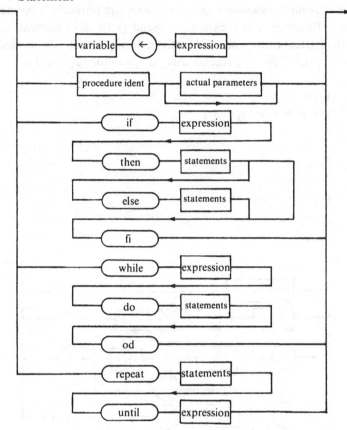

Statement

Notes

1. The assignment statement uses ←.
2. A counting loop 'for...do' is not considered necessary.
3. The syntax rules are drawn to suggest a style of layout.
4. The keywords 'fi' and 'od' are used to delimit the end of 'statements' in an unambiguous way that does not depend on layout. Some other languages use 'begin...end' or {...} to achieve this.

5.4.3   Statements

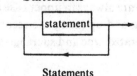

Statements

Notes

1. The individual statements in the sequence are normally separated by 'newline'. However it is occasionally useful (with short statements and when the PDL is being discussed mathematically, e.g. during verification) to separate individual statements using a semicolon (e.g. *S1;S2*).

5.4.4 Type

The primitive types are

$\mathbb{R}$

$\mathbb{Z}$

$\mathbb{N}$

$\mathbb{P}$

$\mathbb{B}$

Char

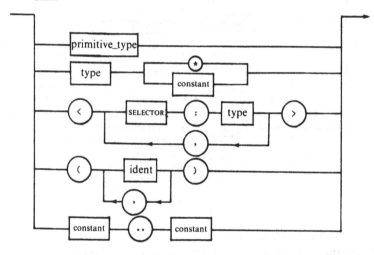

Type

Notes

1. *T** declares a list of type *T* of unrestricted length.

   T^n declares a list of fixed length *n*.

2. $\langle S1:T1,S2:T2,\dots,Sn:Tn \rangle$ declares a record of mixed types *T1,T2,...,Tn* with field names *S1,S2,...,Sn*. The field names are always in upper case and are used as selector functions when accessing and updating the record.

3. The last two type options are called **enumerated** type and **subrange** type respectively.

5.4.5   Variable

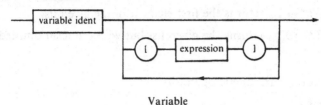

Variable

Notes

1. If a variable is not of primitive type then at the outermost level it will be either a list type or a record type.

(i) List type (T^* or T'')

If the number of elements of a list v is known to be n then $v[1],v[2],\ldots,v[n]$ can be used otherwise use $head(v),tail(v)$.

(ii) Record type

$$\langle S1:T1,S2:T2,\ldots,Sn:Tn\rangle$$

This type defines selector functions $S1(\ ),S2(\ ),\ldots,Sn(\ )$ with result types $T1,T2,\ldots,Tn$ and these functions are used to select the components of the record both for access and update, e.g.

$v:\langle I:\mathbb{Z},R:\mathbb{R},B:\mathbb{B}\rangle$

$I(v)\leftarrow I(v)+1$

if $B(v)$

then $R(v)\leftarrow 1.0$

fi

2. Variable identifiers are written in lower case.

5.4.6   Expressions

An expression is formed from constants, variables, and function calls separated by operators in the usual way.

Constants

    $\langle\ \rangle$ the empty list

    $\langle C1,C2,\ldots,Cn\rangle$ a list if all the Ci are of the same type,
                                     a record otherwise

    $1,+12,-123$

    $1.1,+1.2,-1.23$

    True, False

    $'a','1'$, etc.

Built-in functions

$head: T^* \to T$ returns the first element of the given list

$tail: T^* \to T^*$ returns the given list but with the head omitted

Operators

The normal arithmetic operators

$+ \ - \ * \ /$

The relational operators

$= \ \neq \ < \ > \ \leqslant \ \geqslant$

The append or concatenate operator

$\|$

this produces a list containing all the elements of the first list followed by all the elements of the second list, e.g.

$\langle 1,2 \rangle \| \langle 3,4 \rangle = \langle 1,2,3,4 \rangle$

This completes the basic description of the PDL. Before any more examples are given some more background to the choice of PDL data structures is given.

5.5   PDL data types – list and record

The data types to be used in specifications, PDL and final code are summarised below.

Data Types Available in Specifications, PDL and Final Code

Specification Data Types	PDL Data Types	Final Code Data Types (some or all of...)
Set	List	Array
List	Record	Record
Tuple $- - - \longrightarrow$	Enumerated $- - - \longrightarrow$	Set
Union	Subrange	Pointer
Enumerated		File
Subrange		Union/Variant
		Enumerated
		Subrange
		$\vdots$

Since the data types available at each stage are different we must have a plan for expressing the data structures of the previous stage in the types available in the current stage. We show here how to represent specification data types in PDL data structures. It is left to Chapter 6 to express PDL data types in final code data structures.

5.6 Representing specification data types in PDL

Lists in specifications remain lists in PDL. Tuples in specifications become records in PDL in an obvious way. The only data types which change significantly are sets and unions.

Sets

The chief characteristic of a set of items in comparison to a list of items is that the elements are not ordered in any way in the set. This lack of order is impossible to maintain in reality once the items are stored on a conventional computer. Hence we choose this point to introduce order into the set and this actually helps with the concept of producing an imperative solution. There are two possible representations of a set in PDL one using the lists and the other using records.

First method

If the set of potential members is known (and 'small') then the set can be modelled by a record with Boolean fields. For example

$colourmix : \mathscr{P}(\{red, orange, yellow, green, blue, indigo, violet\})$

$colourmix = \{red, green, blue\}$

can be represented by

$colourmix : \langle RED : \mathbb{B}, ORANGE : \mathbb{B}, \ldots, VIOLET : \mathbb{B} \rangle$

$colourmix \leftarrow \langle \text{True,False,False,True,True,False,False} \rangle$

Second method

This is a universal method but only used when the first method cannot be used. The idea is simply to store the elements belonging to the set in a list.

Thus for example

$telnos : \mathscr{P}(PosInt)$

$telnos = \{377, 418, 297\}$

becomes

$telnos : PosInt^*$

$telnos \leftarrow \langle 377, 418, 297 \rangle$

PDL data representation is chosen on the basis of notational convenience rather than to minimise store occupancy or access time for example. These kinds of consideration are applied at the next stage in deciding whether a list should be represented as an external file, or internally as an array or a collection of records linked by pointers in the final code.

Unions

In general union data type is specified by

$$T::T_1 \cup T_2 \cup \ldots \cup T_n$$

This is represented in PDL by a record with $n+1$ fields. The first field has any type which has n values (often $\mathbb{B}$ for $n=2$) and it is used as the union selector. The other n fields are one for each type in the union (they are assumed to be distinct types). Thus if we have

$$U\_Enum = (U_1, U_2, \ldots, U_n)$$
$$u: \langle\ S:U\_Enum\ ,\ S_1:T_2, \ldots, S_n:T_n\ \rangle$$

then at any one time we are only interested in one field S_i of type T_i when the field S contains U_i. Thus we write assignments like

$$u \leftarrow \langle\ U_1, t_{1}, \ldots, \rangle$$
$$u \leftarrow \langle\ U_2, t_2 \ldots, \rangle$$
$$\vdots$$
$$u \leftarrow \langle\ U_n, \ldots, t_n \rangle$$

with adjacent commas showing that we are not interested in the values of most of the fields and $t_i \in T_i$ for each $i \in 1 .. n$. (In certain languages it is possible to overlay the storage areas occupied by the last n fields so that the 'wasted' space is minimised.)

It is quite common for the types T_i to be themselves records or other structured types as in the example below.

Example

$$Expression::Number \cup$$
$$(Expression \times BinaryOp \times Expression) \cup$$
$$(UnaryOp \times Expression)$$

is a data type with which we could store expressions. For example, $-3+2*5$ would be held as

$$\langle \langle -3 \rangle, +, \langle 2, *, 5 \rangle \rangle$$

The corresponding type in PDL might be

$Bin\_Exp = \langle\ OPND1 : Expression\ ,\ BINOP : BinaryOp\ ,$
$\qquad\qquad\qquad\qquad\qquad OPND2 : Expression\ \rangle$

$Un\_Exp = \langle\ OP : UnaryOp\ ,\ OPND : Expression\ \rangle$

$Expression = \langle\ EXPTYPE : (constant, binexp, unexp),$
$CONST\ EXP : Number\ ,\ BINEXP : Bin\_Exp\ ,\ UNEXP : Un\_exp\ \rangle$

and we might write

$e, f, g, h, i, j : Expression$

$\qquad\qquad e \leftarrow \langle constant, 3,, \rangle$

$\qquad\qquad f \leftarrow \langle constant, 2,, \rangle$

$\qquad\qquad g \leftarrow \langle constant, 5,, \rangle$

$\qquad\qquad h \leftarrow \langle unexp,,, \langle -, e \rangle \rangle$

$\qquad\qquad i \leftarrow \langle binexp,, \langle f, *, g \rangle, \rangle$

$\qquad\qquad j \leftarrow \langle binexp,, \langle h, +, i \rangle, \rangle$

5.7 Examples

These are all taken from specifications given in earlier chapters

(a) function *pos_square_root*

$d : Number \rightarrow psr : Number$

$psr \leftarrow sqrt(d)$

(b) function *dist_from_origin*

$rp : \langle X : \mathbb{R}, Y : \mathbb{R} \rangle \rightarrow dfo : \mathbb{R}$

$dfo \leftarrow pos\_square\_root(sq(X(rp)) + sq(Y(rp)))$

In this case the parameter *rp* is a record and a shorthand which makes references to the individual fields more direct is as follows

function *dist_from_origin*

$x : \mathbb{R}, y : \mathbb{R} \rightarrow dfo : \mathbb{R}$

$dfo \leftarrow pos\_square\_root(sq(x) + sq(y))$

(c) function *average*

$\ell : \mathbb{R}^* \rightarrow a : \mathbb{R}$

$a \leftarrow sum(\ell) / length(\ell)$

where the functions *sum* and *length* are as follows

function *sum*

$\ell:\mathbb{R}^* \to s:\mathbb{R}$

if $\ell=\langle\rangle$

then $s \leftarrow 0$

else $s \leftarrow head(\ell) + sum(tail(\ell))$

fi

function *length*

$\ell:\mathbb{R}^* \to len:\mathbb{P}$

if $\ell=\langle\rangle$

then $len \leftarrow 0$

else $len \leftarrow 1 + length(tail(\ell))$

fi

(d) function *sumlength*

$\ell:\mathbb{R}^* \to s\ell:\langle S:r,L:\mathbb{P}\rangle$

if $\ell=\langle\rangle$

then $s\ell \leftarrow \langle 0,0\rangle$

else $s\ell\_t\ell \leftarrow sumlength(tail(\ell))$

          $S(s\ell) \leftarrow head(\ell) + S(s\ell\_t\ell)$

          $L(s\ell) \leftarrow 1 \quad\quad + L(s\ell\_t\ell)$

fi

(e) function *average*   (a different definition)

$\ell:\mathbb{R}^* \to a:\mathbb{R}$

$s\ell \leftarrow sumlength(\ell)$

$a \leftarrow S(s\ell)/L(s\ell)$

5.8   Other PDL issues

If your PDL is (or is very like) a high-level language for which you have (or have access to) an implementation, then this implementation can be useful in testing before further work on producing the final code is begun.

If your PDL is (or can be made) sufficiently precise then it is possible to write a translator to convert your PDL programs into final code automatically. This may seem a very attractive possibility (cf. other high-level language systems) but of course you do have to be sure that you have got your PDL right before a lot of effort is expended in producing the translator. A notable example of a partial automation is the RATFOR preprocessor for FORTRAN [21] which deals only with control structures.

5.9 PDL summary

A specification produces a declarative solution to the problem. The PDL program produces the first complete imperative solution but is not necessarily executable. The final code produces an imperative solution executable in the chosen language on the chosen machine.

The freedom to choose a PDL suitable to a particular environment combats the stultifying effect of **thinking** in the final coding language.

A possible drawback is that the inclusion of too many advanced features in the PDL may make the translation to final code uncomfortably hard.

Exercises 5

1 Write PDL versions of the operations $MAXL, ALL\_SAME$ which you specified in your answers to questions 2.2 and 2.3.

2 Decide how you wish to represent the sets involved and write PDL versions of the operations $MAXS, CONCATS$ which you specified in your answers to questions 2.1 and 2.4.

3 Write PDL versions of the operations SQ, SUM which you specified in your answers to questions 4.1, 4.2.

4 Write two PDL versions of SUM_SQ, one direct from the specification given in question 4.3 and one from the transformed version you obtained in your answer to the same question.

6
Code generation

In this chapter we address the issues of coding from a PDL into various **real** imperative programming languages. The PDL stage described in the previous chapter contains a complete (imperative) solution to the original problem so that the coding can now be finished without reference to the original problem. The intention in this chapter is to show that the final code generation can be accomplished using coding templates. Coding templates are shown for a variety of programming languages in common use.

6.1   Templates

Coding templates are stylised translations of each feature of a PDL. The methodical application of the templates to the PDL solution will yield the final code.

For any particular final coding language, a set of (coding) templates is created to translate each feature of the PDL in use. This means for example that every 'if' statement in the PDL is translated in the same way. Each time the 'if' statement is met it is coded using the same pattern or **template**. The templates are different for each different final coding language. They are chosen more for generality than for elegance or efficiency. There may well be features of a final coding language that are not used in any template. In this methodology these features will **never** be used. This may seem an unacceptable loss at first sight. However the experience of the authors is that the features which are not used in templates are those which are less widely used anyway or not universally supported or inconsistently supported and so their omission leads to more portable programs.

PDL is closely related to the previous stage of the programming process for two reasons. Firstly the use of a PDL stage between specification and final code makes the gap from stage to stage smaller. Secondly the programmer is not encouraged (or allowed!) to be inventive with the final code. This close relation between stages has the advantage that **testing** or **debugging** can be done while reading a higher level version than the final code. The extra level in the programming process can be viewed as extra documentation which is written **before** the final code!

The problem of producing coding templates for real languages can conveniently be broken down into two parts – the translation of the control structures and the translation of the data structures. Substantial parts of the problem can be quite easy requiring relatively simple templates. However there are usually difficulties with both parts of the problem. An example of a difficult control structure problem is that of translating a recursive PDL solution into a language with no provision for recursion (e.g. FORTRAN). An example of an awkward data structure problem is the modelling of variable length lists (stored in memory) in a language which has no built in dynamic storage allocation (e.g. FORTRAN again). There is of course an advantage in solving these harder coding problems once and for all. It should save programmer time in the long run.

The languages for which templates are given are:

Pascal (Section 6.2)

FORTRAN (Section 6.3)

COBOL (Section 6.4)

A Minicomputer Assembly Language (Section 6.5)

A Microprocessor Assembly Language (Section 6.6)

The sections for each language are written in the same format as far as possible. On a first reading it is suggested that only the section on Pascal is read thoroughly and the others read as required.

None of the template sets given below is complete and the templates that are given are described informally. This is sufficient to describe the technique and demonstrate its effectiveness with a wide variety of final coding languages. If the templates were given in full then what would follow would be the description of five complete compilers. The description would have to be formal to be precise and hence written in some specification language. Since the PDL is not a static language, this level of detail is not appropriate.

6.2 Templates for Pascal

The first real language considered is Pascal. Since it is a high level language and relatively modern compared with FORTRAN and COBOL the templates are the easiest to describe.

6.2.1   Templates for control structures in Pascal

Assignment statement

Taking statements first, we have first of all the assignment statement.

  variable ← expression

has the template translation

  template_code_for_variable:= template_code_for_expression

The only information this actually conveys is that the PDL assignment symbol (←) must be changed to the Pascal assignment symbol (:=). Any other changes that are made are because of some other template. This interdependence of templates is inevitable and appears commonly in what follows. The principal difficulty in applying templates is not that they are individually difficult, but that the applications are nested – sometimes quite deeply.

Procedure call

The only change required is the template translation of the actual parameters which are expressions. If a parameter is a simple variable, a constant number or a constant character or Boolean, then no change at all will be needed.

Statement sequence

Pascal uses semicolon (;) as a statement separator so the PDL statement sequence

  Statement_1

  Statement_2

  ⋮

  Statement_n

has the template translation

  template_code_for_Statement_1 ;

  template_code_for_Statement_2 ;

  ⋮

  template_code_for_Statement_n

If statement

      if   *expression*

      then   *statements_T*

      else   *statements_F*

      fi

has the template translation

      if   *template_code_for_expression*

      then begin

            template_code_for_statements_T

      end

      else begin

            template_code_for_statements_F

      end

Notes

1. In the case where *statements_T* or *statements_F* are not sequences but single *statements*, the corresponding **begin** and **end** can usually be omitted – but see note 2.

2. The **else** portion of the Pascal template is omitted whenever the PDL 'else' portion is not present. However in situations where a compound statement comprises **if** statements both with and without **else** parts, the **begin** and **end** should never be omitted (cf. note 1). This will avoid any ambiguity in the Pascal.

While statement

      while *expression*

      do   *statements*

      od

has the template translation

      while *template_code_for_expression*

      do begin

            template_code_for_statements

      end

Repeat statement

    repeat *statements*

    until   *expression*

has the template translation

    repeat *template_code_for_statements*

    until   *template_code_for_expression*

Example

This example demonstrates the *if* statement, *while* statement, *repeat* statement and *statement-sequence* templates used in combination. The code could be said to multiply two integers x and y producing a result in z. However the PDL to final code stage should not have need to refer to the original problem but merely be a methodical application of the coding templates to the PDL.

    if $y \geqslant 0$

    then $z \leftarrow 0$

          while $y > 0$

          do $z \leftarrow z + x$

               $y \leftarrow y - 1$

          od

    else $z \leftarrow 0$

          repeat $z \leftarrow z - x$

               $y \leftarrow y + 1$

          until $y = 0$

    fi

has the template translation

    if $y \geqslant 0$

    then begin

        z := 0;

        while y > 0

        do begin

            z := z + x;

            y := y - 1

        end

    end

```
    else begin
          z:= 0;
          repeat z:= z − x;
                  y:= y + 1
          until   y = 0
    end
```

Function definition

The template here is superficial in simple cases. Consider a function f with parameter p and result r.

```
function  f
p:type_p → r:type_r
statements
```

has the template translation

```
function   f(p:type_p):type_r;
begin
          template_code_for_statements_
          _with_assignment_to_r_changed_to_
          _assignment_to_f
end
```

For example

```
function letter
c:Char → b:𝔹
b ← ('a' ⩽ c) ∧ (c ⩽ 'z')
```

has the template translation

```
function letter(c:char):boolean;
begin
          letter:= ('a' <= c) and (c <= 'z')
end
```

If the shorthand technique for multiple parameters is being used in the PDL then it should be used in the Pascal too. However Pascal rules restrict the type of a function result to be a primitive data type or a pointer to a data type. Perhaps the easiest approach when faced with this restriction is to convert a function with a result which has (complicated) data type T to a procedure with an extra *variable* parameter of type T. Thus

$r \leftarrow f(p)$

changes to

f(p,r)

where the second parameter is variable and can be the destination of an assignment statement. However, if the function call is embedded in an expression, then

$r \leftarrow \ldots f(p) \ldots$

has to be treated as thought it read as

f(p,r1)

$r \leftarrow \ldots r1 \ldots$

If the result is a record then it may be preferable to define the procedure to have a variable parameter for each component of the record as in the example below. The function *divmod* divides its first parameter by its second parameter and produces as a result a record containing both the quotient and the remainder.

function *divmod*

$p:\langle DIVIDEND:\mathbb{P},DIVISOR:\mathbb{N}\rangle \rightarrow$

$$r:\langle QUOTIENT:\mathbb{P},REMAINDER:\mathbb{P}\rangle$$

$QUOTIENT(r) \leftarrow DIVIDEND(p)$ div $DIVISOR(p)$

$REMAINDER(r) \leftarrow DIVIDEND(p)$ mod $DIVISOR(p)$

has the template translation

type natural_no $= 1 \ldots$ maxint;

pos_int $= 0 \ldots$ maxint;

procedure divmod (dividend:pos_int;divisor:natural_no;

var quotient,remainder:pos_int);

begin

quotient:= dividend **div** divisor;

remainder:= dividend **mod** divisor

end

6.2.2 Templates for data structures in Pascal

Templates for primitive data types in Pascal

$\mathbb{R}$ is modelled by the Pascal type 'real' to a precision which varies from machine to machine and which introduces problems which only a full course in numerical analysis can solve.

$\mathbb{Z}$ is modelled by the Pascal type 'integer' within the range '$-$maxint' to '$+$maxint' where 'maxint' is fixed by each implementation. $\mathbb{P}$ can be modelled by the Pascal subrange type '0..maxint'. $\mathbb{N}$ can be modelled by the Pascal subrange type 1..maxint.

$\mathbb{B}$ is modelled by the Pascal type 'boolean'.

The PDL type 'Char' is the same as the Pascal type 'char'.

Enumerated types and subrange types are available in Pascal and so cause no problem.

Templates for compound data structures in Pascal

We need to model lists and records (including lists of lists, lists of records, records containing lists and records, etc.) both as internal data structures (stored in memory) and as external data structures (stored in files). The choice of internal or external data structures is made when the PDL is complete and before template translation begins.

When modelling lists as internal data structures we anticipate using vectors if the list is of fixed length and using records chained together with pointers for variable length lists. However this does depend on the data structures available in the final coding language and its storage management system. The most obvious and common use of lists as external data structures is for input and output for which sequential files are often used.

Internal data structures

List of fixed length of type T

	Declaration	Use
PDL	$v:T^n$	$v[i]$
Pascal	**var** v:**array**[1..n] **of** T	v[i]

Provided 'n' is not too large for a particular implementation this is the obvious template to choose. The variable reference $v[i]$ in the PDL is unchanged in the Pascal except for the template changes to the expression i. Pascal allows whole array operations so that $vcopy \leftarrow v$ can be translated as 'vcopy:= v' but the assignment of a constant array must be broken down into assignment of individual components. Thus

$$v \leftarrow \langle E1,E2,\ldots,En\rangle$$

has the template translation

v[1]:= E1;

v[2]:= E2;

$\vdots$

v[n]:= En

List of variable length of type T

	Declaration	Use
PDL	$v:T^*$	$head(v)$ $tail(v)$
Pascal	**type** Tlist = ↑domino; domino = **record** head:T; tail:Tlist **end**; **var** v:Tlist;	v↑.head v↑.tail

The PDL can require a list to be constructed from certain given elements, e.g.

$$\langle E1,E2,\ldots,En\rangle$$

or it can require a list to be constructed using the concatenation operator (‖). In both cases the construction of a new list requires the Pascal built-in function *new* to be used to allocate space for the new list. The PDL

$$\langle E1,E2,\ldots,En\rangle$$

has the template translation

rest:= nil; new(p); p↑.head:= En; p↑.tail:= rest;

$\vdots$

rest:= p;   new(p); p↑.head:= E2; p↑.tail:= rest;

rest:= p;   new(p); p↑.head:= E1; p↑.tail:= rest

where 'p' and 'rest' are of type 'Tlist' when the 'Ei' are of type 'T'.

Strictly the concatenation of two lists requires copying from both lists. However cases like

$$\langle c \rangle \| v$$

$$v \leftarrow v \| w$$

where the initial value of the first list involved is no longer required after the concatenation operation ($\langle c \rangle$ in the first case, v in the second) happen so often that the alternative of extending rather than copying the first list is worthwhile. If the lists are modelled by a record for each element with a pointer field to the next record then the second list in a concatenation need never be copied but just pointed to.

The function 'concatenate' given below copies the elements of the list supplied as the first argument and creates the 'join' by pointing to the list supplied as the second parameter.

```
function concatenate(v1,v2:Tlist):Tlist;
var p:Tlist;
begin
        if      v1 = nil
        then    concatenate := v2
        else begin
                new(p);
                p↑.head := v1↑.head;
                p↑.tail := concatenate(v1↑.tail,v2);
                concatenate := p
            end
        end
```

Thus the PDL

$$v \| w$$

has the template translation

```
concatenate(v,w)
```

Record

	Declaration	Use
PDL	$v:\langle S1:T1, S2:T2,\ldots,Sn:Tn \rangle$	$S1(v)$ $S2(v)$, etc.

Pascal	**var** v:**record**
	      S1:T1;
	      S2:T2;
	      $\vdots$
	      Sn:Tn
	end
		v.S1
		v.S2, etc.

External data structures

All lists of fixed or variable length are modelled in the same way. External records are rare but can be modelled if required by separate external data structures for each component in the record.

List of type T

	Declaration	*Use*
PDL	$v:T*$	$v[i]$, *head*(v), *tail*(v)
Pascal	v:**file of** T;	?

Random access files are not available in standard Pascal so there is no direct translation of the PDL list access style $v[i]$. Sequential files are available and these can be used to model **input** lists and **output** lists which are scanned element-by-element once only from the beginning. Thus we have the following translations

PDL	Pascal
newinput $\leftarrow$ *head*(v) $v \leftarrow$ *tail*(v)	read(v,newinput)
$v \leftarrow v \parallel \langle newoutput \rangle$	write(v,newoutput)

Example

$$\ell \leftarrow \langle \rangle$$
$$i \leftarrow 1$$

while $i \leqslant 10$
do $h \leftarrow head(input)$
        $input \leftarrow tail(input)$
        $\ell \leftarrow \langle h \rangle \parallel \ell$
        $i \leftarrow i + 1$
od
$p \leftarrow \ell$
while $p \neq \langle \rangle$
do $output \leftarrow output \parallel head(p)$
        $p \leftarrow tail(p)$
od

has the template translation

$\ell := $ **nil**;
i := 1;
while i <= 10
do begin
        read(input,h);
        new(p);
        p↑.head := h;
        p↑.tail := ℓ;
        $\ell := $ p;
        i := i + 1
end;
p := ℓ;
while p < > **nil**
do begin
        write(output,p↑.head);
        p := p↑.tail
end

6.3   Templates for FORTRAN

FORTRAN is the oldest high level language still in common use.
The restrictions of FORTRAN that have to be overcome in producing a set

of coding templates are
- (i) Control flow is by branching to numerically labelled statements
- (ii) The only data type constructor is 'ARRAY'
- (iii) Storage is statically allocated – hence no run-time storage allocation and no recursion

However the language is still vigorously supported with the latest generally available version being referred to as FORTRAN77 which was standardised in 1978. This version is notable for the 'block-if' statement which brought the keyword 'THEN' into the FORTRAN language for the first time. However the counting loop

DO *label i = start,stop,step*

$\vdots$

label CONTINUE

remains the only specific repetition construct.

6.3.1   Templates for control structures in FORTRAN

Assignment statement

variable ← expression

has the template translation

variable = expression

This template reveals that FORTRAN uses the 'equals' symbol for 'assignment'. This has attracted much criticism based on the frequent appearance of statements such as

I = I + 1

in FORTRAN programs. If this is read as an *equation* (the only reading of '=' known to mathematicians) then we have for example

$2+2$

$=2+(1+1)$

$=2+1$ (using $i=i+1$)

$=2$ (using $i=i+1$)

We deduce that $2+2=2$ which is of course nonsense. So the choice of '=' as the assignment symbol is unfortunate to say the least.

Procedure call
The call of a procedure p with parameters $p1, p2,\ldots,pn$

$p(p1,p2,\ldots,pn)$

has the template translation

    CALL P(P1,P2,…,PN)

Note: FORTRAN is commonly written all in upper case.

Statement sequence

No change is required. FORTRAN requires statements in a statement sequence to be on separate lines. FORTRAN is defined to be written on 80-column cards or card-images. This leads to format restrictions. Numeric labels, if present, occupy the first five columns. A single statement is written in columns 7 to 72 and continued onto the next card if necessary. In this case column six is used as a continuation marker. This folding of lines has produced a tendency in FORTRAN programmers to keep to the left hand margin and avoid indentation. The templates given below for conditional and repetitive control structures encourage indentation as a mechanism to aid reading comprehension.

If statement

Consider the full 'if' statement with 'else'.

    if   *expression*

    then   *statements_T*

    else   *statements_F*

    fi

Using 'pre-FORTRAN77' FORTRAN, where control flow has to be achieved using the GOTO statement, the template translation is

    L0   IF(.NOT.(*expression*))GOTO *L1*

               template_code_for_statements_T

        GOTO *L2*

    L1   CONTINUE

               template_code_for_statements_F

    L2   CONTINUE

$L0$, $L1$, $L2$ are three FORTRAN labels which have to be numeric. It is convenient to choose $L0 = 10*n$ for some $n \in \mathbb{N}$, $L1 = L0 + 1$, and $L2 = L0 + 2$. $L0$ is not intended to be the destination of any 'GOTO' statement. It is there to mark the beginning of an 'if' statement for the benefit of the human reader.

The 'empty-else' form of the statement

    if   *expression*

    then *statements*

    fi

has the template translation

    L0   IF(.NOT.(*expression*))GOTO *L1*

                template_code_for_statements

    L1   CONTINUE

Example

    $m \leftarrow x$

    if $m < 0$

    then $m \leftarrow 0$

    else

        if $m > 15$

        then $m \leftarrow 15$

        fi

    fi

has the template translation

    M = X

  10   IF(.NOT.(M.LT.0))GOTO 11

          M = 0

          GOTO 12

  11   CONTINUE

  20   IF(.NOT.(M.GT.15))GOTO 21

            M = 15

  21   CONTINUE

  12   CONTINUE

The line with label 10 could be rewritten as

  10   IF(M.GE.0)GOTO 11

where the 'not-less-than' relation has been replaced by 'greater-than-or-equal' relation. This is to be resisted if possible so that the original relation in the PDL is present in the final code. Later it will be seen that the templates for repetition also use the 'NOT' explicitly and so the consistency makes the templates easier to use.

FORTRAN77 has the so-called 'block-if' statement which has the form

        IF(*expression*)THEN
                statements
        ELSE
                statements
        ENDIF

and the 'empty-else' form

        IF(*expression*)THEN
                statements
        ENDIF

These can be used as the template translation of the PDL 'if' statement if available. This will avoid the introduction of numeric labels and GOTO statements for the 'if' statement but they will still be needed in the repetition templates (see below).

While statement

        while   *expression*
        do   *statements*
        od

has the template translation

        L0   IF(.NOT.(*expression*))GOTO *L1*
                        template_code_for_statements
                GOTO *L0*
        L1   CONTINUE

Repeat statement

        repeat *statements*
        until *expression*

has the template translation

        L0   CONTINUE
                        template_code_for_statements
                IF(.NOT.(*expression*))GOTO *L0*

Example

This example demonstrates the *if* statement, *while* statement, *repeat* statement and *statement sequence* templates used in combination.

    if $y \geqslant 0$
    then $z \leftarrow 0$
            while $y > 0$
            do $z \leftarrow z + x$
                   $y \leftarrow y - 1$
            od
    else $z \leftarrow 0$
            repeat $z \leftarrow z - x$
                   $y \leftarrow y + 1$
            until $y = 0$
    fi

has the template translation

    10   IF(.NOT.(Y.GE.0))GOTO 11
                Z=0
    20   IF(.NOT.(Y.GT.0))GOTO 21
                    Z=Z+X
                    Y=Y-1
                    GOTO 20
    21   CONTINUE
                GOTO 12
    11   CONTINUE
                Z=0
    30   CONTINUE
                    Z=Z-X
                    Y=Y+1
                    IF(.NOT.(Y.EQ.0))GOTO 30
    12   CONTINUE

Note

FORTRAN programmers would probably like to see a counting loop in the PDL which would have as its template translation the FORTRAN

'DO' loop. It is the experience of the authors that the 'DO' loop is a rich source of incompatibility and errors [7]. For this reason we would encourage counting loops built out of sequencing and pre-check loops of the form below for which the templates already supplied are appropriate.

$$i \leftarrow start$$

while $i \leqslant stop$

do

$$\vdots$$

$$i \leftarrow i + step$$

od

Function definition

The result of a FORTRAN function definition is restricted to a simple value of type REAL, INTEGER or LOGICAL (and DOUBLE PRECISION, COMPLEX, CHARACTER in FORTRAN77). The template given here assumes that the function result is one of these allowed types. For more complicated types the discussion of templates for records and lists provides the basis of the answer.

function f

$p\!:\!type\_p \rightarrow r\!:\!type\_r$

statements

has the template translation

type_r FUNCTION *F(P)*

type_p P

   *template_code_for_statements_*

   *_with_assignment_to_r_changed_to_*

   _assignment_to_F

RETURN

END

For example

function *letter*

$c\!:\!\mathrm{Char} \rightarrow b\!:\!\mathbb{B}$

$b \leftarrow ('A' \leqslant c) \wedge (c \leqslant 'Z')$

has the template translation

LOGICAL FUNCTION LETTER(C)

CHARACTER C

    LETTER = ('A' .LE. C) .AND. (C .LE. 'Z')

RETURN

END

If the shorthand technique for multiple parameters is being used in the PDL then it should be used in the FORTRAN too.

function *dist_from_origin*

$x:\mathbb{R}, y:\mathbb{R} \rightarrow dfo:\mathbb{R}$

$dfo \leftarrow pos\_square\_root(sq(x) + sq(y))$

has the template translation

REAL FUNCTION DFO(X,Y)

REAL X,Y

    DFO = SQRT(X*X + Y*Y)

RETURN

END

6.3.2   Templates for data structures in FORTRAN

Templates for primitive data types in FORTRAN

$\mathbb{R}$ is modelled by the FORTRAN type REAL or possibly DOUBLE PRECISION.

$\mathbb{Z}$ is modelled by the FORTRAN type INTEGER.

There are no equivalents of $\mathbb{N}$, $\mathbb{P}$ in FORTRAN, INTEGER has to be used – see the section on subrange below.

$\mathbb{B}$ is modelled by the FORTRAN type LOGICAL which has two values .TRUE. and .FALSE.

FORTRAN77 was the first version of FORTRAN to have the CHARACTER type included in its definition. In this version it is possible to model the PDL type 'Char' directly. In earlier versions of FORTRAN characters have to be manipulated by storing the numeric codes for the characters in INTEGER (or REAL) variables.

Enumerated types and subrange type are not available in FORTRAN but can be simulated as described below.

Enumerated types

Enumerated types can be simulated in FORTRAN77 using the PARAMETER statement.

	Declaration	Use
PDL	$(ID1,ID2,\ldots,IDn)$	$v \leftarrow IDi$
FORTRAN	PARAMETER(ID$1 = 1$,ID$2 = 2$,$\ldots$,ID$n = n$)	V = IDi

This shows that to a large extent an enumerated type is a collection of symbolic constants.

Subrange types

Declarations which require a subrange type have to be changed to refer to the base type from which the subrange was taken. To maintain the security of the subrange, type checks should be included whenever a value is assigned to a variable with subrange type to make sure that the value is indeed within the subrange.

Templates for compound data structures in FORTRAN

All internal data structures have to be based on ARRAY's of predetermined size. There is no pointer data type so this has to be simulated. There is no dynamic (run-time) storage allocation so, if needed, this has to be simulated too. As a further restriction the elements of an array may only have primitive type.

Internal data structures

List of fixed length of type T

	Declaration	Use
PDL	$v:T^n$	$v[i]$
FORTRAN	T V(n)	V(I)

FORTRAN uses parentheses ( ) where the PDL uses brackets [ ]. The type T has to be primitive – i.e. not itself of ARRAY type. There is no 'whole-array' assignment in FORTRAN so assignment of arrays must proceed element by element.

Lists of variable length and records

An implementation of a variable length list must support insertions at any point in the list. This is possible in a simple array (within the limits imposed by the size of the array) by copying all the elements beyond the point of insertion to a position one place further down the array.

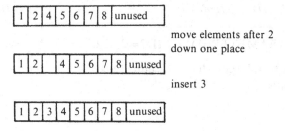

move elements after 2
down one place

insert 3

At the cost of extra store, a faster method is to simulate the domino chain list used in the Pascal templates. For this we need the concept of records which is not available directly in FORTRAN. However since we need a number of similar records we can use arrays again to good effect. The basic idea is to imagine two or more arrays of the same size drawn side by side and then corresponding elements of each array grouped together.

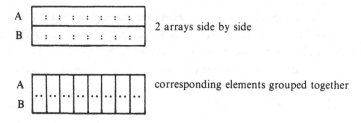

Thus the elements A(1) and B(1) together make up record 1 and we have an array of *n* records each with two fields instead of two arrays each with *n* elements. Using the Data Structure diagrams introduced in Chapter 3 we have converted between the data shapes shown below.

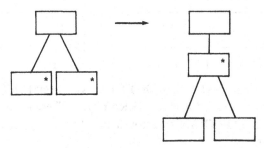

We now have a template translation for an array of records.

	Declaration	Use
PDL	$v:\langle A:T1,B:T2\rangle^n$	$v[i].A$ $v[i].B$
FORTRAN	$T1$ A(n) $T2$ B(n)	A(I) B(I)

In order to manipulate these records as a domino list, the second field of each has to be a pointer to another record. The obvious 'pointer' to use is the subscript of the record to which the pointer is to point. If the subscripts run from *1* to *n* then the value *0* can be used to represent the 'nil' pointer. A suitable name for the first array would now be 'HEADS' and for the second array 'TAILS'.

The dynamic allocation of space (via the procedure *new*) can be simulated by providing a 'heap' of unused records initially and recording the boundary between those that have been allocated for use in the program and those still free.

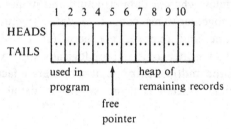

The subroutine NEW which allocates a new record for the program to use could be coded (without error checking) as

```
SUBROUTINE NEW(P)
INTEGER P
P = FREE
FREE = FREE + 1
RETURN
END
```

If the programmer is allowed to 'dispose' of records (return them to the heap) then a slightly more elaborate scheme is needed where all the 'free' records are chained together in a domino list and the variable 'free' becomes a pointer to this free space list.

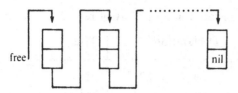

In this case the subroutine NEW could be coded (again without error checking) as

```
SUBROUTINE NEW(P)
INTEGER P
P = FREE
FREE = TAILS(FREE)
RETURN
END
```

This second version of NEW is not correct FORTRAN as it stands because the array identifier TAILS is undefined. The traditional solution is to declare the array TAILS in the main program and then refer to it in a COMMON statement in every subroutine that references it. However we advocate the use of 'modules' where a data structure and its associated operations are grouped together. This confines a data structure (e.g. TAILS) to one subroutine and removes the need for COMMON statements. This gives a much neater solution both logically and textually. The module concept uses the multiple entry point subprogram facility of FORTRAN77. The module concept is demonstrated in detail in the examples which follow.

External data structures

Using the simple 'list-directed' input and output statements we have

PDL	FORTRAN
newinput ← *head*(*input*) *input* ← *tail*(*input*)	READ *,NEWINPUT
output ← *output* ‖ *newoutput*	PRINT *,NEWOUTPUT

Note: In FORTRAN each READ statement begins reading on a new line of data.

Example

This example demonstrates the use of the modular approach to data types. All the internal 'list' activity is confined to FUNCTION LIST which is never actually called but which serves as a heading to the module. The entry STARTL is used just once to initialise the heap. The program reads 10 numbers inserting each one as it is read at the beginning of a list ℓ. When the list is printed out at the end the numbers therefore appear in reverse order.

$$\ell \leftarrow \langle \rangle$$
$$i \leftarrow 1$$
while $i \leqslant 10$
do $h \leftarrow head(input)$
         $input \leftarrow tail(input)$
         $\ell \leftarrow \langle h \rangle \parallel \ell$
         $i \leftarrow i + 1$
od
$$p \leftarrow \ell$$
while $p \neq \langle \rangle$
do $output \leftarrow output \parallel head(p)$
         $p \leftarrow tail(p)$
od

has the template translation

```
C      ****LIST MODULE****
       FUNCTION LIST
         PARAMETER (LSIZE = 10)
         INTEGER HEADS(LSIZE),TAILS(LSIZE),FREE
         INTEGER HEAD,TAIL
         INTEGER P,H,T
       ENTRY STARTL
         FREE = 1
         RETURN
       ENTRY NEW(P)
         P = FREE
         FREE = FREE + 1
         RETURN
```

```
        ENTRY HEAD(P)
          HEAD = HEADS(P)
          RETURN
        ENTRY TAIL(P)
          TAIL = TAILS(P)
          RETURN
        ENTRY MAKEHD(P,H)
          HEADS(P) = H
          RETURN
        ENTRY MAKETL(P,T)
          TAILS(P) = T
          RETURN
        END
C       ****MAIN PROGRAM****
        PARAMETER (NIL = 0)
        EXTERNAL HEAD,TAIL
        INTEGER HEAD,TAIL
        INTEGER H,I,P,L
        CALL STARTL
        L = NIL
        I = 1
10      IF(.NOT.(I.LE.10))GOTO 11
            READ *,H
            CALL NEW(P)
            CALL MAKEHD(P,H)
            CALL MAKETL(P,L)
            L = P
            I = I + 1
            GOTO 10
11      CONTINUE
        P = L
```

```
 20        IF(.NOT.(P.NE.NIL))GOTO 21
           PRINT *,HEAD(P)
           P = TAIL(P)
           GOTO 20
 21        CONTINUE
           STOP
           END
```

This example is repeated with a version of the list module that supports 'disposal' of records. The entry STARTL chains all the records together into a simple list and a pointer to this list is placed in FREE.

```
C ****LIST MODULE****FREE SPACE IS A LIST
           FUNCTION LIST
           PARAMETER (NIL = 0,LSIZE = 10)
           INTEGER HEADS(LSIZE),TAILS(LSIZE),FREE
           INTEGER HEAD, TAIL
           INTEGER P,H,T

           ENTRY STARTL
           I = 1
 10        IF(.NOT.(I.LT.LSIZE))GOTO 11
              TAILS(I) = I + 1
              I = I + 1
              GOTO 10
 11        CONTINUE
           TAILS(LSIZE) = NIL
           FREE = 1
           RETURN

           ENTRY NEW(P)
           P = FREE
           FREE = TAILS(FREE)
           RETURN

           ENTRY DISPOS(P)
           TAILS(P) = FREE
           FREE = P
           RETURN
```

```
ENTRY HEAD(P)
  HEAD = HEADS(P)
  RETURN
ENTRY TAIL(P)
  TAIL = TAILS(P)
  RETURN
ENTRY MAKEHD(P,H)
  HEADS(P) = H
  RETURN
ENTRY MAKETL(P,T)
  TAILS(P) = T
  RETURN
END

PARAMETER (NIL = 0)
EXTERNAL HEAD,TAIL
INTEGER HEAD,TAIL
INTEGER H,I,P,L
CALL STARTL
L = NIL
I = 1
10      IF(.NOT.(I.LE.10))GOTO 11
            READ *,H
            CALL NEW(P)
            CALL MAKEHD(P,H)
            CALL MAKETL(P,L)
            L = P
            I = I + 1
            GOTO 10
11      CONTINUE
        P = L
```

```
20      IF(.NOT.(P.NE.NIL))GOTO 21
            PRINT *,HEAD(P)
            P=TAIL(P)
            GOTO 20
21      CONTINUE
        STOP
        END
```

6.4   Templates for COBOL

COBOL is a language specialised to business applications (COmmon Business Oriented Language). As such it is a language for manipulating large quantities of information which exist primarily in external files. The files consist of sequences of records and the records typically have a very detailed multilevel structure. The computational facilities of COBOL include the ability to perform arithmetic on decimal numbers directly but are otherwise fairly minimal. A COBOL program is built up from words, sentences, paragraphs, sections and divisions. A typical sentence in the procedure division might be

ADD X TO Y GIVING Z.

The **words** ADD, TO, GIVING and the 'full stop' contribute to the unique flavour of COBOL. For the purposes of the templates we can ignore the IDENTIFICATION DIVISION and the ENVIRONMENT DIVISION and concentrate on the DATA DIVISION containing all the declarations and the PROCEDURE DIVISION containing all the executable statements.

6.4.1   Templates for control structures in COBOL

Assignment statement

variable ← expression

has the template translation

COMPUTE *variable = expression.*

The expression can contain the usual arithmetic operators $+$, $-$, $*$, $/$ together with $**$ for exponentiation and parentheses for over-riding operator priorities. Assignments which involve no arithmetic operators and those which use only one type of operator have special forms which are shown below.

PDL	COBOL
$x \leftarrow y$	MOVE Y TO X.
$x \leftarrow x + 1$	ADD 1 TO X.
$x \leftarrow y + 1$	ADD 1 TO Y GIVING X.
$x \leftarrow y + z + 1$	ADD Y, Z, 1 GIVING X.
$x \leftarrow x - 1$	SUBTRACT 1 FROM X.
$x \leftarrow x * 2$	MULTIPLY 2 BY X.
$x \leftarrow x / 2$	DIVIDE 2 INTO X.

Procedure call

Within a single COBOL program there is no concept of a procedure call with parameters. Each paragraph in the PROCEDURE DIVISION is given a name and is said to be a procedure. The statements in the procedure may be executed by using the PERFORM statement. The effect of procedure parameters has to be achieved by explicit copying.

$$p(p1, p2, \ldots, pn)$$

has the template translation

MOVE *P1* TO WS-*P1*.

MOVE *P2* TO WS-*P2*.

$\vdots$

MOVE *PN* TO WS-*PN*.

PEFORM *P*.

The variables WS-*Pi* must be declared in the WORKING-STORAGE section. They take the place of procedure parameters in the procedure *P*.

Statement sequence

Each sentence in COBOL is made up of one or more statements separated by semicolons. Thus strictly a statement sequence is a sentence. However it is more helpful to consider a sentence-sequence in this section.

statement_1

statement_2

$\vdots$

statement_n

has the template translation

> *paragraph-name.*
>> *template_code_for_statement_1.*
>> *template_code_for_statement_2.*
>> ⋮
>> *template_code_for_statement_n.*

Each statement in the PDL is translated to a sentence in COBOL.

If statement

> if   *expression*
>
> then   *statements_T*
>
> else   *statements_F*
>
> fi

has the template translation

> IF-*tag.*
>> IF *template_code_for_expression*
>>
>> THEN PERFORM THEN-*tag*
>>
>> ELSE PERFORM ELSE-*tag.*
>
> THEN-*tag.*
>> *template_code_for_statements_T.*
>
> ELSE-*tag.*
>> *template_code_for_statements_F.*

The *tag* used in the template distinguishes the paragraph names used for this 'if' statement from those used in any other 'if' statement in the program. The *tag* could be a single letter or digit or descriptive string.

If the *statements_T* and *statements_F* each contain a single statement then the following template can be used.

> if   *expression*
>
> then   *statement_T*
>
> else   *statement_F*
>
> fi

has the template translation

> IF   *template_code_for_expression*
>
> THEN   *template_code_for_statement_T*
>
> ELSE   *template_code_for_statement_F.*

The relations used in the translated form of *expression* are as follows

PDL	COBOL
$x = y$	X IS EQUAL TO Y
$x \neq y$	X IS NOT EQUAL TO Y
$x > y$	X IS GREATER THAN Y
$x < y$	X IS LESS THAN Y
$x \geqslant y$	X IS NOT LESS THAN Y
$x \leqslant y$	X IS NOT GREATER THAN Y
$x \wedge y$	X AND Y
$x \vee y$	X OR Y
$x > 0$	X IS POSITIVE
$x = 0$	X IS ZERO
$x < 0$	X IS NEGATIVE

The 'else' portion of the 'if' statement may be omitted in the usual way.

Example

```
m ← x
if      m < 0
then    m ← 0
else
        if      m > 15
        then    m ← 15
        fi
fi
```

has the template translation

```
MOVE X TO M.
IF M IS NEGATIVE
THEN MOVE ZERO TO M
ELSE    IF M IS GREATER THAN 15
        THEN MOVE 15 TO M.
```

While statement

```
while   expression
do      statements
od
```

has the template translation

> PERFORM WHILE-*tag*
> UNTIL NOT *template_code_for_expression.*
> ⋮
> WHILE-*tag.*
>
> > *template_code_for_statements.*

Despite the use of the keyword 'UNTIL' this is indeed a pre-check repetition and the *statements* at paragraph WHILE-*tag* will not be executed at all if the expression is initially false.

Repeat statement

> repeat *statements*
> until   *expression*

has the template translation

> PERFORM REPEAT-*tag.*
> PERFORM REPEAT-*tag* UNTIL *template_code_for_expression.*
> ⋮
> REPEAT-*tag.*
>
> > *template_code_for_statements.*

Example

> if $y \geqslant 0$
> then $z \leftarrow 0$
> > while $y > 0$
> > do $z \leftarrow z + x$
> > > $y \leftarrow y - 1$
> > od
> else $z \leftarrow 0$
> > repeat $z \leftarrow z - x$
> > > $y \leftarrow y + 1$
> > until $y = 0$
> fi

has the template translation

    IF Y IS NOT NEGATIVE
    THEN PERFORM THEN-A
    ELSE PERFORM ELSE-A.
    ⋮
    THEN-A.
        MOVE ZERO TO Z.
        PERFORM WHILE-B UNTIL NOT Y IS POSITIVE.
    ELSE-A.
        MOVE ZERO TO Z.
        PERFORM REPEAT-C.
        PERFORM REPEAT-C UNTIL Y IS ZERO.
    WHILE-B.
        ADD X TO Z.
        SUBTRACT 1 FROM Y.
    REPEAT-C.
        SUBTRACT X FROM Z.
        ADD 1 TO Y.

Function definition

There is no concept of programmer defined functions in COBOL. They may be simulated by 'procedures' which return a result using the opposite mechanism to that used for parameters (see procedure call).

    function f

    $p:type\_p \rightarrow r:type\_r$

    statements

has the template translation

    FUNCTION-f.

        *template_code_for_statements_*
        *_with_references_to_p_changed_to_*WS-p*_and_*
        *_with_assignments_to_r_changed_to_*
        *_assignments_to_*WS-r.

The call of this function is treated as follows

...f(p)..

has the template translation

MOVE *p* TO WS-*p*.

PERFORM FUNCTION-*f*.

...WS-*r*..

6.4.2 Templates for data structures in COBOL

Templates for primitive data types in COBOL

ℝ is not modelled directly. Fixed format real numbers are modelled using PICTUREs with a sign (S), some digits (99999) with a decimal point (V) included, e.g. PICTURE S999V99.

ℤ is not modelled directly. Fixed format integers are modelled using PICTUREs with a sign, some digits but no decimal point, e.g. PICTURE S999.

ℕ, ℙ are not modelled directly. Fixed format integers are modelled using PICTUREs with digits but no sign, e.g. PICTURE 999.

𝔹 is not available in COBOL. It is modelled by using two values of another type, e.g. 'T' and 'F' from the letter subrange of Char.

The type 'Char' in PDL is modelled in COBOL by the type PICTURE X.

COBOL has no programmer defined constants so the usual way of simulating enumerated types is not possible. The use of variables with values that are not (supposed to be) altered is possible but unsafe.

Subrange types have to be simulated as for FORTRAN except that 'PICTURE 99' could be said to be a subrange type $00..99$.

PDL	COBOL
ℝ	PICTURE S999V99.
ℤ	PICTURE S999.
ℙ	PICTURE 999.
𝔹	PICTURE A. (value 'T' or 'F')
Char	PICTURE X.
'0'..'9'	PICTURE 9.
'A'..'Z'	PICTURE A.

For $\mathbb{R}$, $\mathbb{Z}$ and $\mathbb{P}$ the number of 9's defines the number of decimal digits stored and is selected to encompass the range required in a program. For $\mathbb{R}$ the 'V' shows the place of the implied decimal point.

Templates for compound data structures in COBOL

Internal data structures

List of fixed length of type T

	Declaration	Use
PDL	$v : T^n$	$v[i]$

COBOL	L1 V-TABLE.
	  L2 V OCCURS n TIMES
	    template_code_for_type_T
		V(I)

L1, L2 are level numbers which are two digit decimal numbers with L2 > L1 (see Records).

If T is type 'Char' and the list is always used as a whole then the alternative template is

	Declaration	Use
PDL	$v : T^n$	v
COBOL	V PICTURE X(n).	V

Lists of variable length of type T
If required the style introduced in the section on FORTRAN templates can be used.

Record
If a data structure diagram is used to show the structure of a record then the diagram will display a number of levels. In COBOL each level is numbered and named. Consider the example shown in the diagram below

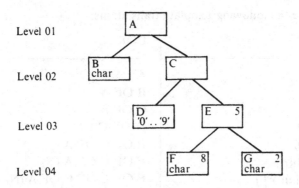

This would have a PDL declaration as follows

$a:\langle\ B:Char\ ,\ C:C\_type\ \rangle$

$C\_type=\langle\ D:'0'..'9'\ ,\ E:E\_type\ \rangle$

$E\_type=E1\_type^5$

$E1\_type=\langle\ F:Char^8\ ,\ G:Char^2\ \rangle$

and translated into COBOL it becomes

```
01  A.
    02  B                    PICTURE X.
    02  C.
        03  D                PICTURE 9.
        03  E    OCCURS 5 TIMES.
            04  F            PICTURE X(8).
            04  G            PICTURE X(2).
```

The basic template translation of a selection of a field from a record is

PDL	COBOL
S(r)	S OF R

and so we have the following template translations

PDL	COBOL
a	A
$B(a)$	B OF A
$C(a)$	C OF A
$D(C(a))$	D OF C OF A
$E(C(a))$	E OF C OF A
$E(C(a))[n]$	E OF C OF A (N)
$F(E(C(a))[n])$	F OF E OF C OF A (N)
$G(E(C(a))[n])$	G OF E OF C OF A (N)

Note: Irrespective of which level contains an 'OCCURS' clause any subscript is always written at the end. In the case of multiple subscripts they are written comma-separated in one pair of parentheses, e.g. (1,2,3). COBOL allows up to three subscripts.

External data structures

An external file is described in a file-description (FD) entry in the FILE SECTION of the DATA DIVISION of a COBOL program. The FD entry shows the structure of each record in the file. A one record buffer is created for each file with an FD entry. The COBOL verbs for input and output are READ and WRITE. So the statements

> READ *file-name* RECORD.

> WRITE *record-name*.

read a record from the named file and place it in the input buffer and write a record from the named output buffer to the corresponding file. Thus values are typically READ into an input buffer, MOVEd from the input buffer into WORKING-STORAGE areas, undergo some computation and are then MOVEd to some output buffer before the WRITE statement is used to transfer the contents of the output buffer to the output file. Input files must be OPENed for INPUT before READing from them. Output files must be OPENed for OUTPUT before WRITEing to them. All files should be CLOSEd before STOPping the program RUN.

Example

$$card\_record = \langle EMPLOYEE\_NAME:Char^{15},$$
$$HOURS\_WORKED:0..99 \rangle$$

$$data\_file = card\_record*$$

$payroll\_record = \langle EMPLOYEE\_NAME:\text{Char}^{15} ,$
$\qquad\qquad HOURS\_WORKED:0..99, GROSS\_PAY:\mathbb{R}\rangle$

$payroll\_file = payroll\_record*$

$cr \leftarrow head(data\_file)$

$data\_file \leftarrow tail(data\_file)$

$payroll\_file \leftarrow payroll\_file \parallel$
$\qquad\langle EMPLOYEE\_NAME(cr), HOURS\_WORKED(cr),$
$\qquad\qquad\qquad 10.5*HOURS\_WORKED(cr)+20\rangle$

has the template translation

DATA DIVISION.

FILE SECTION.

FD DATA-FILE

⋮

01	CARD-RECORD.	
	02 EMPLOYEE-NAME	PICTURE X(15).
	02 HOURS-WORKED	PICTURE 99.

FD PAYROLL-FILE.

⋮

01	PAYROLL-RECORD.	
	02 EMPLOYEE-NAME	PICTURE X(15).
	02 HOURS-WORKED	PICTURE 99.
	02 GROSS-PAY	PICTURE £999.99.

⋮

WORKING-STORAGE SECTION.

77	WS-GROSS-WAGE	PICTURE 999V99

⋮

PROCEDURE DIVISION.

MAIN-PROGRAM.

    PERFORM OPEN-FILES.

⋮

    PERFORM READ-RECORD.

    PERFORM PROCESS-RECORD.

    PERFORM WRITE-RECORD.

:

PERFORM CLOSE-FILES.

STOP RUN.

OPEN-FILES.

OPEN INPUT DATA-FILE.

OPEN OUTPUT PAYROLL-FILE.

READ-RECORD.

READ DATA-FILE RECORD.

PROCESS-RECORD.

MOVE EMPLOYEE-NAME OF CARD-RECORD

TO EMPLOYEE-NAME OF PAYROLL-RECORD.

MOVE HOURS-WORKED OF CARD-RECORD

TO HOURS-WORKED OF PAYROLL-RECORD.

COMPUTE WS-GROSS-WAGES =

10.5*HOURS-WORKED OF CARD-RECORD.

ADD 20 TO WS-GROSS-WAGES.

MOVE WS-GROSS-WAGES

TO GROSS-WAGES OF PAYROLL-RECORD.

WRITE-RECORD.

WRITE PAYROLL-RECORD.

CLOSE-FILES.

CLOSE DATA-FILE.

CLOSE PAYROLL-FILE.

6.5   Templates for a minicomputer assembly language

The minicomputer on which the language is based has eight 16-bit registers. The names of the registers are r0, r1,..., r7 except that r6 is usually known by the alternative name of sp and is the 'stack pointer' and r7 is usually known by the alternative name of pc and is the 'program counter'.

The machine has eight addressing modes as shown in the table below

Written in program	Mode name	Mode number
R	Register	0
R↑	Register Deferred	1
R↑ +	Autoincrement	2
R↑↑ +	Autoincrement Deferred	3
− R↑	Autodecrement	4
− R↑↑	Autodecrement Deferred	5
X[R]	Index	6
X[R]↑	Index Deferred	7

Modes 2, 3, 6 and 7 are used with register pc so often that special abbreviations are used in the program and the modes are given special names.

Written as	Short for	Mode name	Mode number
.n	pc↑ +	Immediate	2
.A↑	pc↑↑ +	Absolute	3
A	X[pc]	Relative	6
A↑	X[pc]↑	Relative Deferred	7

In the tables above

> R is a general purpose register
> X is a vector base address (written as a label or a number)
> n is a number
> A is an address (written as a label or a number)

The instructions occupy one word (2 bytes) or two words or three words and can have from zero to two operands as shown in the following table. The information is given in the form

> *instruction   op-code   flags   explanation*

The op-code is the octal form of the first (or only) word of the instruction. SS stands for a full source-operand and DD stands for a full destination-operand. A full operand is made up of a mode-number (one octal digit) and a register number (one octal digit). R stands for a half operand and is made up of a register-number (one octal digit). In this case Register Mode (Mode 0) is assumed.

The *flags* information given for each instruction uses the following notation

↑ flag may be set or reset according to operands
0 flag is always reset by the instruction
1 flag is always set by the instruction
− flag is never affected by the instruction

The flag information is given in the order NZVC. The four flags show Negative, Zero, oVerflow, and Carry conditions.

Zero operand instructions

halt	000000	- - - -	stop
nop	000240	- - - -	do nothing

Half operand instructions

exit R	00020R	- - - -	pc ← R↑

One operand instructions

swab D	0003DD	↑↑00	swap bytes in D
not D	0051DD	↑↑00	every bit of D inverted
neg D	0054DD	↑↑↑↑	value in D is negated

Branch instructions (*XXX* stands for the last 8 bits of the instruction)

brn L	0004XXX	- - - -	branch unconditionally to label L
b <> L	0010XXX	- - - -	branch if Z = 0
b = L	0014XXX	- - - -	branch if Z = 1
b > = L	0020XXX	- - - -	branch if N = 0
b < L	0024XXX	- - - -	branch if N = 1
b > L	0030XXX	- - - -	branch if Z = 0 and N = 0
b < = L	0034XXX	- - - -	branch if Z = 1 or N = 1
bvc L	1020XXX	- - - -	branch if V = 0
bvs L	1024XXX	- - - -	branch if V = 1
bcc L	1030XXX	- - - -	branch if C = 0
bcs L	1034XXX	- - - -	branch if C = 1

One-and-a-half operand instructions

call R,L	004RDD	- - - -	call subroutine at label L, saving R on stack
mul R,S	070RSS	↑↑0↑	R ← R∗S

if R is an even register (r0,r2,r4,r6), double-length result in R,R + 1 div R,S   071RSS   ↑↑↑↑   R ← R div S

      if R is an even register (r0,r2,r4,r6), next odd register ← R mod S

sℓℓ R,D   072RDD   ↑↑00   R is shifted left logically D places

srℓ R,D   172RDD   ↑↑00   R is shifted right logically D places

sℓc R,D   073RDD   ↑↑00   R is shifted left circularly D places

src R,D   173RDD   ↑↑00   R is shifted right circularly D places

Two operand instructions

mov S,D   01SSDD   ↑↑00   copy source value to destination address

cmp S,D   02SSDD   ↑↑↑↑   compute S − D, set flags

and S,D   03SSDD   ↑↑00   D ← D and S

er S,D   04SSDD   ↑↑00   D ← D xor S   (exclusive or)

or S,D   05SSDD   ↑↑00   D ← D or S

add S,D   06SSDD   ↑↑↑↑   D ← D + S

sub S,D   16SSDD   ↑↑↑↑   D ← D − S

movb S,D   11SSDD   ↑↑00   copy source byte to destination address

cmpb S,D   12SSDD   ↑↑00   compare source byte with destination byte

andb S,D   13SSDD   ↑↑00   D ← D and S

erb S,D   14SSDD   ↑↑00   D ← D xor S   (exclusive or)

orb S,D   15SSDD   ↑↑00   D ← D or S

6.5.1   Templates for control structures

Assignment statement

      variable ← expression

has the template translation

      *template_code_to_evaluate_expression_*

      _and_place_the_result_in_register_R

      mov *R,variable*

If *expression* is a literal constant or a simple variable then no evaluation is necessary and the 'mov' can take place directly. Some simple operations on a variable can be achieved without the 'mov' operation – see $x ← x + 1$ below.

     If the assignment involves a byte value rather than a word value then the move byte instruction 'movb' is used.

Examples

PDL	Assembler
$x \leftarrow 1$	mov .1,x
$x \leftarrow y$	mov y,x
$x \leftarrow y + 1$	mov y,r0; add .1,r0; mov r0,x
$x \leftarrow y * 2$	mov y,r0; mul r0,.2; mov r0,x
$x \leftarrow x + 1$	add .1,x
$ch \leftarrow \text{'}1\text{'}$	movb .'1',ch

Procedure call

    $p(p1,p2,\ldots,pn)$

has the template translation

    push pn

    $\vdots$

    push p2

    push p1

    call pc,*p*

    pop all parameters

where the code to *push* a parameter onto the stack is

    mov $w,-$sp↑ (for a word value *w*, decreases sp by 2)

    movb $b,-$sp↑ (for a byte value *b*, decreases sp by 1)

The parameters must be evaluated (in a register) before being stacked if they are complex expressions. The code required to 'pop' all the parameters off the stack is

    add   .*x*,sp

where *x* is the number required to bring the stack pointer back to its value before stacking the parameters. (N.B. The machine has a 'backwards' growing stack so that sp should be initialised to a high value at the start of the program.)

Example

    $p(v,7)$

has the template translation

```
mov .7, - sp↑
mov v, - sp↑
call pc,p
add .4,sp
```

Statement sequence

Each statement in the PDL is begun on a new line in the assembly language version. However multiple instructions emanating from the template code for a single PDL statement may be written on one line with semicolon separation.

> *statement_1*
>
> *statement_2*
>
> :
>
> *statement_n*

has the template translation

> *template_code_for_statement_1*
>
> *template_code_for_statement_2*
>
> :
>
> *template_code_for_statement_n*

If statement

> if   *expression*
>
> then   *statements_T*
>
> else   *statements_F*
>
> fi

has the template translation

> if*tag:*
>
> > *template_code_to_branch_to_the_else_label_*
> > *_if_the_expression_is_False*
>
> then*tag*:
>
> > *template_code_for_statements_T*
> >
> > brn fi*tag*
>
> else*tag*:
>
> > *template_code_for_statements_F*
>
> fi*tag*:

In this template *tag* is an identifying suffix associated with this 'if' statement to distinguish it from other 'if' statements in the program. The *tag* is usually an upper-case letter (although it could be any letter or digit or combination). The composite labels if*tag*, then*tag*, else*tag*, fi*tag* are used to mark strategic points in the program text for the benefit of the human reader. Only the last two are used as the destination of a branch instruction.

The most common form of *expression* in an 'if' statement is

  if   *operand_1 relop operand_2* then ...

where *operand_1* and *operand_2* are literal constants or simple variables and *relop* is a relational operator.

In this case the template code to branch to the 'else' label is

  cmp *operand_1,operand_2*

  branch_*if_not_condition* else*tag*

This gives rise to the following table of translations:

relop	branch_if_not_condition
=	b<>
≠	b=
<	b>=
>=	b<
>	b<=
<=	b>

The 'else' portion of the 'if' statement may be omitted in the obvious way. If the condition is compound (e.g. if...and...then, if...or...then) the same template ideas can be used and it is convenient to include extra labels (e.g. and*tag*, or*tag*) at the appropriate points in the template code.

Example

    m ← x
    if   *m < 0*
    then   *m ← 0*
    else
           if   *m > 15*
           then   *m ← 15*
           fi
    fi

has the template translation

```
        mov x,m
    ifA:        cmp m,.0
                b> = elseA
    thenA:      mov .0,m
                brn fiA
    elseA:
            ifB:        cmp m,.15
                        b< = fiB
            thenB:      mov .15,m
            fiB:
    fiA:
```

While statement

```
        while   expression
        do      statements
```

has the template translation

```
    whiletag:
            template_code_to_branch_to_od_label
                    _if_the_expression_is_False
    dotag:
            template_code_for_statements
            brn whiletag
    odtag:
```

Repeat statement

```
        repeat statements
        until   expression
```

has the template translation

```
    repeattag:
            template_code_for_statements
    untiltag:
            template_code_to_branch_to_repeat_label_
                    _if_the_expression_is_False
```

Example

        if $y \geqslant 0$
        then $z \leftarrow 0$
                while $y > 0$
                do $z \leftarrow z + x$
                        $y \leftarrow y - 1$
                od
        else $z \leftarrow 0$
                repeat $z \leftarrow z - x$
                       $y \leftarrow y + 1$
                until $y = 0$
        fi

has the template translation

        ifA: cmp y,.0
                    b< elseA
        thenA: mov .0,z
                    whileB: cmp y,.0
                             b<= odB
                    doB: add x,z
                             sub .1,y
                             brn whileB
                    odB:
                    brn fiA
        elseA: mov .0,z
                    repeatC: sub x,z
                             add .1,y
                    untilC: cmp y,.0
                             b< > repeatC
        fiA:

Function definition

        function f
        $p{:}type\_p \rightarrow r{:}type\_r$
        statements

has the template translation

    f:

        symbolic_constants_for_p_and_r

        *template_code_for_statements_*

        *_with_references_to_p_changed_to_p[sp]_and_*

        _with_assignment_to_r_changed_to_assignment_to_r[sp]

        exit pc

If the shorthand technique for multiple parameters is being used in the PDL it should be used in the assembly version too.

    The function result is treated by the template as a parameter in reverse. Thinking of the function result as a fictitious last parameter leads to the idea of stacking a dummy value as a place holder on the stack during the call of the function. The function can then place its result at this special place on the stack from where it can be retrieved during the 'popping' operation. Thus

    $\ldots f(p1,p2,\ldots,pn)\ldots$

has the template translation

    push_dummy_value_as_place_holder_for_function_result

    push pn

    $\vdots$

    push p2

    push p1

    call pc,f

    pop_all_genuine_parameters

    pop_function_result_into_R

    $\ldots R \ldots$

The 'call' instruction stacks the return address of the function so that the stack just after a function call may be drawn as

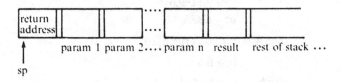

The parameters and result are accessed using Index Mode addressing (Mode 6) with register 'sp'. For each parameter and for the result, its offset

from where the stack pointer is pointing is calculated. This offset is then encapsulated in a symbolic constant so that the name of the parameter can be used in the addressing mode. The first parameter always has an offset of two bytes (since the return address occupies one word = two bytes) so it can be referred to by the addressing mode '2[sp]'. Using the symbolic constant definition

> p1 = 2

this may be rewritten conveniently as

> p1[sp]

The parameter pack (including the result) must always be an even number of bytes long so that the return address is on a word boundary. Word parameters must also be placed on word boundaries. This means that when byte and word parameters are mixed or when an odd number of byte parameters are present dummy byte parameters have to be inserted. This is not required in the example below.

Example

> function *letter*
>
> c:Char $\rightarrow$ b:$\mathbb{B}$
>
> $b \leftarrow ('a' \leqslant c) \wedge (c \leqslant 'z')$

has the template translation

> False = 0
>
> True = 1

> letter:
>
>   c = 2
>
>   b = 3

```
    ifA:      cmpb .'a',c[sp]
              b>  elseA
    andA:     cmpb c[sp],.'z'
              b>  elseA
    thenA:    movb .True,b[sp]
              brn fiA
    elseA:    movb .False,b[sp]
    fiA:
    exit pc
```

A call of this function

> if   *letter(ch)*
>
> then   ...

has the template translation

        ifB: movb .0, − sp↑   {dummy byte for result}

                    movb ch, − sp↑

                    call pc,letter

                    add .1,sp   {pop genuine parameter}

                    movb sp↑ + ,r0   {pop result into r0}

                    cmpb r0,.True

                    b < > elseB

        thenB: ...

If the function contains any 'local' variables then these are allocated space to the 'left' of the return address and parameters. Thus they have negative addresses relative to the stack pointer 'sp'. Symbolic constants are introduced for each (negative) offset as required.

Special care has to be taken to protect these local variables if a further function (or procedure) is called during the execution of a function (or procedure) with local variables. Unless the stack pointer is moved, the stacking of more parameters and another return address would cause the local variables to be 'overwritten'. It is often the case (especially with recursive calls) that the parameters required for the further call depend on the parameters and/or local variables of the calling routine. The template solution is to have (temporarily) two stack pointers (r5 as well as sp). First 'sp' is copied into 'r5', then 'sp' is moved to the 'left' of the local variables (if present).

> mov sp,r5
>
> sub .x,sp

where x is a number expressing the size in bytes of the local variable pack in the stack picture.

Now parameters can be stacked for the further call using 'sp', while the original parameters and local variables can be accessed using Index Mode and 'r5'.

After the further call and the popping of the parameters (and result) the instruction

> add .x,sp

restores 'sp' to its original value.

Example

Write_natural is a recursive output procedure. The variables q and r stand for quotient and remainder.

> function write_natural
>
> $n: \mathbb{P} \to$
>
> if $n = 0$
>
> then $output \leftarrow output \,\|\, \langle '0' \rangle$
>
> else $q \leftarrow n$ div 10
>
> $r \leftarrow n$ mod 10
>
> $output \leftarrow output \,\|\, write\_natural(q)$
>
> $\|\, chr(r + ord('0'))$
>
> fi

has the template translation

```
writenatural:
    n = 2                          {symbolic constant for parameter}
    q = -2                         {symbolic constants for locals}
    r = -4
ifA:    cmp n[sp],.0               {if n = 0}
        b < > elseA
thenA:  movb .'0',output           {output ← output ‖ ⟨'0'⟩}
        brn fiA
elseA:  mov n[sp],r0
        div r0,.10
        mov r0,q[sp]               {q ← n div 10}
        mov r1,r[sp]               {r ← n mod 10}
        mov sp,r5                  {copy sp}
        sub .4,sp                  {protect locals}
        mov q[r5], -sp↑            {stack parameter for procedure}
        call pc,writenatural
        add .2,sp                  {pop parameter}
        add .4,sp                  {reinstate locals}
        mov r[sp],r0
        add .'0',r0                {ord('0')}
        movb r0,output
fiA:
```

6.5.2 Templates for data structures

Templates for primitive data types

On the minicomputer a real number is stored in a double-word as a record containing an exponent in one byte and a fraction part in three bytes. Four special arithmetic instructions (fadd, fsub, fmul, fdiv) are available via an option. In the absence of these, functions with records representing real numbers as parameters and results have to be written to simulate the hardware instructions. $\mathbb{R}$ is not considered further here.

$\mathbb{Z}$ is modelled by 16-bit patterns stored in words giving a range of

$$-2^{15} \text{ to } +2^{15} - 1$$

$\mathbb{N}$, $\mathbb{P}$ have to be modelled as subrange types.

$\mathbb{B}$ has to be modelled as an enumerated type.

The PDL type 'Char' is modelled by 8-bit patterns stored in bytes.

Enumerated types

Enumerated types can be simulated in assembler using symbolic constants.

	Declaration	Use
PDL	$(ID1,ID2,\ldots,IDn)$	$v \leftarrow IDi$
Assembler	$ID1=0; ID2=1; \ldots IDn=n$	mov .IDi,v

Subrange types

The type from which the subrange was taken has to be used and checks included to test the validity of assignments to subrange types.

Templates for compound data structures

Space for a compound data structure is allocated by including a size in brackets after a label. The label becomes a label of the first byte of the space.

vec[20]: .0

allocates 20 words (40 bytes) of store (and initialises them to zero). The label 'vec' addresses the first byte. Index mode 'X[R]' is used with fixed 'X' and variable 'R' to access arrays. Index mode 'X[R]' is used with fixed 'R' and variable 'X' to access records. The Deferred modes (e.g. R↑) are used for pointers.

Internal data structures

List of fixed length of type T

	Declaration	Use
PDL	$v:T^n$	$v[i]$
Assembler	v[N]:.0	mov i,R; *map_R* ; ...v[R]..

The value of 'N' is the number of words taken up by n values of type T. The subscript 'i' in the PDL has to be mapped to a byte offset in assembler. The offset required is the number of bytes from the start address of the vector to the start of the i'th value of type T. If each value of type T has size t bytes and the subscripts range from 1 to n then *map_R* is

mov i,R

sub .1,R

mul R,.t

Example

$v:\mathbb{Z}^{10}$

$v[i] \leftarrow v[i+1]$

has the template translation

v[10]:.0

mov i,r1; add .1,r1	{i + 1}
sub .1,r1; mul r1,.2	{map subscript}
mov v[r1],r0	
mov i,r1	
sub .1,r1; mul r1,.2	{map subscript}
mov r0,v[r1]	

Lists of variable length

If the instructions are imagined as occupying the beginning of the store allocated to the program and the stack is imagined as growing from the end of the store towards the instructions then there is a piece of store of indeterminate size from the end of the program to the top of the stack. This piece of store is conveniently used as a 'heap'. By attaching the label 'heap:' to the first byte after the end of the program and by using a variable 'free' to record the free space, the heap may be accessed conveniently. A procedure 'new' may be defined to allocate space from the heap and thus domino records with pointer fields to other dominos can be created and linked into variable length lists as for Pascal. Thus

$$v \leftarrow \langle newelt \rangle \,\|\, v$$

has the template translation

	head = 0; tail = 2	{symbolic field offsets for domino record}
free:	.heap	{free pointer initialised to start of heap}
p:	.0	{a pointer variable}
new:		
	mov free,2[sp]↑	{address of next free space into 1st param}
	add 4[sp],free	{add size of space required (2nd param) to free}
	exit pc	
begin:		{start of program}
	⋮	
	mov .4, −sp↑	{size of record}
	mov .p, −sp↑	{variable parameter requires address of p}
	call pc,new	{new(p,4)}
	add .4,sp	{pop parameters}
	mov p,r0	
	mov v,tail[r0]	{p.tail ← v}
	mov newelt,head[r0]	{p.head ← newelt}
	mov p,v	{v ← p}
	⋮	
end:	halt	{end of program}
heap:	.0	{heap}
	↓	
	↑	
	{stack}	

Record

The template requires the total size of each field to be worked out and then the offset in bytes of each field from the beginning of the record. Symbolic constants are declared for the offset of each field.

	Declaration	Use
PDL	$v:\langle S1:T1,S2:T2,\ldots,Sn:Tn\rangle$	$S1(v)$ $S2(v)$, *etc.*
Assembler	$S1 = offset\_1$ $S2 = offset\_2$ $\vdots$ $Sn = offset\_n$	*move_address_of_v_to_R* $\ldots S1[R]\ldots$ $\ldots S2[R]\ldots$ etc.

Example

$rec:\langle I:\mathbb{Z}\ ,\ C:\text{Char},\ B:\mathbb{B}\ ,\ V:\mathbb{Z}^5\rangle$

$I(rec) \leftarrow 2$

$C(rec) \leftarrow '2'$

$B(rec) \leftarrow \text{True}$

$V(rec)[3] \leftarrow 2$

has the template translation

    rec[7]:.0   {total size 14 bytes}

    $I = 0; C = 2; B = 3; V = 4$

    mov .rec,r0   {address of rec into r0}

    mov .2,I[r0]

    mov .rec,r0   {strictly according to template}

    movb .'2',C[r0]

    mov .rec,r0; movb .True,B[r0]

    mov .3,r1; sub .1,r1; mul r1,.2   {map subscript}

    mov .rec,r0; add .V,r0; add r1,r0; mov .2,r0↑

In the last two lines the final destination of the value 2 is an address computed from three components

    the base address of the vector,

the offset of the field 'V', and

the offset of element 3 from the start of the array V.

The Register Deferred mode (R↑) was used to place the value in the computed address.

External data structures
The (non-standard) support for input and output used in the examples is

PDL	Assembler
newinput ← head(input)	mov input,newinputi {for integers}
input ← tail(input)	movb input,newinputc {for characters}
output ← output ‖ newoutput	mov newoutputi,output {for integers}
	movb newoutputc,output {for characters}

6.6   Templates for a microprocessor assembly language

The particular microprocessor considered here is known as the Z80. The templates follow the same pattern as those for the minicomputer assembler and so are not given in full. However the Z80 instruction set is not as powerful as the minicomputer in certain critical cases. For example the minicomputer 'mov' instruction can move any addressable object to any addressable destination. However the corresponding load (LD) instruction on the Z80 can only be said to move any addressable object to or from a register. Thus some 'mov'es take two 'LD's.

The Z80 has eight 8-bit registers which may be grouped in pairs as shown

A	F
B	C
D	E
H	L

There are four 16-bit registers including the stack pointer and the program counter.

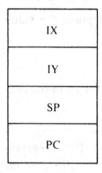

The Z80 can address
  (a) the registers A, F, B, C, D, E, H, L
  (b) a literal number n (one byte) or nn (two bytes)
  (c) the contents of a named store location (nn)
  (d) the contents of a store location pointed to by a double length register (modified in the case of IX, IY)

$$(BC), (DE), (HL), (SP), (IX+d), (IY+d)$$

  (e) the contents of a double length register

$$BC, DE, HL, SP, IX, IY$$

The load (LD) instruction has two operands, one of which must be the name of a single or double length register.

Apart from 'INC' and 'DEC' which add-1-to or take-1-from any register and a 16-bit add and subtract on 'IX' and 'IY' all the 8-bit arithmetic and logical operations use register 'A' and all the 16-bit operations use 'HL'.

There are no multiply or divide instructions.

6.6.1   Templates for control structures

Assignment

> *variable ← expression*

has the template translation

> *template_code_to_evaluate_expression_*
>
> *_and_place_the_result_in_register_R*
>
> LD (*variable*),R

The register pair 'HL' is used for 16-bit values, the register 'A' for 8-bit values.

Examples

PDL	Z80
$x \leftarrow 1$	LD HL,1
	LD (x),HL
$x \leftarrow y$	LD HL,(y)
	LD (x),HL
$x \leftarrow y+3$	LD HL,(y)
	LD BC,3
	ADD HL,BC
	LD (x),HL
$x \leftarrow y*2$	LD HL,(y)
	ADD HL,HL
	LD (x),HL
$x \leftarrow x+1$	LD HL,(x) {byte version: LD HL,x }
	INC HL { INC (HL)}
	LD (x),HL
$ch \leftarrow '1'$	LD A,'1'
	LD (ch),A

Procedure call

$$p(p1,p2,\ldots,pn)$$

has the template translation

> *push pn*
>
> $\vdots$
>
> *push p2*
>
> *push p1*
>
> CALL *p*
>
> *pop all parameters*

where the code to *push* a 16-bit parameter onto the stack is

> LD HL,...
>
> PUSH HL

and the code to push two 8-bit parameters onto the stack together is

        LD H,...
        LD L,...
        PUSH HL

The code required to pop all the parameters off the stack is

        LD HL,x
        ADD HL,SP
        LD SP,HL

where x is the number of bytes taken up by all the parameters taken together.

Example

        $p(v,7)$

has the template translation

        LD HL,7
        PUSH HL
        LD HL,(v)
        PUSH HL
        CALL P
        LD HL,4
        ADD HL,SP
        LD SP,HL

If statement

The template used is essentially that described for the minicomputer but the 'comparison-and-branch' code is different.

There are only 4 conditional branch instructions corresponding to $x = y$, $x \neq y$, $x < y$ and $x \geqslant y$ so that the two relations $x > y$ and $x \leqslant y$ are tested in reverse, i.e. $y < x$ and $y \geqslant x$.

Minicomputer	Z80	
cmp x,y	AND A	{trick to clear the carry flag}
	LD HL,(x)	
	LD BC,(y)	
	SBC HL,BC	{subtract with carry}
b = label	JP Z,label	{Z stands for Zero}
⋮	⋮	
b < > label	JP NZ,label	{NZ stands for Not Zero}
⋮	⋮	
b < label	JP M,label	{M stands for Minus}
⋮	⋮	
b >= label	JP P,label	{P stands for Positive}
cmp x,y	AND A	
	LD HL,(y)	
	LD BC,(x)	
	SBC HL,BC	{y − x}
b> label	JP M,label	
cmp x,y	AND A	
	LD HL,(y)	
	LD BC,(x)	
	SBC HL,BC	{y − x}
b <= label	JP P,label	

If the jumps are local (less than 128 bytes away) then 'JR' can be used in place of 'JP'.

If 8-bit values are involved then the compare instruction 'CP' is used

Minicomputer	Z80	
cmpb x,y	LD A,(x)	
	LD HL,y	
	CP (HL)	{flags set according to A-(HL)}
b = label	JP Z,label	
etc.,...	etc.,...	

If 'y' is a constant then the form is even more direct

        LD A,(x)

        CP y

        JP ...

Example

        $m \leftarrow x$

        if $m < 0$

        then $m \leftarrow 0$

        else

                if $m > 15$

                then $m \leftarrow 15$

                fi

        fi

has the template translation (assuming 'byte' variables)

        LD A,(x)

        LD (m),A

        ifA: LD A,(m)

                   CP 0 $\{(m) - 0\}$

                   JR P,elseA

        thenA: LD A,0

                   LD (m),A

                   JR fiA

        elseA:

                ifB: LD A,15

                           LD HL,m

                           CP (HL) $\{15 - (m)\}$

                           JR P,fiB

                thenB: LD A,15

                           LD (m),A

                fiB:

        fiA:

Templates for the *while* statement and the *repeat* statement follow similarly.

Function definition

function f

$p:type\_p \rightarrow r:type\_r$

statements

has the template translation

f:

symbolic_constants_for_p_and_r

*template_code_for_statements_*

_with_references_to_p_and_r_suitably_changed

RET

The basic template given for the minicomputer is used but the references to parameters and local variables are written differently.

Minicomputer	Z80
...x[sp]...	LD IX,x
	ADD IX,SP
	...(IX+0)...
	...(IX+1)... {for 2nd byte, if required}

The capturing of the function result by popping it off the stack also changes as follows

Minicomputer	Z80
mov sp↑+,r0	POP HL

Example

function *letter*

$c:\text{Char} \rightarrow b:\mathbb{B}$

$b \leftarrow ('a' \leqslant c) \wedge (c \leqslant 'z')$

has the following template translation using EQU to define symbolic constants (cf. '=' in Section 6.5.1) as shown

False: EQU 0

True: EQU 1

c: EQU 2

b: EQU 3

```
letter: ifA:    LD IX,c
                ADD IX,SP
                LD A,(IX+0)
                LD B,'a'
                CP B            {c-'a'}
                JR M,elseA
       andA:    LD A,'z'
                LD IX,c
                ADD IX,SP
                LD B,(IX+0)
                CP B            {'z'-c}
                JR M,elseA
       thenA:   LD A,True
                LD IX,b
                ADD IX,SP
                LD (IX+0),A     {b←True}
                JR fiA
       elseA:   LD A,False
                LD IX,b
                ADD IX,SP
                LD (IX+0),A     {b←False}
       fiA:
                RET
```

A call of this function

> if   *letter(ch)*
>
> then   ...

has the template translation

```
ifA:    LD H,0      {to show dummy byte for result}
        LD L,(ch)   {genuine parameter}
        PUSH HL     {push parameter and 'result' together}
        CALL letter
        POP HL      {pop parameter and result together}
```

```
        LD A,H
        LD B,True
        CP B
        JP NZ,elseA
thenA:  ...
```

6.6.2   Templates for data structures

Templates for primitive data structures

The Z80 instruction set supports decimal arithmetic performed two digits at a time. Each digit occupies four bits in BCD (Binary Coded Decimal) so that a pair occupies a byte. This facility may be used to support 'real' numbers or the 'exponent & fraction' style in binary may be used. $\mathbb{R}$ is not considered further here.

$\mathbb{Z}$, $\mathbb{N}$, $\mathbb{P}$, $\mathbb{B}$, Char are as for the minicomputer.

Enumerated types

Enumerated types can be simulated in Z80 assembler using symbolic constants created by the 'EQU' pseudo operator.

	Declaration	Use
PDL	$(ID1,ID2,,..,IDn)$	$v \leftarrow IDi$
Z80	$ID1:$ EQU 0 $ID2:$ EQU 1 $\vdots$ $IDn:$ EQU $n-1$	LD A,IDi LD (v),A

Templates for compound data structures

Internal data structures

List of fixed length of type T

There is no true indexing available for arrays. Two values must be added with an ADD instruction to find the address of an element given a subscript.

$$v[i]$$

has the template translation

    LD HL,(i)

    map_HL

    LD BC,HL

    LD IX,v

    ADD IX,BC

    ...(IX + 0)...

    ...(IX + 1)...   {for 2nd byte, if required}

Example

$$v:\mathbb{Z}^{10}$$

$$v[i] \leftarrow v[i + 1]$$

has the template translation

    v: DEFS 20   {20 bytes required}

    LD HL,(i)

    INC HL   {i + 1}

    DEC HL   {map − require $v + 2*((i + 1) - 1)$}

    ADD HL,HL

    LD BC,HL

    LD IX,v

    ADD IX,BC

    LD HL,(i)

    DEC HL   {map − require $v + 2*(i - 1)$}

    ADD HL,HL

    LD BC,HL

    LD IY,v

    ADD IY,BC

    LD A,(IX + 0)   {move 1st byte}

    LD (IY + 0),A

    LD A,(IX + 1)   {move 2nd byte}

    LD (IY + 1),A

Record

The 'd' in the addressing mode (IX + d) can be viewed as the offset for accessing fields within records.

    Si(v)

has the template translation

    LD IX,*v*

    ...(IX + *Si*)...

Example

    rec:⟨*I*:$\mathbb{Z}$, *C*:Char , *B*:$\mathbb{B}$, *V*:$\mathbb{Z}^5$⟩

    I(rec) ← 2

    C(rec) ← '2'

    B(rec) ← True

    V(rec)[3] ← 2

has the template translation

rec:	DEFS 14	{total size 14 bytes}
iL:	EQU 0	{low byte of i}
iH:	EQU 1	{high byte of i}
c:	EQU 2	
b:	EQU 3	
v:	EQU 4	

    LD IX,rec
    LD A,2
    LD (IX + iL),A
    LD A,0
    LD (IX + iH),A

    LD IX,rec
    LD A,'2'
    LD (IX + c),A

    LD IX,res
    LD A,True
    LD (IX + b),A

```
        LD HL,3
        DEC HL              {map}
        ADD HL,HL
        LD BC,HL
        LD IX,rec
        ADD IX,BC
        LD BC,v
        ADD IX,BC
        LD A,2
        LD (IX+0),A
        LD A,0
        LD (IX+1),A
```

External data structures

The main I/O instructions in Z80 assembler are

     IN A,(n)   {read a byte from port 'n' into register A}

     OUT (n),A   {output a byte to port 'n' from register A}

Thus the byte I/O templates are

PDL	Assembler
newinputc ← head(input) input ← tail(input)	IN A,(input) LD (newinputc),A
output ← output ‖ newoutputc	LD A,(newoutputc) OUT (output),A

Exercises 6

1 By now you should have eight PDL functions from your answers to the questions in Chapter 5 and you now have templates for five languages so there are 40 coding tasks to choose from!

7
Verification

Having been very particular about how we write our specifications, we are now in a position to check that associated code segments actually satisfy these specifications. Moreover the techniques presented below can be applied at any intermediate stage in the overall translation process – along any arrow in the schematic diagram (Figure 7.1) – and more generally at any stage within the stepwise refinement process.

Taking small steps is the safest approach, justifying each translation as we go. We usually 'trust' the final code generator in the same way as most programmers 'trust' compilers but we shall say more about this later (Chapter 8). To make matters a little more concrete we shall focus attention on the translation from an implementation-orientated specification (Specification II) to a PDL realisation. In the current chapter we shall also presume that the PDL treats its integer arithmetic in an idealised way – no errors, no limitations – and that we know how to manipulate expressions without explicit reference to the relevant algebraic rules. These matters will be addressed in due course but ignoring them for the time being allows us to concentrate on the logical aspects of the problem which are, in any case, of more general application.

Recall that for the specification of $f:D \to R$ given by

> type: $D \to R$
> pre--$f(x) \triangleq \ldots$
> post-$f(x,y) \triangleq \ldots$

any realisation, F, is valid provided that we can prove the theorem 'for all elements x in the set D, satisfaction of the pre-condition implies that the

Fig. 7.1

realisation gives the result $F(x)$ and the pair $(x,F(x))$ satisfies the post-condition'. Symbolically this can be written:

$$(\forall x \in D)(\text{pre-}f(x) \Rightarrow \text{post-}f(x,F(x))).$$

If D was small then it might be feasible to check the implication for each individual element but usually this is impracticable so we proceed by treating the input value purely symbolically, paying no regard to which value we actually have. We shall therefore often avoid explicit mention of D but it is important to remember that in this situation D is not only a set but, by association, often has standard operators defined upon it. For example if $x \in \mathbb{Z}$ and $y \in \mathbb{B}$ then $x + 2$ is sensible but $y + 2$ is not. When examining proofs 'by hand' this is no problem but automating such a process requires that the operators and their properties should be properly defined. As already noted these matters will be discussed later.

We are now left with implication ($\Rightarrow$). This logical operator is central to the verification techniques but is less common than the familiar *and-or-not* logic found elsewhere in Computer Science and hence we introduce it (Section 7.1) in some considerable depth before applying it to proofs about program segments.

Proving the correctness of a non-trivial program is a very complex task. We shall therefore seek ways in which specifications and programs can be dissected into subparts that are easier to use separately and can be recombined in standard ways to yield the sought logical interrelationships. In Section 7.2 we consider how we might unify the concepts of operations and functions so as to obtain the best of both worlds. This also necessitates discussion of parameter passing and the correspondence between *control* flow and *data* flow diagrams.

Having made certain simplifying assumptions, we can then apply our knowledge of the logical operators to relate the standard *structured-programming* constructs to specifications of their submodules. In Section 7.3 we deal with sequencing and alternation and then in Section 7.4 we tackle the more difficult problems associated with recursion and iteration. In that section we shall have to overcome the conflict that arises from the absence of iteration in specifications and the absence of (or at least opposition to the use of) recursion in many high-level programming languages. We shall also include more material on logic, notably proof by induction. Some concluding remarks are given in Section 7.5.

7.1   The implication operator

We shall be concerned with implications between predicates. Predicates (about numbers, sets, lists, strings or whatever) are functions which, depending on their inputs, yield the value True or False. The classical Boolean algebra involving the constants True and False, and the operators ∧ (pronounced *and*, so $p \wedge q$ is read as 'p and q'), ∨ (pronounced *or*) and ⌐ (pronounced *not*, so ⌐p is read as 'not p', which is also written – in this section only – as p′) satisfy the following axioms

1. $p \vee q = q \vee p$
2. $p \vee (q \vee r) = (p \vee q) \vee r$
3. $p \vee \text{False} = p$
4. $p \vee p' = \text{True}$
5. $p \wedge q = q \wedge p$
6. $p \wedge (q \wedge r) = (p \wedge q) \wedge r$
7. $p \wedge \text{True} = p$
8. $p \wedge p' = \text{False}$
9. $p \wedge (q \vee r) = (p \wedge q) \vee (p \wedge r)$
10. $p \vee (q \wedge r) = (p \vee q) \wedge (p \vee r)$

These axioms are consistent with the usual definition table given in Figure 7.2 and give rise to the consequential laws.

11. $p \vee \text{True} = \text{True}$
    $p \wedge \text{False} = \text{False}$
12. (idempotence)
    $p \wedge p = p$
    $p \vee p = p$
13. (involution)
    $(p')' = p$
14. (absorption)
    $p \wedge (p \vee q) = p$
    $p \vee (p \wedge q) = p$
15. (de Morgan's laws)
    $(p \wedge q)' = p' \vee q'$
    $(p \vee q)' = p' \wedge q'$

Fig. 7.2

p	q	$p \wedge q$	$p \vee q$	p'
True	True	True	True	False
True	False	False	True	False
False	True	False	True	True
False	False	False	False	True

The identities, or rules, numbered 1–15 will be quoted only when necessary to justify a particularly tedious or new piece of maniulation.† Now for implication. The easiest way to motivate the definition of $p \Rightarrow q$, in terms of *and-or-not*, is to refer back to the expression

$$\text{pre-}f(x) \Rightarrow \text{post-}f(x,F(x))$$

and to consider ways in which the realisation F might not be acceptable. Recall that if pre-$f(x)$ is not satisfied then we are not going to execute F and hence we do not care what F would do with x; any action would be acceptable (and totally irrelevant) – we would not reject a piece of code because it gave the 'wrong' answer from an invalid data value! On the other hand, if pre-$f(x)$ were True we would definitely reject F if post-$f(x,F(x))$ was False. Thus we have the table in Figure 7.3.

Fig. 7.3

p	q	$p \Rightarrow q$
True	True	True
True	False	False
False	True	True
False	False	True

This definition often causes problems; students simply do not believe that it is sensible. It is however very important to spend time convincing yourself of its validity. In 'programming language style' $p \Rightarrow q$ can also be read as

> if p then q fi

or, if you worry about having no *else* clause,

> if p then q else True fi

(But see also Exercises 7.1.7 and 7.1.8.)

Investigation of the truth tables in Figures 7.2 and 7.3 will reveal that

$$(p \Rightarrow q) \triangleq p' \vee q$$

From this algebraic definition we can properly deduce the properties of the implication operator. The first group of these is very simple.

† Note. It may help in following the logic arguments to come to regard **all** free-standing Boolean statements as being True. So p means 'p is True'; $\neg p$ means '$\neg p$ is True' and therefore, by rule 13, 'p is False'. Of course there will be situations when a Boolean expression has to be evaluated and should not be presumed to be True; such cases should be clear by their context, usually within a proof.

Theorem 1

For arbitrary predicates p and q –

    (a) $(\text{True} \Rightarrow q) = q$

    (b) $(\text{False} \Rightarrow q) = \text{True}$

    (c) $(p \Rightarrow \text{True}) = \text{True}$

    (d) $(p \Rightarrow \text{False}) = p'$

Proofs

    (a) $(\text{True} \Rightarrow q)\ = \text{False} \vee q$ (definition)

                       $= q$ (rule 3)

    (b) $(\text{False} \Rightarrow q) = \text{True} \vee q$ (definition)

                      $= \text{True}$ (rule 11)

    (c) $(p \Rightarrow \text{True}) = p' \vee \text{True}$ (definition)

                    $= \text{True}$ (rule 11)

    (d) $(p \Rightarrow \text{False}) = p' \vee \text{False}$ (definition)

                    $= p'$ (rule 3)   □

These proofs were represented as a succession of equalities and utilised the transitive property of the equality relation (i.e. if $a = b$ and $b = c$ then $a = c$). Such an approach is not always applicable since it is not always possible to reverse logical arguments ($x = 3$ implies x is odd but x being odd does not imply that $x = 3$). Subsequently we shall now use implication as part of the proof mechanism as well as a component of the expression about which facts are being proved. This is not really as bad as it sounds, if we use '$\rightarrow$' as a higher level implication operator and note the following argument:

$$(p \Rightarrow q) \wedge (q \Rightarrow r)$$

$$= (p' \vee q) \wedge (q' \vee r)$$

$$= (p' \wedge (q' \vee r)) \vee (q \wedge (q' \vee r))$$

$$= (p' \wedge q') \vee (p' \wedge r) \vee (q \wedge q') \vee (q \wedge r)$$

$$= (p' \wedge q') \vee (p' \wedge r) \vee \text{False} \vee (q \wedge r) \qquad \text{(rule 8)}$$

$$= (p' \wedge q') \vee (p' \wedge r) \vee (q \wedge r) \qquad \text{(rule 3)}$$

Now notice that:

    if $s \wedge t = \text{True}$

    then $s = s \vee (s \wedge t)$ (rule 14)

               $= s \vee \text{True}$ (assumption)

             $= \text{True}$ (rule 11)

so   (i) $(p' \wedge q') = \text{True} \rightarrow p' = \text{True}$

                      $\rightarrow p' \vee r = \text{True}$

                      $\rightarrow (p \Rightarrow r)$

(ii) $(q \wedge r) = \text{True} \rightarrow r = \text{True}$
$$\rightarrow p' \vee r = \text{True}$$
$$\rightarrow (p \Rightarrow r)$$
and (iii) $(p' \wedge r) = \text{True} \rightarrow p' \vee r = \text{True}$
$$\rightarrow (p \Rightarrow r)$$

So, if $(p \Rightarrow q)$ and $(q \Rightarrow r)$ then $(p \Rightarrow q) \wedge (q \Rightarrow r)$ is True and so is $(p' \wedge q') \vee (p' \wedge r) \vee (q \wedge r)$. Therefore at least one of the factors $(p' \wedge q')$, $(p' \wedge r)$ or $(q \wedge r)$ must also be true and each of these imply that $(p \Rightarrow r)$. Thus we deduce that if $p \Rightarrow q$ and $q \Rightarrow r$ then $p \Rightarrow r$. So transitivity also holds for implication. This allows us to put together *direct proofs* by constructing a finite progression of intermediate predicates $p_0, \ldots, p_n$ where

$$p_0 \Rightarrow p_1, p_1 \Rightarrow p_2, \ldots, \text{and } p_{n-1} \Rightarrow p_n,$$

then, if $p = p_0$ and $q = p_n$, we may use transitivity (n times) to deduce that $p \Rightarrow q$. Such a progression of implications is often written:

$$p_0 \Rightarrow p_1 \Rightarrow p_2 \Rightarrow \ldots \Rightarrow p_{n-1} \Rightarrow p_n$$

but must be interpreted as n separate (but related) implications as above.

Our earlier use of equality, sometimes written as $\equiv$ or $\leftrightarrow$ or $\Leftrightarrow$ to avoid confusion with non-logical equality operations, can be easily explained by the definition

$$(p \Leftrightarrow q) \triangleq (p \Rightarrow q) \wedge (q \Rightarrow p)$$

Before utilising direct proofs to obtain some results concerning implication we remark that one useful way of demonstrating that p implies q is to prove that the expression $p \Rightarrow q$ is True. This follows from a mathematical deduction law called *modus ponens* which essentially says that if p is True and $p \Rightarrow q$ is also True then we can deduce that q is also True.

Similarly, the predicates p and q are equivalent if the expression $p \Leftrightarrow q$ is True.

We put these ideas to immediate use in the next theorem.

Theorem 2

For arbitrary predicates p, q and r

(a) $(p \Rightarrow q) \Leftrightarrow (q' \Rightarrow p')$

(b) $(p \Rightarrow q) \Rightarrow (p \Rightarrow (q \vee r))$

(c) $(p \Rightarrow q) \Rightarrow ((p \wedge r) \Rightarrow q)$

(d) $((p \Rightarrow q) \wedge (p' \Rightarrow q')) \Leftrightarrow (p \Leftrightarrow q)$

Proof

(a) $(p \Rightarrow q) \Leftrightarrow (q' \Rightarrow p')$

$\leftrightarrow (p' \vee q) \Leftrightarrow (q'' \vee p')$

$\leftrightarrow$ $(p' \vee q) \Leftrightarrow (q \vee p')$

$\leftrightarrow$ $x \Leftrightarrow x$

where $x = p' \vee q$

But $\quad x \Leftrightarrow x$

$\leftrightarrow$ $(x \Rightarrow x) \wedge (x \Rightarrow x)$

$\leftrightarrow$ $(x' \vee x) \wedge (x' \vee x)$

$\leftrightarrow$ True $\wedge$ True

$\leftrightarrow$ True

(b) $(p \Rightarrow q) \Rightarrow (p \Rightarrow (q \vee r))$

$\leftrightarrow$ $(p' \vee q) \Rightarrow (p' \vee (q \vee r))$

$\leftrightarrow$ $(p' \vee q)' \vee (p' \vee q \vee r)$

$\leftrightarrow$ $(p \wedge q') \vee (p' \vee q \vee r)$

$\leftrightarrow$ $(p \vee p' \vee q \vee r) \wedge (q' \vee p' \vee q \vee r)$

$\leftrightarrow$ $(\text{True} \vee q \vee r) \wedge (\text{True} \vee p' \vee r)$

$\leftrightarrow$ True $\wedge$ True

$\leftrightarrow$ True

(c) similarly

$(p \Rightarrow q) \Rightarrow ((p \wedge r) \Rightarrow q)$

$\leftrightarrow$ $(p \wedge q') \vee ((p \wedge r)' \vee q)$

$\leftrightarrow$ $(p \wedge q') \vee (p' \vee r' \vee q)$

$\leftrightarrow$ $(p \vee p' \vee r' \vee q) \wedge (q' \vee p' \vee r' \vee q)$

$\leftrightarrow$ True $\wedge$ True

$\leftrightarrow$ True

(d) $((p \Rightarrow q) \wedge (p' \Rightarrow q')) \Leftrightarrow (p \Leftrightarrow q)$

$\leftrightarrow$ $((p \Rightarrow q) \wedge (p' \Rightarrow q')) \Leftrightarrow ((p \Rightarrow q) \wedge (q \Rightarrow p))$

But by (a) $(p' \Rightarrow q') \Leftrightarrow (q \Rightarrow p)$ so both sides of the equivalence are identical and hence the result follows. $\qquad \square$

Most of the implications we shall need to prove can be schematically demonstrated by progressively restricting the left-hand side (using Theorem 2(c)) or extending the right-hand side (Theorem 2(b)) and reducing the implication to the form $p \Rightarrow p$ which is known to be True.

Of course, when investigating $p \Rightarrow q$ it is unlikely that p and q will be simple predicates; they will be expressions having components linked by other logical connectives, typically *and-or-not* operators or *if-then-else-fi* constructs. Several useful results concerning the evaluation of expressions and their subexpressions now follow – then we can forget about justifying our logical rules and get back to programs and specifications.

Theorem 3(a)

> If $p \Rightarrow q$
>
> and $p = p_1 \vee p_2 \vee \ldots \vee p_n$ for some $n \in \mathbb{N}$
>
> then $(p \Rightarrow q) \leftrightarrow ((p_1 \Rightarrow q) \wedge (p_2 \Rightarrow q) \wedge \ldots \wedge (p_n \Rightarrow q))$

Proof

We give the case when $n = 3$; the general proof is similar.

$$p \Rightarrow q$$
$$\leftrightarrow (p' \vee q) = \text{True}$$
$$\leftrightarrow ((p_1 \vee p_2 \vee p_3)' \vee q) = \text{True}$$
$$\leftrightarrow ((p_1' \wedge p_2' \wedge p_3') \vee q) = \text{True}$$
$$\leftrightarrow ((p_1' \vee q) \wedge (p_2' \vee q) \wedge (p_3' \vee q)) = \text{True}$$
$$\leftrightarrow ((p_1 \Rightarrow q) \wedge (p_2 \Rightarrow q) \wedge (p_3 \Rightarrow q)) = \text{True}$$
$$\leftrightarrow (p_1 \Rightarrow q) \wedge (p_2 \Rightarrow q) \wedge (p_3 \Rightarrow q) \qquad \square$$

Using the notations

$$\bigvee_{i=1}^{n} p_i \quad \text{for } p_1 \vee \ldots \vee p_n,$$

$$\bigvee_{i \in A} p_i \quad \text{(where } i \text{ is allowed to range over some finite set } A \subset \mathbb{N}$$
which may or may not be stated explicitly),

$$\bigwedge_{i=1}^{n} p_i \quad \text{for } p_1 \wedge \ldots \wedge p_n$$

and

$$\bigwedge_{i \in A} p_i,$$

we can represent the conclusion of the theorem by

$$\left(\left(\bigvee_{i \in A} p_i \right) \Rightarrow q \right) \leftrightarrow \bigwedge_{i \in A} (p_i \Rightarrow q)$$

This theorem is particularly useful in two kinds of situation. Firstly if r is some decidable predicate then $r \vee r' = \text{True}$ and

$$(r \Rightarrow q) \wedge (r' \Rightarrow q)$$
$$\rightarrow ((r \vee r') \Rightarrow q)$$
$$\rightarrow (\text{True} \Rightarrow q)$$
$$\rightarrow q$$

Secondly, and of more general application, if $p = \bigvee_{i \in A} p_i$ and $p_j \not\Rightarrow q$ (p_j does not imply q) for some value of $j \in A$ then $p \not\Rightarrow q$. More precisely

$$(p_j \not\Rightarrow q) \triangleq (p_j \Rightarrow q)'$$

So if $p_j \Rightarrow q$ is False then by rule 11 and theorem 3(a) we have:

$$p \Rightarrow q \leftrightarrow \left(\bigwedge_{i \in A \setminus \{j\}} (p_i \Rightarrow q) \right) \wedge (p_j \Rightarrow q)$$

$$\leftrightarrow \text{False}$$

So we conclude that $p \not\Rightarrow q$ without reference to the components $p_i \Rightarrow q$ when $i \neq j$. Similarly we have:

Theorem 3(b)

$$\left(\bigwedge_{i \in A} p_i \right) \Rightarrow q$$

$$\leftrightarrow \bigvee_{i \in A} (p_i \Rightarrow q) \qquad \qquad \square$$

Thus, again by rule 11, $(p_j \Rightarrow q) \to (p \Rightarrow q)$ for any suitable $j \in A$; other terms can be ignored.

Theorem 3(c)

$$p \Rightarrow \bigwedge_{j \in A} q_j$$

$$\leftrightarrow \bigwedge_{j \in A} (p \Rightarrow q_j)$$

Theorem 3(d)

$$p \Rightarrow \bigvee_{j \in A} q_j$$

$$\leftrightarrow \bigvee_{j \in A} (p \Rightarrow q_j) \qquad \qquad \square$$

Just as parts (a) and (b) can be used to shorten the evaluation of $p \Rightarrow q$ when p is expressible in the form $\bigwedge p_i$ or $\bigvee p_i$, similar consequences follow from parts (c) and (d) when q is representable in the conjunctive or disjunctive form, i.e. $\bigwedge q_j$ or $\bigvee q_j$.

As already noted, the implication operator is closely linked with the incomplete conditional expression 'if...then...fi'. We have also seen that the complete construct *if...then...else...fi* occurs naturally both in specifications and in PDL. This construct can now be properly defined using logical operators and hence we obtain methods of dissecting proofs involving conditionals.

Firstly the definition:

$$\text{if } \alpha \text{ then } p \text{ else } q \text{ fi} \triangleq (\alpha \Rightarrow p) \wedge (\alpha' \Rightarrow q)$$

Now for the theorems.

Theorem 4(a)

$$(\text{if } \alpha \text{ then } p \text{ else } q \text{ fi}) \Rightarrow r$$
$$\leftrightarrow \text{if } \alpha \text{ then } (p \Rightarrow r) \text{ else } (q \Rightarrow r) \text{ fi} \qquad \square$$

The proof of 4(a) is left as an exercise to the reader.

Theorem 4(b)

$$p \Rightarrow (\text{if } \beta \text{ then } q \text{ else } r \text{ fi})$$
$$\leftrightarrow \text{if } \beta \text{ then } (p \Rightarrow q) \text{ else } (p \Rightarrow r) \text{ fi}$$

Proof

$$p \Rightarrow (\text{if } \beta \text{ then } q \text{ else } r \text{ fi})$$
$$\leftrightarrow p' \vee ((\beta' \vee q) \wedge (\beta \vee r))$$
$$\leftrightarrow (p' \vee \beta' \vee q) \wedge (p' \vee \beta \vee r)$$
$$\leftrightarrow (\beta' \vee (p' \vee q)) \wedge (\beta \vee (p' \vee r))$$
$$\leftrightarrow (\beta \Rightarrow (p \Rightarrow q)) \wedge (\beta' \Rightarrow (p \Rightarrow r))$$
$$\leftrightarrow \text{if } \beta \text{ then } (p \Rightarrow q) \text{ else } (p \Rightarrow r) \text{ fi} \qquad \square$$

We can now forget about details of these proofs and quote the theorems as appropriate without recourse to handwaving.

Exercises 7.1

1. Show
   (a) by construction of the appropriate truth table, and
   (b) by a proper algebraic proof using the numbered axioms and laws, that $(a \wedge (a \Rightarrow b)) \to b$ is always true.
2. State the four parts of Theorem 2 in non-mathematical language and construct simple examples (arithmetic or otherwise) to illustrate each of them.
3. Provide full proofs of Theorems 3(b), (c) and (d) for the case when $A = \{1,2,3\}$.
4. Show that
   $$(p \Rightarrow (q \Rightarrow r)) \to ((p \wedge q) \Rightarrow r)$$
   and hence, by writing True as $p \vee \neg p$, that
   $$(q \Rightarrow r) \leftrightarrow ((p \wedge q) \Rightarrow r) \wedge ((\neg p \wedge q) \Rightarrow r).$$

5. Prove that

$$(a \wedge b) \rightarrow (a \Rightarrow b)$$

and hence deduce that another way of verifying that $a \Rightarrow b$ is by seeing whether $a \wedge b$ evaluates to True.

Show also that

$$(a \Rightarrow b) \rightarrow (a \wedge b)$$

is not always True.

6. Notwithstanding the conclusion of question 5, show that

$$(\text{if } p \text{ then } t \text{ else } f \text{ fi}) \Leftrightarrow ((p \wedge t) \vee (p' \wedge f))$$

The astute reader will have noticed an operational discrepancy between the sequential perception of $a \Rightarrow b$ and the static, and total, evaluation of its defining expression $a' \vee b$. If a were False then we would like to conclude that the implication was True without even considering the value of b. We may wish to do this in certain circumstances where b may not even be defined when a is False. For instance, we might wish to define a function value y in terms of the real number x by

$$\text{if } x = 0 \text{ then } y = 1 \text{ else } y = 1/x \text{ fi}$$

Using our standard definition this reduces to

$$(\neg(x = 0) \vee (y = 1)) \wedge ((x = 0) \vee (y = 1/x))$$

which should give True for suitable values of x and y, and False otherwise. However, consider $x = 0$, $y = 2$. This requires us to obtain a Boolean value for the expression $(2 = 1/0)$, but $1/0$ is not a real number so the value of the expression is neither True nor False; it is Undefined. Oops!

We cannot avoid this problem so we must extend our logic from $\mathbb{B}$ to $\mathbb{E}$ (extended, three-valued logic) where $\mathbb{E} = \{\text{True, Undefined, False}\}$ with operations defined thus:

$\vee$	T	U	F		$\wedge$	T	U	F		$\neg$	
T	T	T	T		T	T	U	F		T	F
U	T	U	U		U	U	U	F		U	U
F	T	U	F		F	F	F	F		F	T

In the table T,U,F stand for True, Undefined and False respectively. Compare these with *logical arithmetic* in [8] p. 126.

7. Determine which of the logic rules (1–15) are valid over $\mathbb{E}$.

8. Consider the definition of implication and justify that provided that *a* is not Undefined then $a \Rightarrow b$ works properly over $\mathbb{E}$. Show also that, under a similar proviso for each value immediately preceding an implication operator, transitivity holds and that conditionals behave predictably.

7.2   Control-flow diagrams and data-flow specification diagrams

In what follows we shall usually ignore the *type* line of a specification and regard all changes caused by an operation as acting on the background state. (The choice between state/parameter and state/result for input and output values helps to clarify the main aspects of the specification but the parameter/result components are essentially cosmetic in that they allow a degree of parameterisation of the specification.) Restricting specifications in this way allows us to give a proper functional description of processes – but these functions are much more powerful than those commonly available in conventional programming languages.

Consider a general specification:

$$OP$$

$$\vdots$$

$$\text{post-}OP(\sigma,\pi,\sigma',\rho) \triangleq \dots$$

Recall that

σ is a list of variables which can be accessed and changed by *OP*,

π is a list of variables, the 'values' of which are, in general, derived from expressions before being made available to *OP*, and

ρ is a list of variables to which *OP* assigns values.

From *OP* we can derive *OP'*, an 'equivalent' operation in that it does exactly the same calculations but acts on a general state vector, Σ. This is done as follows; first note that *OP* can be refined from:

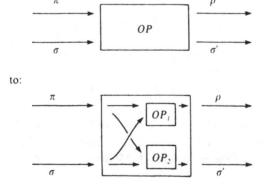

to:

where OP_1 produces the results (effects) and OP_2 causes any required side-effects which are represented as changes in the state (from σ to σ').

Now let Σ be the set of globals (i.e., variables generally accessible **outside** of OP). Σ can be partitioned into disjoint sets

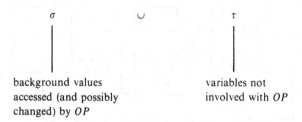

Σ then relates to OP as follows:

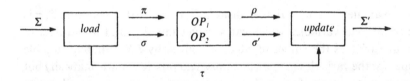

This is a *data flow* diagram. Information, in the form of (name, value) pairs flows along **all** these paths, each process obtaining its data from (name,value) pairs on the input lines and broadcasting its effect by making appropriate (name,value) pairs available on the output lines. To see how it works consider the following specification:

EX

states: $\mathbb{Z}$

type: $\mathbb{Z} \to \mathbb{Z}$

pre--$EX(y,x) \triangleq$ True

post-$EX(y,x,y',r) \triangleq (r = x + y) \wedge (y' = y + 2x)$

Now suppose that the global set is $\{a,b,y:\mathbb{Z}\}$ and that EX is used in the statement

$b \leftarrow EX(a+b)$

The context of an assignment statement gives rise to explicit actions for *load* and *update*. (Precise details of how these processes are defined in other contexts will not be considered but it is important to realise that corresponding actions are **always** present.) Hence we have for example:

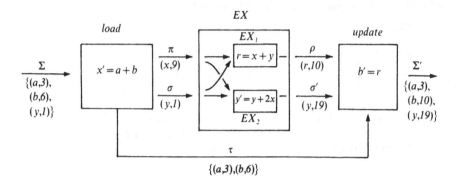

π and ρ are new sets of variables, disjoint from each other and from Σ; π is the set of load variables which carry values into EX and ρ is the set of output variables the values of which are given by EX. (Finding suitable names for the variables in these sets causes no problem mathematically but allocation of names for local quantities within your proposed target language may not be so simple.)

Now, with reference to the example, it is easy to see what has to happen in the general case. The *load* process has no effect on σ or τ, their values merely being passed through, but using the expressions quoted as actual parameters of OP (or EX) values for π are computed from Σ ($=\sigma \cup \tau$). In the EX example we have $x' = a + b$ and by implication $y' = y$, $a' = a$ and $b' = b$. The values for π and σ are then made available to OP (or EX) and the outputs ρ and σ' produced accordingly. Finally, in *update*, appropriate values in τ are overwritten by values from ρ which are subsequently discarded.

The processes *load* and *update* can be described mathematically but we shall not do this because we now wish to ignore the details of the interconnections between *load/OP/update* and replace the combination with

$$OP' : \Sigma \to \Sigma'$$

thus extending the operation OP to an operation (or process) OP'. Using a suitable Σ then allows operations to be plugged together. Moreover, we can regard OP' as an implicit function and indicate the state change from σ_1 to σ_2

caused by OP' by writing $\sigma_2 = OP'(\sigma_1)$. Diagrammatically this is

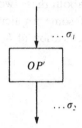

Therefore there is no need to use special names (such as OP' instead of OP) nor do we need to specify which data flows in each part of the diagram – **all** flow lines carry data values for the entire state. We can therefore turn our attention to the more common *control* flow diagrams (i.e. flowcharts).

Later we shall consider the standard flowchart shapes in some detail but to conclude these more general introductory remarks we make some brief comments on how processes are connected in arbitrary flowcharts.

We shall assume that Σ is the state on which the program acts, that σ, σ', σ_1, etc. represent particular values of Σ and all tests are binary. Diagrammatically we have only to consider the following five features:

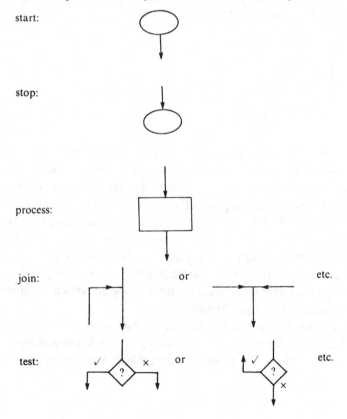

To aid program synthesis and analysis it is desirable that we only have a single start and a single stop but nothing else need be said about these two components. A process *SUB* is a correct realisation of some implicit function *F* if it changes states in accordance with the specification of *F*.

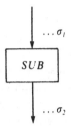

So $\sigma_2 = SUB(\sigma_1)$ and we require that post-$F(\sigma_1,\sigma_2)$ = True whenever pre-$F(\sigma_1)$ = True. This then gives an implicit relation between the predicate valid at σ_1 (i.e. the facts which are guaranteed to hold at σ_1) and that valid at σ_2. It is the only way in which new knowledge about Σ can arise.

At a join, information is rationalised. Let us annotate a join with predicates *P*, *Q* and *R* (each of type $\Sigma \to \mathbb{B}$).

There are two observations to make here. Firstly if we look at (say) the left-hand side of the diagram, notice that there is no computation between the points annotated by *P* and *R*. So no information can be gained while moving between these two points. If *R* was a pre-condition for some process we may not need all the information in *P* and we may therefore choose to lose some. Logically we require the relationship $P \Rightarrow R$ (or $P(\sigma) \Rightarrow R(\sigma)$). Taking the whole diagram into account it is obvious that we also need $Q \Rightarrow R$, and from the rules of logic it follows that $(P \vee Q) \Rightarrow R$. This is perfectly reasonable since when we reach *R* we do not know whether we came via the left or right branch.

At a (binary) test the situation is similar, we have done no further calculation which would change values in Σ but we do know more by virtue of our current position in the flowchart which was determined by a test evaluated with reference to Σ. Again consider an example.

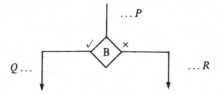

As before, we might choose to lose information between P and Q or R but we must have

$$(P \wedge B) \Rightarrow Q$$

and

$$(P \wedge \neg B) \Rightarrow R$$

Typically, knowing whether B is True or False enables us to simplify information given in P.

The problem of analysing a given flowchart is non-trivial and is secondary to our main task of program synthesis and verification. However we shall briefly return again to the subject in Chapter 11. Next we look at natural ways of relating specifications of processes to specification of their subprocesses.

Exercises 7.2
1. By constructing suitable dataflow diagrams, consider how you would split a specification (post-condition) of an arbitrary OP into specification of OP_1 – delivering ρ – and OP_2 – delivering σ'.
2. Show that

$$((P \Rightarrow R) \wedge (Q \Rightarrow R)) \Rightarrow ((P \vee Q) \Rightarrow R)$$

7.3   Sequencing and alternation
Proving that a single simple statement in a given programming language satisfies an appropriate specification amounts to little more than straightforward symbol manipulation – it is almost impossible to manufacture small examples which are particularly convincing. So let us combine processes (or equivalently dissect specifications) as a first attempt to move to realistic programs/problems. We begin by considering non-repetitive processes – in which any piece of code is executed at most once.

Suppose we compose two program segments one after the other as in Figure 7.4. If the segments $SUB1$ and $SUB2$ execute to termination (i.e. given the state σ_1 then the states σ_2 and σ_3 **are** achieved) then we have the relationships

$$\sigma_2 = SUB1(\sigma_1)$$

and

$$\sigma_3 = SUB2(\sigma_2)$$

and therefore

$$\sigma_3 = SUB2(SUB1(\sigma_1))$$

In terms of functional composition this is written as

$$\sigma_3 = SUB2 \circ SUB1(\sigma_1)$$

and in PDL as

$$\sigma_3 = (SUB1;SUB2)(\sigma_1)$$

Notice the order reversal. This is an accident of notation; it is not of fundamental importance but can lead to mistakes so be careful.

Fig. 7.4

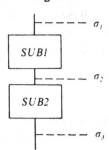

In some cases we will require functions (as implemented by *SUB1* and *SUB2*, say) to be perfectly matched so that all the processing done by the first exactly fits the input requirements of the second. However some slack is usually allowed and logically this means that parts of the system are linked by implication rather than equality (i.e. ⇔). To see how this works we need to relate *SUB1* and *SUB2* to the specifications of the functions they satisfy: let them be *F1* and *F2*.

So

$$\text{pre-}F1(\sigma) \Rightarrow \text{post-}F1(\sigma, SUB1(\sigma))$$

and

$$\text{pre-}F2(\sigma) \Rightarrow \text{post-}F2(\sigma, SUB2(\sigma))$$

Suppose we wish to implement *F*, having the appropriate pre- and post-conditions, and that *SUB1;SUB2* is offered as a solution. Rather than working directly from the PDL segment we shall use annotated flowcharts so as to facilitate indication of post-conditions. Recall that these relate two distinct arcs in the control flow of the program. To keep the names in step we shall refer to the combination *SUB1;SUB2* as *SUB* as indicated in Figure 7.5.

Fig. 7.5

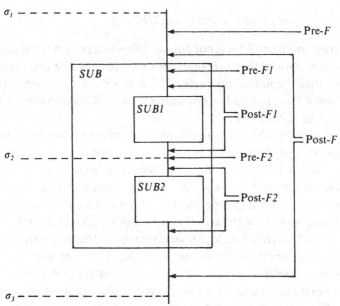

Now, regardless of what *SUB1* actually does, all we can guarantee is that under the constraint pre-*F1* the state σ_1 is altered, by *SUB1*, to become σ_2 and (σ_1,σ_2) together satisfy post-*F1*. Similarly for the logical relationship between σ_2 and σ_3, the change here being caused by *SUB2*.

On the other hand, we require that

$$\text{pre-}F(\sigma_1) \Rightarrow \text{post-}F(\sigma_1, SUB(\sigma_1))$$

Progressing **down** Figure 7.5 we can see how the changes of state relate to the specifications.

$$\text{pre-}F(\sigma_1) \Rightarrow \text{pre-}F1(\sigma_1)$$

– we can only start the process *SUB* if we can start *SUB1*,

$$\text{pre-}F1(\sigma_1) \land \text{post-}F1(\sigma_1,\sigma_2) \Rightarrow \text{pre-}F2(\sigma_2)$$

– the state change caused by *SUB1* must result in a state, σ_2, which allows us to start *SUB2*, and

$$\text{pre-}F(\sigma_1) \wedge \text{post-}F1(\sigma_1,\sigma_2) \wedge \text{post-}F2(\sigma_2,\sigma_3) \Rightarrow \text{post-}F(\sigma_1,\sigma_3)$$

– the state change caused by *SUB1* followed by *SUB2* is strong enough to meet the post-condition (i.e. the real specification) of *F*.

These three requirements should be clear from the figure; if all three hold then the combination *SUB1;SUB2* does indeed satisfy the correctness theorem for *F*, i.e.

$$\text{pre-}F(\sigma) \Rightarrow \text{post-}F(\sigma,(SUB1;SUB2)(\sigma))$$

Referring to Figure 7.5 it is not difficult to see where each of the conditions came from. Notice that here there are two types, the first two implications ensure that the individual parts of *SUB* can begin $(\ldots \Rightarrow \text{pre-}F1(\sigma_1))$ and $(\ldots \Rightarrow \text{pre-}F2(\sigma_2))$ and the last one relates the overall state change (σ_1 to σ_3) to the post-condition of *F*.

We can collect these conditions together and rationalise our notation. In particular, since the states are 'variables' we can use any names we like; suffices will be dropped except when useful to indicate progression through several different states. We are also unconcerned about (unaware of) any discrepancy between the specification of a process and the actual process and hence we can use the same name for both *SUB* and *F* (in fact we shall refer to both as *OP*). Finally, because we require that any state satisfying a specific pre-condition should be such that complete execution of the associated operation is guaranteed – mathematically the state is in the *domain* of the operation – conditions implying the validity of pre-conditions are called *domain rules*. Similarly, the other conditions relate initial to final states and the final states are elements of the *range*; the conditions are therefore known as *range rules*.

In the case of sequencing there are two domain rules (d_1,d_2) and a single range rule (r_1) and we can state that if *OP1* and *OP2* satisfy their respective pre- and post-conditions then $OP \triangleq OP1;OP2$ satisfies pre-*OP* and post-*OP* providing the following rules hold.

d_1: $\text{pre-}OP(\sigma) \Rightarrow \text{pre-}OP1(\sigma)$

d_2: $\text{pre-}OP1(\sigma_1) \wedge \text{post-}OP1(\sigma_1,\sigma_2) \Rightarrow \text{pre-}OP2(\sigma_2)$

r_1: $\text{pre-}OP(\sigma_1) \wedge \text{post-}OP1(\sigma_1,\sigma_2) \wedge \text{post-}OP2(\sigma_2,\sigma_3)$
$$\Rightarrow \text{post-}OP(\sigma_1,\sigma_3)$$

The proof of correctness of *OP1;OP2* against the specification of *OP* can then be tackled indirectly by proving d_1, d_2 and r_1.

Our notation is now in line with that to be found in [20].

Example 7.3.1
Consider an ordered pair of assignment statements acting on a state consisting of a pair of integers identified by the names *total* and *n*. Individually the assignments are

$$OP1 \triangleq total \leftarrow total + n$$

and

$$OP2 \triangleq n \leftarrow n - 1$$

which trivially satisfy the specifications

OP1

states: $\mathbb{Z} \times \mathbb{Z}$

pre--$OP1(\langle total,n \rangle) \triangleq$ True

post-$OP1(\langle total,n \rangle,\langle total',n' \rangle) \triangleq \quad (total' = total + n)$
$$\wedge (n' = n)$$

and

OP2

states: $\mathbb{Z} \times \mathbb{Z}$

pre--$OP2(\langle total,n \rangle) \triangleq$ True

post-$OP2(\langle total,n \rangle,\langle total',n' \rangle) \triangleq \quad (total' = total)$
$$\wedge (n' = n - 1)$$

For use in a future example we require to show that $OP1;OP2$ satisfies the specification

OP

states: $\mathbb{Z} \times \mathbb{Z}$

pre--$OP(\sigma) \triangleq n > 0$

post-$OP(\sigma,\sigma') \triangleq \quad \left(total' + \sum_{i=0}^{n'} i = total + \sum_{i=0}^{n} i \right)$
$$\wedge (0 \leqslant n' < n)$$

where $\sum_{i=a}^{b} i \triangleq a + (a+1) + (a+2) + \ldots + (b-1) + b$ with $a \leqslant b$, and $a,b \in \mathbb{Z}$,

$$\sigma \triangleq \langle total,n \rangle$$

and

$$\sigma' \triangleq \langle total',n' \rangle$$

Here, and subsequently, we shall adopt the convention that once a state has been (locally) defined its 'decorated' variants follow automatically by convention. So, given σ, we can presume σ' is as defined above. Also $\sigma_1 = \langle total_1, n_1 \rangle$, $\sigma_2 = \ldots$, etc.

So much for notation, now let us apply the three rules to show that *OP1;OP2* is a suitable implementation of *OP*.

d_1:   pre-$OP(\sigma) \Rightarrow$ pre-$OP1(\sigma)$

$(\rightarrow)$ $n > 0 \Rightarrow$ True

$(\rightarrow)$ True   (Theorem 1(c))

d_2:   pre-$OP1(\sigma_1) \wedge$ post-$OP1(\sigma_1, \sigma_2) \Rightarrow$ pre-$OP2(\sigma_2)$

$(\rightarrow)$ True $\wedge\, (total_2 = total_1 + n_1) \wedge (n_2 = n_1) \Rightarrow$ True

$(\rightarrow)$ True

r_1:   pre-$OP(\sigma_1) \wedge$ post-$OP1(\sigma_1, \sigma_2) \wedge$ post-$OP2(\sigma_2, \sigma_3) \Rightarrow$
$$\text{post-}OP(\sigma_1, \sigma_3)$$

$(\rightarrow)$ $(n_1 > 0) \wedge (total_2 = total_1 + n_1) \wedge (total_3 = total_2) \wedge$
$$(n_2 = n_1) \wedge (n_3 = n_2 - 1)$$

$$\Rightarrow \left(total_3 + \sum_{i=0}^{n_3} i = total_1 + \sum_{i=0}^{n_1} i \right) \wedge (0 \leqslant n_3 < n_1)$$

But, by exercise 7.1.5, the validity of the implication $(a \Rightarrow b)$ follows from evaluating the conjunction of both sides $(a \wedge b)$.

And:

$$(total_3 = total_1 + n_1) \wedge (n_3 = n_1 - 1) \wedge (n_1 > 0) \wedge$$

$$\left(total_3 + \sum_{i=0}^{n_3} i = total_1 + \sum_{i=0}^{n_1} i \right) \wedge (0 \leqslant n_3 < n_1)$$

$(\rightarrow)$ $\left(total_1 + n_1 + \sum_{i=0}^{n_1 - 1} i = total_1 + \sum_{i=0}^{n_1} i \right) \wedge (0 \leqslant n_1 - 1 < n_1)$

$(\rightarrow)$ $\sum_{i=0}^{n_1} i = \sum_{i=0}^{n_1} i$

$(\rightarrow)$ True

Hence the code does satisfy the specification. $\square$

Within the three parts of the proof in the above example we have used many logical and arithmetic manipulations; where do these come from and how do we know which to use? Where they come from will be explained more fully in Chapter 10 but put simply, we can only use rules which are inherent in the proper (algebraic) definition of the objects we are manipulating. Choosing which rules to use is more difficult; indeed to answer the question properly would require us to tackle the topic of automatic theorem proving. To cover that subject would need a text significantly larger than the one you are currently reading. So, what can we do?

Turning to the example we see that steps d_1 and d_2 are trivial because of the inclusion of the constant *True* in convenient places (the occurrence of really simple logical expressions such as these is not uncommon). The range condition (r_1) is more of a problem. Since the rule is associated with state changes from σ_1 to σ_3 via σ_2 an obvious first move is to use substitution to remove all occurrences of σ_2 variables. Once this has been done we can focus attention on trying to arrange to have terms of the form $x \Rightarrow x$ or $y = y$, etc. which we know to be true. Without reference to the relevant algebra we can say little more except to point out an essential consequence of rules such as d_1, d_2 and r_1.

If information is lost or discarded as the proof proceeds, then we may fail to reach an affirmative conclusion. Of course the implication under consideration may actually be false and so we ought not to be able to prove that it is true. However, if we have missed out something essential then we must retrace our steps and rework the later stages of the proof. What **can** be guaranteed is that logically inadequate data, will **not** lead to a successful conclusion.

In terms of a correctness proof this means that we may reject valid code (because we have not been clever enough to prove its correctness) but we will never accept incorrect code. This is what statisticians call a *type 2 error* or *false acceptance*; our methodology is based on the requirement that the probability of such an error is **zero**. In Example 7.3.1 the code did satisfy the specification and hence cannot illustrate incorrectness, however consideration of the range rule can be used to illustrate how a reduction can be inconclusive. Picking out the terms associated with the variable n, we have

$$(n_1 > 0) \wedge (n_2 = n_1) \wedge (n_3 = n_2 - 1)$$
$$(\rightarrow)\ (n_1 > 0) \wedge (n_3 = n_1 - 1)$$
$$(\rightarrow)\ (n_1 > 0) \wedge (n_3 < n_1)$$
$$(\nrightarrow)\ 0 \leqslant n_3$$

Yes, it is true that $n_3 < n_1$ but in this particular proof we need to know by how much so as to be able to convert from $<$ to $\leqslant$ (and, incidentally, rely heavily on the fact that n is an *integer* variable, not a *real*). So much for sequential composition. It was important to spend quite a long time looking at sequencing because, although it is relatively simple it is also very common. Indeed, since a purely sequential (straight-line) program is essentially the same as the only computation it can perform, and **any** computation through **any** program can be represented by a (possibly very long but nevertheless finite) straight-line program; all that is left to do is to overlay and fold-up such programs and introduce decisions (which do not contribute to the computation but select between different computations). Needless to say this is not trivial. However the first step to more complex combinations is not too bad.

We shall tackle alternation† directly from a suitably annotated diagram, Figure 7.6, and trace the inherent state changes which are achieved by the sub-processes as required by the overall specification. Given that *OP1* and *OP2* satisfy their respective pre- and post-conditions what conditions must hold to ensure that

$$OP \triangleq \text{if } b \text{ then } OP1 \text{ else } OP2 \text{ fi}$$

satisfies pre-*OP* and post-*OP*?

Fig. 7.6

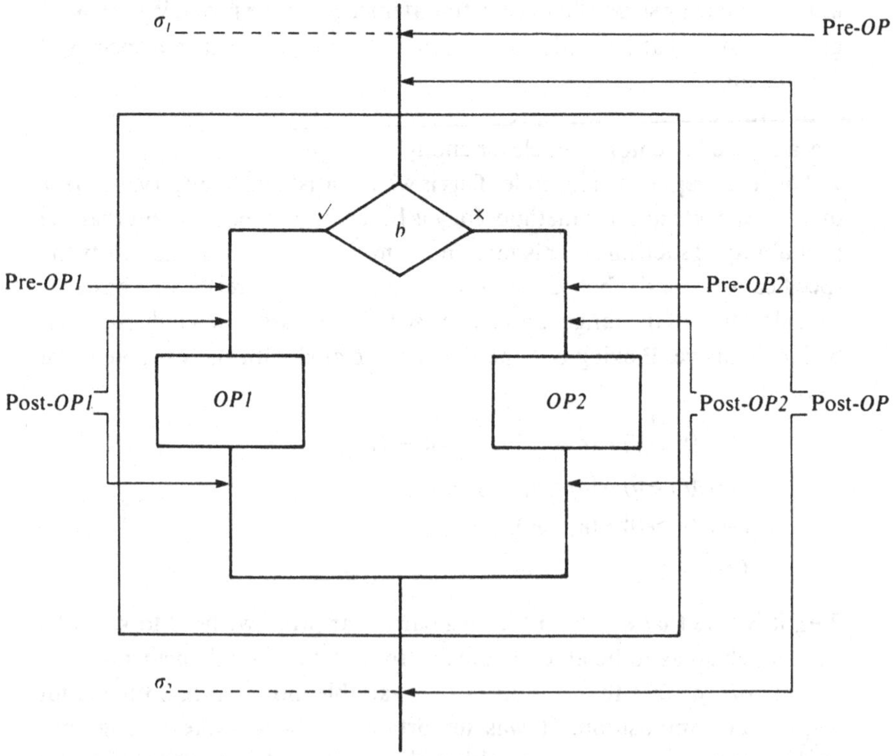

† Alternation indicates a choice between 2 alternatives, rather than a selection from 2 or more.

First we stipulate that b is a function of type State $\rightarrow \mathbb{B}$, there are no side-effects – no change in state – and the result is internal to the *if-then-else-fi* control mechanism.

Thus we have:

d_1:   pre-$OP(\sigma_1) \wedge b(\sigma_1) \Rightarrow$ pre-$OP1(\sigma_1)$

d_2:   pre-$OP(\sigma_1) \wedge \neg b(\sigma_1) \Rightarrow$ pre-$OP2(\sigma_1)$

r_1:   pre-$OP(\sigma_1) \wedge b(\sigma_1) \wedge$ post-$OP1(\sigma_1,\sigma_2) \Rightarrow$ post-$OP(\sigma_1,\sigma_2)$

r_2:   pre-$OP(\sigma_1) \wedge \neg b(\sigma_1) \wedge$ post-$OP2(\sigma_1,\sigma_2) \Rightarrow$ post-$OP(\sigma_1,\sigma_2)$

Reading each of these rules in conjunction with Figure 7.6 should convince you that they are necesary but are they sufficient and could we use any other rules instead?

The domain rules suffice because they justify all routes (i.e. both routes) **to** the subprocesses *OP1* and *OP2*. Similarly, since there are only two paths **through** the combination, the range rules are also adequate. So far, the rules pertaining to changes of state have been written down directly from the flowchart. However notice that, although

pre-$OP(\sigma_1) \wedge b(\sigma_1) \Rightarrow$ pre-$OP1(\sigma_1)$

it is not appropriate to use

pre-$OP1(\sigma_1) \wedge$ post-$OP1(\sigma_1,\sigma_2) \Rightarrow$ post-$OP(\sigma_1,\sigma_2)$

instead of r_1. Without going into detail as to why this will not always work (it is in fact too restrictive) notice that *OP1* is only required to work when b is True. Hence this rule would force a state change in *OP* which was consistent with that of *OP1* even when *OP2* was executed! How do we avoid this? The clue is back in the diagram. Since *OP* relates to the change from σ_1 to σ_2, and even though b does not cause a state change, we must relate back to a point where both $b(\sigma)$ and $\neg b(\sigma)$ are feasible (but of course for any **actual** σ only one of these terms **is** True) and hence we are forced to the point labelled by σ_1.

An example of alternation on its own must be fairly simple and is of little use in itself. However the style of the data flow and control flow graphs of both the alternation construct and certain forms of recursion are very similar, and this similarity extends to their proofs from first principles. Now, in practical cases, we would not attempt to prove correctness of alternation 'from scratch' but use the four implications (d_1, d_2, r_1 and r_2). Nevertheless as a preliminary to subsequent work on recursion, we now consider a small example and use it to illustrate how the four rules relate to a direct correctness proof.

Example 7.3.2

Suppose that our target operation is *ASSIGN_MAX_TO_I* which acts on a state $\mathbb{Z}^3$ (i.e. $\mathbb{Z} \times \mathbb{Z} \times \mathbb{Z}$), has a pre-condition which is identically True and has a post-condition:

$$\text{post-}ASSIGN\_MAX\_TO\_I(\langle x,y,i\rangle,\langle x',y',i'\rangle) \triangleq ((i' = x) \vee (i' = y))$$
$$\wedge (i' \geqslant x) \wedge (i' \geqslant y)$$

An obvious realisation, presuming the availability of assignment, would be

    if $x > y$
    then $i \leftarrow x$
    else $i \leftarrow y$
    fi

This works but is certainly not the only answer, let us be more general and write:

    if $x > y$
    then *I_TAKES_VALUE_X*
    else *I_TAKES_VALUE_Y*
    fi

where the two new operations are specified on $\mathbb{Z}^3$ by post-conditions:

$$\text{post-}I\_TAKES\_VALUE\_X(\sigma,\sigma') \triangleq i' = x$$
$$\text{post-}I\_TAKES\_VALUE\_Y(\sigma,\sigma') \triangleq i' = y$$

$$\text{where } \sigma = \langle x,y,i\rangle$$

These operations allow x' and y' to assume any values, a property also permitted by the specification of *ASSIGN_MAX_TO_I*.

Before turning our attention to proofs we convert the expression $x > y$ into a predicate acting on an arbitrary state vector σ, viz $X\_GREATER\_THAN\_Y(\sigma) \triangleq (x > y)$.

So far so good, these names are fine for documentation or even for coding but they are rather long to be written out repeatedly in mathematical arguments. Therefore we use straightforward abbreviations which result in the problem being stated as an attempt to prove correctness of

    $AMTI \triangleq$ if $XGTY$
           then $ITVX$
           else $ITVY$
           fi

i.e.   post-$AMTI(\sigma,\sigma')$

where $\sigma' =$ if $XGTY(\sigma)$
then $ITVX(\sigma)$
else $ITVY(\sigma)$
fi

First we prove that the code is acceptable by recourse to our four rules,

d_1:   pre-$AMTI(\sigma_1) \wedge XGTY(\sigma_1) \Rightarrow$ pre-$ITVX(\sigma_1)$

($\rightarrow$)   True $\wedge (x_1 > y_1) \Rightarrow$ True

($\rightarrow$)   True

d_2:   pre-$AMTI(\sigma_1) \wedge \neg XGTY(\sigma_1) \Rightarrow$ pre-$ITVY(\sigma_1)$

($\rightarrow$)   True $\wedge \neg(x_1 > y_1) \Rightarrow$ True

($\rightarrow$)   True

r_1:   pre-$AMTI(\sigma_1) \wedge XGTY(\sigma_1) \wedge$ post-$ITVX(\sigma_1,\sigma_2) \Rightarrow$
$$\text{post-}AMTI(\sigma_1,\sigma_2)$$

($\rightarrow$) True $\wedge (x_1 > y_1) \wedge (i_2 = x_1) \Rightarrow$
$$((i_2 = x_1) \vee (i_2 = y_1)) \wedge (i_2 \geqslant x_1) \wedge (i_2 \geqslant y_1)$$

Now $(x_1 > y_1) \wedge (i_2 = x_1)$

$\Rightarrow (i_2 > y_1) \wedge (i_2 = x_1)$
$\Rightarrow (i_2 \geqslant y_1) \wedge (i_2 = x_1)$
$\Rightarrow (i_2 \geqslant y_1) \wedge (i_2 \geqslant x_1) \wedge (i_2 = x_1)$
$\Rightarrow (i_2 \geqslant y_1) \wedge (i_2 \geqslant x_1) \wedge ((i_2 = x_1) \vee (i_2 = y_1))$

and hence r_1 is True. Notice that here we have numerous applications of theorem 2(b) such as

$(i_2 > y_1) \Rightarrow (i_2 > y_1) \vee (i_2 = y_1)$
$\Leftrightarrow (i_2 \geqslant y_1)$

The validity of r_2 follows in an almost identical fashion.

Now, what happens if we attempt a direct proof rather than using the domain and range rules? What exactly do we have to do?

We need to show that

pre-$AMTI(\sigma) \Rightarrow$ post-$AMTI(\sigma,\sigma')$

where $\sigma' =$ if $XGTY(\sigma)$
then $ITVX(\sigma)$
else $ITVY(\sigma)$
fi

Now, by exercise 7.1.4, we can replace an implication $Q \Rightarrow R$ by

$$((P \wedge Q) \Rightarrow R) \wedge ((\neg P \wedge Q) \Rightarrow R)$$

for any predicate P and hence use P to split the proof of $Q \Rightarrow R$ into two parts. In order to simplify the proof, the predicate P needs to relate directly to either a predicate in the specification or in the realisation – if they both have conditional forms there ought to be some natural connection between the two conditions and hence with P. In our example the realisation is conditional so we use the predicate $XGTY$, and hence the first part of the proof begins with:

$$XGTY(\sigma) \wedge \text{pre-}AMTI(\sigma) \Rightarrow \text{post-}AMTI(\sigma,\sigma')$$

To investigate the validity of this implication we need only evaluate post-$AMTI(\sigma,\sigma')$ assuming pre-$AMTI(\sigma)$ and $XGTY(\sigma)$.†

i.e. $\text{post-}AMTI(\sigma,\sigma') = ((i' = x) \vee (i' = y)) \wedge (i' \geqslant x) \wedge (i' \geqslant y)$

$$\text{where } \sigma' = ITVX(\sigma) \text{ since } XGTY(\sigma)$$

Now, recall that the where clause quoted here really means

$$\text{pre-}ITVX(\sigma) \wedge \text{post-}ITVX(\sigma,\sigma')$$

and hence we have:

$$((i' = x) \vee (i' = y)) \wedge (i' \geqslant x) \wedge (i' \geqslant y)$$

$$\text{where } (i' = x)$$

Thus

$(i' = x) \vee (i' = y)$ is True,

$(i' \geqslant x)$ is True

and, since $XGTY(\sigma)$, i.e. $x > y$, we also have that

$(i' \geqslant y)$ is True and hence post-$AMTI(\sigma,\sigma')$ is True

For the second part:

$$\text{post-}AMTI(\sigma,\sigma') = ((i' = x) \vee (i' = y)) \wedge (i' \geqslant x) \wedge (i' \geqslant y)$$

$$\text{where } (i' = y) \wedge \neg(x > y)$$

but

$(i' = y) \Rightarrow ((i' = x) \vee (i' = y)),$

$(i' = y) \Rightarrow (i' \geqslant y)$

and

$$((i' = y) \wedge \neg(x > y)) \Rightarrow ((i' = y) \wedge (y \geqslant x))$$

$$\Rightarrow (i' \geqslant x)$$

† Note. This is exercise 7.1.5 yet again, but expressed slightly differently.

Therefore, once again we have

post-$AMTI(\sigma,\sigma')$ = True

Of course the work involved here is essentially the same as before, the *XGTY* case relating to the rules d_1 and r_1, and $\neg XGTY$ to the rules d_2 and r_2. The advantage of using the rules is that the proof is more mechanical and requires less thought to get started. The direct approach is indicative of methods that must be applied when a suitable set of rules are not readily available.

Exercises 7.3

1. Prove that

   $SEG1 \triangleq y \leftarrow y+1; x \leftarrow x-1$

   satisfies the specification

   SEG1

   states: $\mathbb{Z} \times \mathbb{Z}$

   pre--$SEG1(\langle x,y \rangle) \triangleq y < 0$

   post-$SEG1(\langle x,y \rangle, \langle x',y' \rangle) \triangleq \quad (x'+y'=x+y)$
   $$\wedge (0 \leqslant -y' < -y)$$

2. Similarly verify that

   $SEG2 \triangleq x \leftarrow x-1; z \leftarrow z+y$

   is correct with respect to the specification

   SEG2

   states: $\mathbb{Z} \times \mathbb{Z} \times \mathbb{Z}$

   pre--$SEG2(\langle x,y,z \rangle) \triangleq x > 0$

   post-$SEG2(\langle x,y,z \rangle, \langle x',y',z' \rangle) \triangleq \quad (z+x*y=z'+x'*y')$
   $$\wedge (0 \leqslant x' < x)$$

3. Devise a specification over $\mathbb{Z} \times \mathbb{Z} \times \mathbb{Z} \times \mathbb{Z} \times \mathbb{Z} \times \mathbb{Z}$ which places the initial values of x, y and z into *low*, *mid* and *high* in appropriate order of magnitude. Use nested alternation in a realisation to implement the operation, called *SORT3*.

7.4   Repetition

Repetition within a program may be achieved by folding segments of flowchart to form loops or embedding segments within other, not necessarily distinct, segments to permit recursion. Although looping, or iteration, is a common feature of both *high-* and *low-level* programming languages, we must first deal with recursion. This is because specifications are recursive; due to their functional, or relational, nature recursion is the only way in which repetition can be indicated.

Proofs of repetitive constructs (their correctness proofs) are more complex than sequencing and alternation due to the need to consider termination. We have all seen, and possibly even written, loops which never – legally – terminate. Consider

$$\text{while} \quad y \neq 0$$
$$\text{do} \quad y \leftarrow y + 1$$
$$\text{od}$$

and

$$\text{while} \quad y \neq 0$$
$$\text{do} \quad y \leftarrow 1$$
$$\text{od}$$

The first statement will either exit immediately because the value of y is zero, or after a finite number of repetitions if the initial value is a negative integer. The other reasonable possibilities are that y has no proper initial value, in which case the evaluation of $y \neq 0$ or $y + 1$ should cause execution to terminate in an error; or the initial value is a strictly positive integer, in which case the value of y should eventually overflow and again give rise to an error.

The second statement will loop forever providing that y has a valid non-zero initial value.

Now whilst 'non-terminating' processes may be acceptable or even necessary in certain process-control applications, such behaviour is generally not required of conventional programs. We need to be assured that execution of the program is actually 'getting somewhere', and that progress towards the goal is sufficiently fast to ensure that the goal is actually achieved.

The need to guarantee termination complicates the correctness proof and requires us to look at proof by induction. However to get matters off the ground we look at a simple form of recursion, Section 7.4.1, before digressing to discuss quantifiers and simple induction (in Section 7.4.2), finally extracting iterative proof rules in Section 7.4.3.

7.4.1   Simple recursion

Procedurally repetition can be represented in many ways;

functionally it can only be represented as recursion. Many forms of recursion are possible and in general they do not correspond explicitly to any of the standard forms of flow diagrams so far considered. However, taking one of the simplest non-trivial forms and writing it as a state transformation not only isolates the essential computational features which relate to the correctness proof, but also suggests how equivalent iterative realisations may be achieved.

Consider the function

$$F(\sigma) \triangleq \text{if} \qquad b(\sigma)$$
$$\text{then} \quad G(\sigma)$$
$$\text{else} \quad H(\sigma)$$

Either G or H may include embedded Fs but there must be at least one 'escape' which can, under appropriate conditions, be followed and which does not include further calls of F. Subject only to this proviso, the number and position of embedded Fs is not restricted; however the description of computations associated with all but the most simple cases is incredibly difficult.† To simplify matters, suppose that in the above case H does not include F and that

$$G(\sigma) \triangleq G_1(F(G_2(\sigma)))$$

Diagrammatically this is equivalent to taking the data/control flowchart in Figure 7.7 and, from it, extracting the computation sequence in Figure 7.8.

This means that F computes a result of the form

$$G_1^n(H(G_2^n(\sigma)))$$

for a given value of σ and where n is the smallest positive integer such that

$$\neg b(G_2^n(\sigma)) - \text{if such an } n \text{ exists}$$

(Clearly the value of n depends on σ but writing $n(\sigma)$ everywhere merely serves to clutter up the picture.)

Here the calculation recurses **inwards**, eventually reaching a state in which b is False, and then **unwinds** to give the final answer.

The progression of states is therefore

$$\sigma, G_2\sigma, G_2^2\sigma, \ldots, G_2^n\sigma,$$
$$HG_2^n\sigma,$$
$$G_1 H G_2^n\sigma, G_1^2 H G_2^n\sigma, \ldots, G_1^n H G_2^n\sigma$$

---

† Note. There is one crumb of comfort to be gained from this rather off-putting statement. Experience suggests that such complexity is usually not required and probably indicates unclear reasoning and/or errors. Backtracking to reconsider the specification or realisation is advised.

Notice that the Boolean test, *b*, in Figure 7.7 becomes a sequence of annotations (*b* is True or *b* is False) in Figure 7.8 and these play no part in the calculation of the result.

Fig. 7.7

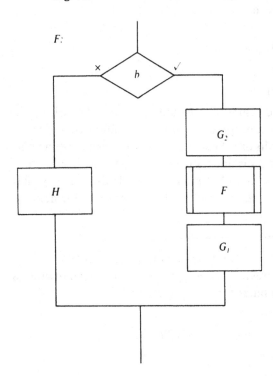

Fig. 7.8

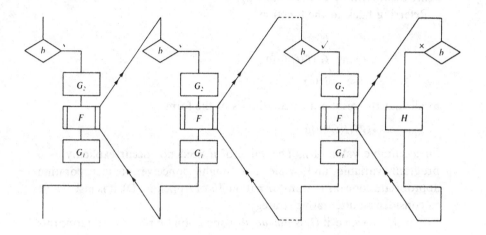

Providing that the appropriate value of n can be preserved (as is done automatically in block-structured languages that support recursion) so as to ensure the correct 'power' of G_1, the progression can be achieved by combining the three state changes

$$\sigma \mapsto G_2^n \sigma \qquad \text{(i.e. } \sigma \text{ is changed into } G_2^n \sigma \text{)},$$

$$\sigma \mapsto H \sigma$$

and

$$\sigma \mapsto G_1^n \sigma$$

In certain, fortunately fairly common, situations the appropriate annotated computation sequence can be achieved by other, non-recursive, flow diagrams. A reasonably comprehensive collection of such transformations is given in Appendix D; however, since specifications are inherently recursive and there are many non-recursive target languages we cannot defer the topic totally. Luckily there is one variant of the problem which is easily dealt with in an informal way.

Referring back to the function

$$F: \sigma \mapsto \text{if} \qquad b(\sigma)$$
$$\text{then} \quad G_1(F(G_2(\sigma)))$$
$$\text{else} \quad H(\sigma)$$

recall that the resultant calculation is of the form

$$\sigma \mapsto G_1^n(H(G_2^n(\sigma)))$$

for a suitable value of n. The value of n need not occur explicitly as a program variable and while one might conceive of incorporating appropriate code (as in transformation T7 of Appendix D), it is instructive to consider an alternative strategy.

If $G_1: \sigma \mapsto \sigma$, i.e. if G_1 is the *identity* operation (in procedural terms this means that there is no operation at all!) then $G_1^m: \sigma \mapsto \sigma$ for all positive integer values of m.

Diagrammatically we have Figure 7.9 which, for the appropriate value of n yields the following progression of states and assertions.

$$\sigma, \qquad b(\sigma)$$
$$G_2(\sigma), \qquad b(G_2(\sigma))$$
$$G_2^2(\sigma), \qquad b(G_2^2(\sigma))$$
$$\vdots \qquad \qquad \vdots$$
$$G_2^{n-1}(\sigma), \qquad b(G_2^{n-1}(\sigma))$$
$$G_2^n(\sigma), \qquad \neg b(G_2^n(\sigma))$$
$$H(G_2^n(\sigma))$$

Those with some programming experience should easily recognise that this is exactly the same computation as that generated by the statements

$$\text{while } b \text{ do } G_2 \text{ od}; H$$

the flowchart of which appears in Figure 7.10.

In technical terms the two program schemes in Figures 7.9 and 7.10 are strongly equivalent in that provided that the names b, G_2 and H are replaced by consistent, yet arbitrary, pieces of code in both schemes they will yield the same values. The subject of strong equivalence is studied at some depth in [5] and we shall say more about the relationship between the two forms in Section 7.4.3. We conclude this section with an example which uses the transformation and highlights the need for a repetitive process to make

Fig. 7.9

F:

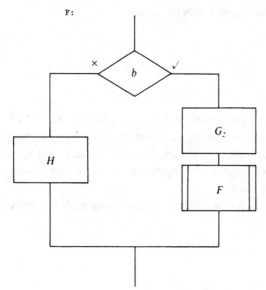

Fig. 7.10

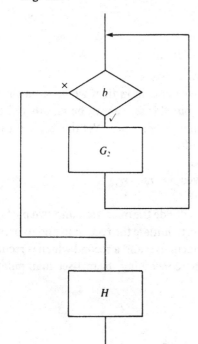

adequate progress to its goal. It also illustrates how simple flowchart factorisation can be used to simplify specifications.

Example 7.4.1

Consider the construction of the specification of an operation *SETMAX* intended to find the maximal element of a non-empty set of real numbers. The idea behind the specification is to reduce the set of elements still to be considered until it becomes empty. The repetitive nature of this process necessitates the use of recursion.

A reasonable (but incorrect) first attempt at specifying such a process would be

> *SETMAX1*
>
> states: $\mathbb{R}$-Set $\times \mathbb{R}$
>
> pre--$SETMAX1(\langle rs,max \rangle) \triangleq \neg(rs = \varnothing)$
>
> post-$SETMAX1(\langle rs,max \rangle,\langle rs',max' \rangle) \triangleq$
>
> > if $rs = \varnothing$
> >
> > then   ...
> >
> > else   ...$SETMAX1(...)$

This post-condition must indicate that

(i) if we have looked at all elements in rs then we have finished (so some set is now empty – but this set cannot be rs, otherwise the recursion would violate the pre-condition. Yet the test in the post-condition **is** what we want!!)

(ii) max' should be in rs, and

(iii) the set should be preserved, i.e. $rs' = rs$,

so how can we reduce rs?

The way round this impasse is to divide the operation into **two** parts, one to ensure validity of the initial state, to initiate the recursion and to preserve the real-set, but which is not itself recursive; and a second which is recursive but not subject to the restrictions concerning its real-set manipulation. Here is our second version:

> *SETMAX2*
>
> states: $\mathbb{R}$-Set $\times \mathbb{R}$
>
> pre--$SETMAX2(\langle rs,max \rangle) \triangleq \neg(rs = \varnothing)$

$$\text{post-}SETMAX2(\langle rs,max\rangle,\langle rs',max'\rangle) \triangleq \quad (x \in rs)$$
$$\wedge (copy = rs\backslash\{x\})$$
$$\wedge (\langle copy',x'\rangle =$$
$$TRY(\langle copy,x\rangle))$$
$$\wedge (rs' = rs)$$
$$\wedge (max' = x')$$

which requires a specification of *TRY*:

TRY

states: $\mathbb{R}$-Set $\times$ $\mathbb{R}$

pre--$TRY(\langle copy,x\rangle) \triangleq$ True

post-$TRY(\langle copy,x\rangle,\langle copy',x'\rangle) \triangleq$

    if $copy = \varnothing$

    then $(x' = x)$

          $\wedge (copy' = copy)$

    else $(y \in copy)$

          $\wedge (newcopy = copy\backslash\{y\})$

       $\wedge$ if $y > x$

          then $\langle copy',x'\rangle = TRY(\langle newcopy,y\rangle)$

          else $\langle copy',x'\rangle = TRY(\langle newcopy,x\rangle)$

The dataflow diagrams associated with these specifications are depicted in Figures 7.11 and 7.12.

From Figure 7.12 we quickly see that post-*TRY* is not in the form required for immediate transformation into a *while* loop. However by introducing a further intermediate state variable (or as many of its constituent variables as required) we can use a 'downwards' factorisation of the flow diagram as drawn in Figure 7.13 to yield

TRY2

states: $\mathbb{R}$-Set $\times$ $\mathbb{R}$

pre--$TRY2(\langle copy,x \rangle) \triangleq$ True

post-$TRY2(\langle copy,x \rangle, \langle copy',x' \rangle) \triangleq$

      if $copy = \varnothing$

      then $(x' = x)$

            $\wedge (copy' = copy)$

      else $(y \in copy)$

            $\wedge (newcopy = copy \backslash \{y\})$

            $\wedge ($if $y > x$

              then $z = y$

              else $z = x)$

            $\wedge (\langle copy',x' \rangle = TRY2(\langle newcopy,z \rangle))$

Fig. 7.11. Data dependencies in SETMAX 2.

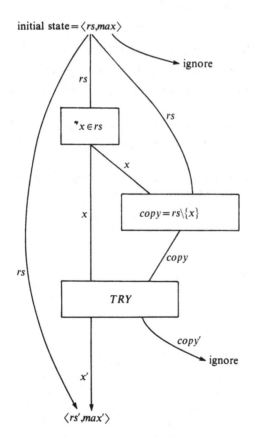

Now *TRY2* is of the form

$$TRY2 : \sigma \mapsto \text{if} \quad X(\sigma)$$
$$\text{then} \quad Y(\sigma)$$
$$\text{else} \quad TRY2(Z(\sigma))$$

where $X : \sigma \mapsto (copy = \varnothing)$

   i.e. $\langle copy, x \rangle \mapsto (copy = \varnothing)$, a Boolean result,

   $Y : \sigma \mapsto \sigma$, no change

and $Z : \sigma \mapsto \langle copy \backslash \{y\}, z \rangle$

   with $\sigma = \langle copy, x \rangle$

   $\wedge (y \in copy)$

   $\wedge (\quad ((z = x) \wedge (y \leqslant x))$

   $\vee ((z = y) \wedge (y > x)))$

Correspondingly we have the PDL scheme

   while $\neg X$ do Z od; Y □

Fig. 7.12. Data dependencies in TRY (following the control flow to cope with conditionals).

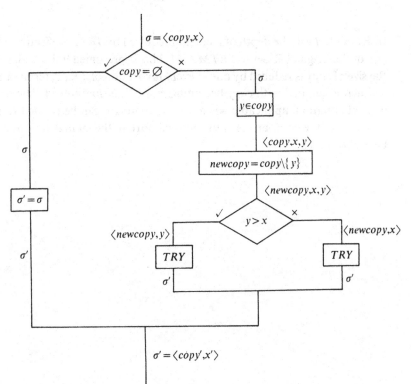

Fig. 7.13. Tail-factorisation in specifications.

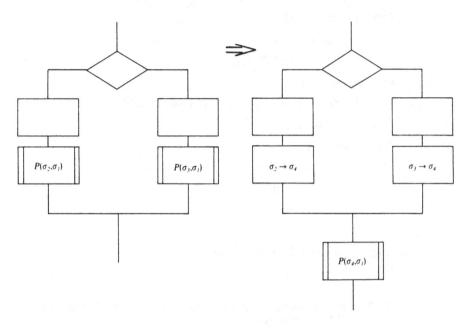

In Example 7.4.1, the depth of recursion required by *TRY2* is effectively the size of the original ℝ-Set in *SETMAX2*. This is presumed finite and, since the size of *copy* is reduced by one at every invocation of *TRY2*, termination – which is equated with *copy* becoming empty – is guaranteed. The more general situation, applicable whenever all recursion can be pushed to the end of **all** of the alternatives of the non-exit fork in the main definition, can be expressed as

$P: \sigma \mapsto \text{if} \quad end\_reached(\sigma)$

$\qquad \text{then} \quad extract\_result(\sigma)$

$\qquad \text{else} \quad progress(\sigma \text{ to } \sigma') \text{ and } P(\sigma')$

This form, called *tail recursion*, then gives rise to the iterative construct

while $\neg end\_reached$

do $\quad progress$

od

extract_result

Unfortunately that is not the whole story. By virtue of the properties of positive integers the *progress* step in Example 7.4.1 ensured that *end_reached* was eventually True. As we shall see, integers are the key to solving this problem; but first we need some more logic.

7.4.2 Quantifiers and induction

In Section 7.1 we introduced the logical versions of the summation and product symbols namely $\bigvee$ and $\bigwedge$. These symbols were used because of their natural association with $\vee$ and $\wedge$ but two other symbols commonly used in logic are inspired by their spoken forms. We have already met one of these. The *universal quantifier* – 'for all' – is written $\forall$, an upside-down capital A, and is defined by

$$(\forall x \in X)(p(x)) \triangleq \bigwedge_{x \in X} p(x)$$

for all $x \in X$, $p(x)$, i.e. $p(x)$ is True,....

We shall allow such forms to be written even when X is not finite but, as will become obvious later, we are only really interested in finite subsets of $\mathbb{P}$, the set of positive integers. The other quantifier, the so-called *existential quantifier* – 'there exists' – is written as a backwards E, and its predictable definition is:

$$(\exists x \in X)(p(x)) \triangleq \bigvee_{x \in X} p(x)$$

The symbols $\forall$ and $\exists$ **are** valid replacements for the informal operators *for_all* and *there_exists* which we might use in specifications and which now have a proper definition; at least over finite sets.

In fact, as an immediate consequence of the definitions in terms of $\bigwedge$ and $\bigvee$, we have

$$(\forall x \in \emptyset)(p(x)) = \text{True}$$

and

$$(\exists x \in \emptyset)(p(x)) = \text{False}$$

for any predicate p. Moreover, over a finite set A, we can give a recursive specification of the quantifiers. Writing $FOR\_ALL(p,A)$ for $(\forall x \in A)(p(x))$, etc., we have

> post-$FOR\_ALL(p,A) \triangleq$
> > if $A = \emptyset$
> > then   True
> > else $(y \in A \Rightarrow (p(y) \wedge FOR\_ALL(p, A \backslash \{y\})))$

and

> post-$THERE\_EXISTS(p,A) \triangleq$
> > if $A = \emptyset$
> > then   False
> > else $(y \in A \Rightarrow (p(y) \vee THERE\_EXISTS(p, A \backslash \{y\})))$

As is to be expected, these quantifiers are related by an extended form of de Morgan's Laws;

$$(\forall x \in X)(p(x)) \Leftrightarrow \neg(\exists x \in X)(\neg p(x))$$

and

$$(\exists x \in X)(p(x)) \Leftrightarrow \neg(\forall x \in X)(\neg p(x))$$

We can also use the symbols to indicate the logical validity of disproof by counter-example:

$$(\exists x \in X)(\neg p(x)) \Rightarrow \neg(\forall x \in X)(p(x))$$

Thus, if there exists some value x such that $p(x)$ is False, then it is **not** True that $p(x)$ holds for all x in X.

We now turn to proof by induction. Suppose we wish to prove the validity of some statement, p say, which expresses some characteristic (some property) of an arbitrary object from a set X. In other words, we want to prove $(\forall x \in X)(p(x))$. The essential idea behind proof by induction is that each x should have a 'size' and that we prove the validity of $p(x)$ for some arbitrary x by presuming the validity of $p(y)$ for all elements, y, which are 'smaller' than x. If we can then prove that $p(a)$ is true for the smallest value, a, in X then we may deduce that p holds for all elements in X. As it stands this chain of argument is not quite correct. We need to be more particular about 'size', but an example will help identify the tacit assumptions which need to be made more explicit.

Example 7.4.2
The factorial function is nearly always included in discussions about recursion; and, as often as not, it is ridiculed for being a silly function to compute recursively. However, for our purposes it is ideal. It is familiar, and, since it involves repetition, it **must** be specified recursively. Moreover, in its most obvious form, it is not directly amenable to tail recursion so structurally it is not that simple.

Later we shall consider the usual iterative realisation but to keep matters straightforward here we use PDL recursion. However, so as to preserve some distinction between the specification and the code, we shall presume existence of the appropriate operator within the specification (i.e. $x!$ meaning x factorial where

$0!$ is defined to be 1,

$1! = 1$

$2! = 2*1 = 2$

$3! = 3*2*1 = 6$

$4! = 24 \ldots$ etc)

The operator is not available in PDL and, in any case, is itself defined by recursion (!!)

$FACT$

type: $\mathbb{P} \to \mathbb{N}$

pre--$FACT(x) \triangleq$ True

post-$FACT(x,r) \triangleq r = x!$

Now suppose

$FACT(x) \triangleq$ if $\quad x = 0$

then $\quad 1$

else $\quad x * FACT(x-1)$

fi

If this realisation is to satisfy the preceding specification we must show that

pre-$FACT(x) \Rightarrow$ post-$FACT(x,FACT(x))$

for all values $x \in \mathbb{P}$. Since pre-$FACT(x)$ is True, we must show that post-$FACT(x,FACT(x))$ is True. The form of the flowgraph is superficially similar to alternation (Figure 7.6) and hence we can use the condition, $x = 0$, to partition the proof in a useful way. Following the scheme used in the last part of Exercise 7.3.2, we need first to evaluate post-$FACT(x,FACT(x))$ assuming $(x = 0)$.

$$\text{post-}FACT(x,FACT(x)) \Leftrightarrow \text{post-}FACT(0,1)$$

$$\Leftrightarrow 1 = 0!$$

$$\Leftrightarrow \text{True}$$

by the definition of factorial.

The case when $\neg(x = 0)$ is where the recursion occurs and where induction must be used. For an arbitrary value of x (> 0) we shall presume that $FACT$ computes the required result when the input value is $x - 1$ – this assumption is called the *induction hypothesis*.

The second part of the correctness proof now requires the evaluation of post-$FACT(x,FACT(x))$ when $\neg(x = 0)$

$$\text{post-}FACT(x,FACT(x)) \Leftrightarrow \text{post-}FACT(x,x * FACT(x - 1))$$

$$\Leftrightarrow x * FACT(x - 1) = x!$$

$$\Leftrightarrow x * (x - 1)! = x!$$

by the hypothesis

$$\Leftrightarrow x! = x!$$

from the definition of '!'

$$\Leftrightarrow \text{True}$$

On the face of things we have assumed something which we do not know to be true (the induction hypothesis) and, in any case, we have only considered two cases so how can this justify that $FACT$ works for all values in $\mathbb{P}$?

Closer examination will reveal that we have only considered one case explicitly, $(x = 0)$; this is called the *base step*. The second part, called the *induction step*, merely related any non-zero value to the immediately preceding one – but this is enough! Take the case when $x = 4$. We know $FACT$ works for $x = 0$, and if it works for 0 it works for 1; hence it also works for 2 by the same argument, hence for 3 and also for 4. In fact we have

$$\text{post-}FACT(0,FACT(0)) \Rightarrow \text{post-}FACT(1,FACT(1))$$

$$\Rightarrow \text{post-}FACT(2,FACT(2))$$

$$\Rightarrow \text{post-}FACT(3,FACT(3))$$

$$\Rightarrow \text{post-}FACT(4,FACT(4))$$

The same logical argument can be used to show that $FACT$ is valid for any finite value in $\mathbb{P}$ – and all values in $\mathbb{P}$ are finite.   □

The form of inductive argument used here can be expressed symbolically by the statement

$$(p(0) \wedge (n \in \mathbb{P} \Rightarrow (p(n) \Rightarrow p(n+1)))) \Rightarrow (\forall n \in \mathbb{P})(p(n))$$

$$\text{where } p : \mathbb{P} \to \mathbb{B}$$

But what about a function such as *ODD*, defined recursively by

```
ODD
type: P ⇒ B
pre--ODD(x) ≜ True
post-ODD(x,b) ≜ if      x=0
                then  False
                else  if      x=1
                      then  True
                      else  ODD(x-2)
```

and realised by the PDL segment

```
ODD(x) ≜ if      x<2
         then  if      x=0
               then  False
               else  True
               fi
         else  ODD(x-2)
         fi
```

This 'obviously' works but on first impressions cannot be proved using the inductive form

$$p(0) \wedge (\forall n \in \mathbb{P})(p(n) \Rightarrow p(n+1)).$$

Surely we need something like:

$$(p(0) \wedge p(1)) \wedge (\forall n \in \mathbb{P})(p(n) \Rightarrow p(n+2))$$

In fact we can use the simpler form provided we choose the predicate p appropriately. In effect the n required is a measure of recursive depth (the number of recursions before the exit condition is reached, see Figure 7.8). In both the above cases if we start with an arbitrary $x \in \mathbb{P}$ and decrease it repeatedly we achieve a finite progression which eventually yields a value.

The problem is similar to the convergence of series. Try to reach a value greater than 3 by computing successive terms in the series

(a) *1,*
    1+1/2,
    1+1/2+1/4,
    *1+1/2+1/4+1/8,...,*etc.

and

(b) *1,*
    1+1/2,
    1+1/2+1/3,
    *1+1/2+1/3+1/4,...,*etc.

The series (a) never reaches 2 and hence the search for an appropriate value will not succeed. On the other hand, despite some similarities between these series, the values in (b) grow without limit and by taking enough terms we can exceed any given positive number. The eleventh term is just greater than 3. The mathematical notion associated with this problem is called *well-ordering*. An ordered set (a set, together with some ordering like $<$, see [8] for more details) is *well-ordered* if it does not contain any infinite decreasing sequences.

Our illustration using the series (a) and (b) is then explained by considering the sets (i)

$$\{3-1, 3-(1+1/2), 3-(1+1/2+1/4),...\} \cap \{x:0 \leqslant x \wedge x \in \mathbb{R}\}$$

and (ii)

$$\{3-1, 3-(1+1/2), 3-(1+1/2+1/3),...\} \cap \{x:0 \leqslant x \wedge x \in \mathbb{R}\}$$

The first of these is not well-ordered, the second is.

For an inductive proof to work we need to ensure that for an arbitrary data value x, the set of values that descend from it is well-ordered and that the smallest values in the set satisfy the premise.

The main use to which we shall put induction is in the proof of iterative realisations of recursive specifications. So, to explain these requirements we return again to the recursive scheme.

$$F : \sigma \mapsto \text{if} \quad b(\sigma)$$
$$\text{then} \quad G_1(F(G_2(\sigma)))$$
$$\text{else} \quad H(\sigma)$$
$$\text{fi}$$

For this scheme to give rise to a result for a given initial state, σ, the set

$$\{\rho : (\rho = \sigma) \vee (\rho = G_2^{m+1}(\sigma) \wedge b(G_2^m(\sigma)) \wedge m \in \mathbb{P})\}$$

must be well-ordered. The functions need not necessarily be numeric so the order relation may not be the familiar *less than* and we therefore use the symbol $\prec$ rather than $<$.

This can be read as 'in some sense less than'. Since a well-ordered set has no infinite decreasing sequences we must obviously achieve successively smaller values and hence for some finite $n \in \mathbb{P}$, we have

$$G_2^n(\sigma) \prec G_2^{n-1}(\sigma) \prec \ldots \prec G_2(\sigma) \prec \sigma$$

with $\quad \neg b(G^n(\sigma))$, and $b(G_2^m(\sigma))$ for all $m < n$

Moreover, because we have a proper *else*-clause, we are guaranteed a base case which can begin the induction and will reach σ.

So, for a proper inductive proof we need to have an acceptable base case, we need to ensure that any other initial value gives rise to a well-ordered set of descendants which reaches the base case, and we must prove that the induction step ensures the validity of a particular value from the validity of its descendants.

In practice we shall always seek a characterisation of size (and hence $\prec$) in terms of positive integers (and, correspondingly, $<$). This fits with the notion of counting the depth of recursion and benefits from the fact that since $\mathbb{P}$ is well-ordered so are all its non-empty subsets. We can also make matters easier still by 'sliding' any suitable subset of $\mathbb{P}$ down to 0; the value of 0 corresponding to exit from the recursion.

Using an inductive proof in cases that admit tail recursion yields sets of implications (rules!) which are similar to those used to verify the sequencing and alternation constructs and which significantly simplify the correctness proofs of iterative constructs. This topic is the subject matter of the final section of this chapter.

Other, more complex, recursion schemes which cannot be unravelled as in Figure 7.8 lead to more complicated conditions to guarantee well-ordered value sets (see for example the conditions associated with transformation rule T4 in Appendix D). Correctness proofs related to such recursion schemes should be tackled from first principles.

7.4.3 Iteration

Using the flowchart transformations given in Section 3.2 it is clear that we need only consider one form of iterative loop in any great detail. We shall concern ourselves with the pre-check loop, modelled in PDL by

$$LOOP \triangleq \text{while } b \text{ do } BODY \text{ od}$$

This may be defined recursively in many different ways. The method used here follows directly from the verification rules for sequencing and alternation, and adopts the two level scheme (with only the lower one involving recursion) that was introduced in Section 7.4.1.

The flowchart for *LOOP* may be manipulated in numerous, strongly equivalent, ways, some of which are depicted in Figure 7.14. In this figure, diagram (*a*) is the usual flowchart for a pre-check loop. Parts (*b*) and (*c*) of the diagram duplicate progressively more parts of (*a*) until, in (*c*), we have the original diagram as a subpart. This is a manifestation of recursion and is explicitly represented as such in diagram (*d*).

Hence, an alternative definition of *LOOP*, is

$$LOOP \triangleq \text{if} \qquad b$$
$$\text{then} \quad LOOP(BODY)$$
$$\text{else} \quad \text{exit}$$
$$\text{fi}$$

So

$$LOOP(\sigma) \triangleq \text{if} \qquad b(\sigma)$$
$$\text{then} \quad (LOOP(BODY))\sigma \dots$$

and

$$(LOOP(BODY))\sigma = (LOOP \circ BODY)(\sigma)$$
$$= LOOP(BODY(\sigma))$$

which might look more familiar. We can juggle the brackets because functional composition is associative, but are forced to use an unusual form here because we are manipulating a function (*LOOP*) without direct reference to its data (σ).

This is recursive but is not a two-level scheme. One obvious way to make it so is:

$$LOOP \triangleq \text{if} \qquad b$$
$$\text{then} \quad INNER(BODY)$$
$$\text{else} \quad \text{exit}$$
$$\text{fi}$$

where

$$INNER \triangleq \text{if} \qquad b$$
$$\text{then} \quad INNER(BODY)$$
$$\text{else} \quad \text{exit}$$
$$\text{fi}$$

Now we have a two-level description and only the lower level is recursive.

Fig. 7.14. Equivalent forms of LOOP.

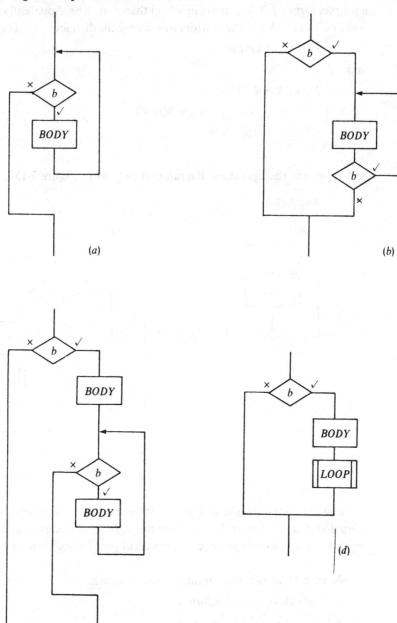

(a)

(b)

(c)

(d)

However, although this satisfies our stipulation, it is over-complex – there is a simpler form – *LOOP* is more involved than it need be. Apparently *LOOP* is equivalent to *INNER* so in order to preserve the distinct levels let us write

$\qquad$ *LOOP* $\triangleq$ *INNER*

and

$\qquad$ *INNER* $\triangleq$ if $\qquad$ *b*

$\qquad\qquad\qquad$ then $\quad$ *INNER(BODY)*

$\qquad\qquad\qquad$ else $\quad$ exit

$\qquad\qquad\qquad$ fi

and represent the operators diagrammatically as in Figure 7.15.

Fig. 7.15

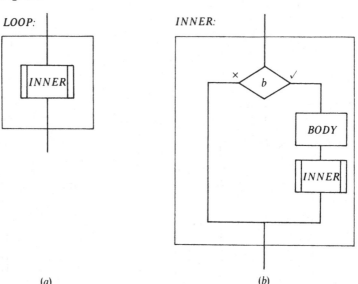

$\qquad\qquad$ (a) $\qquad\qquad\qquad\qquad\qquad\qquad\qquad$ (b)

Now taking the scheme in Figure 7.15(b) and introducing new names to help distinguish between *INNER* and the embedded reference to the same operation, we have to provide a correctness proof associated with Figure 7.16.

We wish to isolate the conditions under which

$\qquad$ pre-$I(\sigma) \Rightarrow$ post-$I(\sigma,I(\sigma))$

Case 1: $\neg b(\sigma)$ i.e. *b* is False for σ.

$\qquad$ pre-$I(\sigma) \wedge \neg b(\sigma) \Rightarrow$ post-$I(\sigma,I(\sigma))$

$\qquad\qquad\qquad\qquad = $ post-$I(\sigma,\sigma)$

So our first requirement is:

$$\text{pre-}I(\sigma) \wedge \neg b(\sigma) \Rightarrow \text{post-}I(\sigma,\sigma)$$

Case 2: $b(\sigma)$

$$\text{pre-}I(\sigma) \wedge b(\sigma) \Rightarrow \text{post-}I(\sigma,I(\sigma))$$

But when $b(\sigma)$, $I(\sigma) = J(B(\sigma))$, so we require

$$\text{pre-}I(\sigma) \wedge b(\sigma) \Rightarrow \text{pre-}B(\sigma),$$

and

$$\text{pre-}B(\sigma_1) \wedge \text{post-}B(\sigma_1,\sigma_2) \Rightarrow \text{pre-}J(\sigma_2).$$

Now for the induction step. The hypothesis is that the embedded body of *INNER* (here called *J*) works correctly and satisfies its post-condition: it therefore follows that *I* will work correctly if the post-conditions of *I* and *J* satisfy the (over restrictive) implication:

$$\text{pre-}B(\sigma_1) \wedge \text{post-}B(\sigma_1,\sigma_2) \wedge \text{post-}J(\sigma_2,\sigma_3) \Rightarrow \text{post-}I(\sigma_1,\sigma_3)$$

But *I* and *J* are both incarnations of *INNER* so our four conditions can be restated as:

r_1: $\quad \text{pre-}INNER(\sigma) \wedge \neg b(\sigma) \Rightarrow \text{post-}INNER(\sigma,\sigma)$

d_1: $\quad \text{pre-}INNER(\sigma) \wedge b(\sigma) \Rightarrow \text{pre-}BODY(\sigma)$

d_2: $\quad \text{pre-}BODY(\sigma_1) \wedge \text{post-}BODY(\sigma_1,\sigma_2) \Rightarrow \text{pre-}INNER(\sigma_2)$

r_2: $\quad \text{pre-}BODY(\sigma_1) \wedge \text{post-}BODY(\sigma_1,\sigma_2) \wedge \text{post-}INNER(\sigma_2,\sigma_3) \Rightarrow$
$$\text{post-}INNER(\sigma_1,\sigma_3)$$

Fig. 7.16

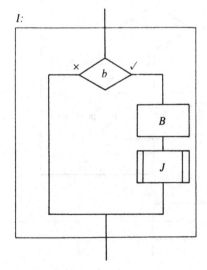

Connecting *INNER* with *LOOP* we also have:

d_3:   pre-*LOOP*$(\sigma) \Rightarrow$ pre-*INNER*(σ)

r_3:   pre-*LOOP*$(\sigma_1) \wedge$ post-*INNER*$(\sigma_1,\sigma_2) \Rightarrow$ post-*LOOP*(σ_1,σ_2)

Now recall that when tail recursion is wrapped into a *while* loop (Figures 7.9 and 7.10) the 'process' *INNER* actually disappears. So which parts of the flowchart do pre-*INNER* and post-*INNER* relate to, and what do they mean? Well, with reference to Figure 7.15, the first state (σ_1 in pre-*INNER*(σ_1) and post-*INNER*(σ_1,σ_2)) must come after pre-*LOOP*, after *BODY* and before b. Similarly the second state must be before the final state of post-*LOOP* but after the final processing of *BODY*. Hence we have Figure 7.17.

It is apparent looking at this annotated flowchart that the names pre-*INNER* and post-*INNER* have no obvious significance within the while loop. We therefore change them to *invar*, denoting an invariant which holds

Fig. 7.17

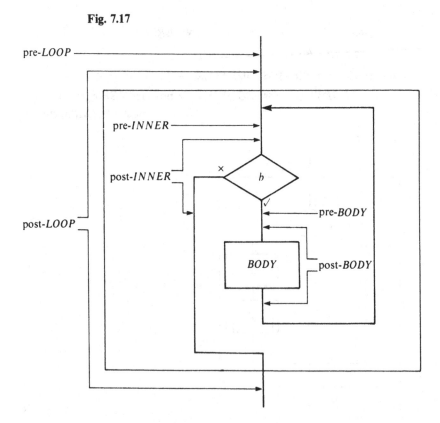

on every iteration of the loop, and *to_end*, which relates the current intermediate state before the test to the state at the end of the *LOOP*.

We have not yet said anything about convergence of the iteration to the exit condition (well-orderings, etc.) but we can collect together the domain and range conditions and describe their significance in terms of

(i) progressing through the loop, and

(ii) working backwards from the expected final state.

So, to prove the so-called partial correctness of

$$LOOP \triangleq \text{while } b \text{ do } BODY \text{ od}$$

we must find functions

$$invar: \text{state} \to \mathbb{B}$$

and

$$to\_end: \text{state} \times \text{state} \to \mathbb{B}$$

which, when associated with the flowchart segments as indicated in Figure 7.18, satisfy the following conditions:

d_1: $invar(\sigma) \wedge b(\sigma) \Rightarrow \text{pre-}BODY(\sigma)$

(don't exit)

d_2: $\text{pre-}BODY(\sigma_1) \wedge \text{post-}BODY(\sigma_1,\sigma_2) \Rightarrow invar(\sigma_2)$

(continue round the loop, executing the *BODY*)

d_3: $\text{pre-}LOOP(\sigma) \Rightarrow invar(\sigma)$

(enter *LOOP*)

r_1: $invar(\sigma) \wedge \neg b(\sigma) \Rightarrow to\_end(\sigma,\sigma)$

(exit with final state)

r_2: $\text{pre-}BODY(\sigma_1) \wedge \text{post-}BODY(\sigma_1,\sigma_2) \wedge to\_end(\sigma_2,\sigma_3) \Rightarrow$

$$to\_end(\sigma_1,\sigma_3)$$

(relate final state to the state one iteration further back)

r_3: $\text{pre-}LOOP(\sigma_1) \wedge to\_end(\sigma_1,\sigma_2) \Rightarrow \text{post-}LOOP(\sigma_1,\sigma_2)$

(link back to initial state)

Unfortunately, satisfaction of these six conditions only leads to **partial correctness** of *LOOP*. They guarantee that 'if you get to the end then the resultant state change is correct', but you may never reach the end.

By now it should be obvious that we require a suitable well-ordered set the elements of which are associated with successive states encountered by repeated execution of the loop body. This set can conveniently be viewed as a subset of $\mathbb{P}$, being the results of evaluating a function, *term* (for termination) where *term*: state → $\mathbb{P}$,

the state is that associated with *invar* and

t_1:   pre-*LOOP*$(\sigma) \Rightarrow (term(\sigma) \geqslant 0)$

(initial value)

t_2: $invar(\sigma) \land (term(\sigma) > 0) \Rightarrow b(\sigma)$

t_3: $invar(\sigma) \land (term(\sigma) = 0) \Rightarrow \neg b(\sigma)$

$(\neg b(\sigma) \Leftrightarrow term(\sigma) = 0)$

t_4:   pre-*BODY*$(\sigma_1) \land$ post-*BODY*$(\sigma_1, \sigma_2) \Rightarrow (term(\sigma_2) < term(\sigma_1))$

(values strictly decrease)

So *term*(σ) is a crude measure of how close we are to reaching an exit state. Since $\mathbb{P}$ is well-ordered the decreasing progression must reach zero (and hence $\neg b$).

The function *term* may simply yield the value of a program variable, or the size of a set, the length of a list or the height of a tree, etc. Notice also

Fig. 7.18

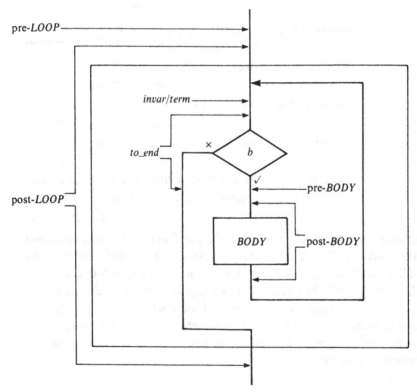

that, relating this function to the program rather than the computation (subtle distinction here, but read on) allows the possibility of the integer values decreasing by amounts greater than one. Computation depths increase one at a time but suppose we have a sorting program with *term* defined to give the length of the 'still_to_be_sorted' list. Clearly, with suitable data, this list can shrink in a non-uniform fashion and it is to cope with such situations that rule t_4 is formulated as shown. Remember that *term* has to be invented as part of the proof and relating it directly to the program does make this easier. Now for some examples.

Examples 7.4.3

Given the specification of an operation *MULTP*

> *MULTP*
>
> states: $\mathbb{P} \times \mathbb{P} \times \mathbb{P}$
>
> pre--$MULTP(\langle x,y,z \rangle) \triangleq \text{True}$
>
> post-$MULTP(\langle x,y,z \rangle, \langle x',y',z' \rangle) \triangleq z' = x * y,$

we are required to show the validity of the realisation

> $MULTP \triangleq z \leftarrow 0$
>
> > while $\quad \neg(x=0)$
> >
> > do $\quad x \leftarrow x-1$
> >
> > $\quad\quad\quad z \leftarrow z+y$
> >
> > od

Trivially, the specification satisfied by $z \leftarrow 0$ includes $z' = 0$ within its post-condition. Also, in Exercises 7.3.2, you showed that

> $BODY \triangleq x \leftarrow x-1;\ z \leftarrow x+y$

satisfies the specification

> states: $\mathbb{P} \times \mathbb{P} \times \mathbb{P}$
>
> pre--$BODY(\sigma) \triangleq x > 0$
>
> post-$BODY(\sigma,\sigma') \triangleq (z' + x' * y' = z + x * y) \wedge (0 \leqslant x' < x)$
>
> > > > > > > where $\sigma \triangleq \langle x,y,z \rangle$.

Hence the problem reduces to showing that

> $LOOP \triangleq$ while $\quad \neg(x=0)$
>
> > do $\quad x \leftarrow x-1$
> >
> > $\quad\quad\quad z \leftarrow z+y$
> >
> > od

satisfies

$$\text{pre--}LOOP(\sigma) \triangleq z = 0$$

$$\text{post-}LOOP(\sigma,\sigma') \triangleq z' = x * y$$

over states $\sigma \in \mathbb{P} \times \mathbb{P} \times \mathbb{P}$.

Before we proceed we need to invent *invar*, *term* and *to_end*. The exit condition is $x = 0$, initially $x \geqslant 0$ and *BODY* reduces the value of x so take $term(\sigma) \triangleq x$; invar is not so easy, there are many reasonable choices. If we involve z then we must relate back to the original values of x and y but this is not allowed in a predicate of *1* variable (i.e. the current state); y is invariate so although it could be included it serves no useful purpose; so we are therefore left with x and all we can say about x is $(x \geqslant 0)$. Use this for *invar*.

The prediate *to_end* relates the state at the stage associated with *invar* and the state σ_2 in post-$LOOP(\sigma_1,\sigma_2)$; $z' = z$ would be a reasonable guess but we must not presume that we are on the last iteration and hence $\neg(x = 0)$ is false.

In which case $z' = z + x * y$ (see post-*BODY* and recall that on the last iteration $x * y = 0$) is more generally valid.

So, with

$$invar(\sigma) \triangleq x \geqslant 0$$

$$to\_end(\sigma,\sigma') \triangleq z' = z + x * y$$

$$term(\sigma) \triangleq x$$

We have†

d_1: $invar(\sigma) \wedge b(\sigma) \Rightarrow \text{pre-}BODY(\sigma)$

$(\rightarrow)$ $(x \geqslant 0) \wedge \neg(x = 0) \Rightarrow (x > 0)$

$(\rightarrow)$ True

d_2: $\text{pre-}BODY(\sigma_1) \wedge \text{post-}BODY(\sigma_1,\sigma_2) \Rightarrow invar(\sigma_2)$

$(\rightarrow)$ $(x_1 > 0) \wedge \ldots \wedge (0 \leqslant x_2 < x_1) \Rightarrow (x_2 \geqslant 0)$

$(\rightarrow)$ True

d_3: $\text{pre-}LOOP(\sigma) \Rightarrow invar(\sigma)$

$(\rightarrow)$ $(z = 0) \wedge (x \geqslant 0) \wedge \ldots \Rightarrow (x \geqslant 0)$

$(\rightarrow)$ True

---

† Note. In this and other examples you might find it useful to draw yourself an appropriate flowchart annotated with pre-*BODY*, post-*BODY*, *to_end*, etc., to help follow the substitutions into the general forms of the various domain, range and termination rules.

[Clauses such as $x \geqslant 0$ apply to all variables in σ by virtue of their type, $\mathbb{P}$. If this seems like cheating consider the type as $\mathbb{Z}$ and include $x \geqslant 0$ as an extra pre-condition of *MULTP*.]

r_1: $\mathrm{invar}(\sigma) \wedge \neg b(\sigma) \Rightarrow \mathrm{to\_end}(\sigma, \sigma)$

$(\rightarrow)$ $(x \geqslant 0) \wedge (x = 0) \Rightarrow z = z + x * y$

$(\rightarrow)$ True

r_2: $\mathrm{pre\text{-}BODY}(\sigma_1) \wedge \mathrm{post\text{-}BODY}(\sigma_1, \sigma_2) \wedge \mathrm{to\_end}(\sigma_2, \sigma_3) \Rightarrow$
$$\mathrm{to\_end}(\sigma_1, \sigma_3)$$

$(\rightarrow)$ $(x_1 > 0) \wedge (z_2 + x_2 * y_2 = z_1 + x_1 * y_1) \wedge \ldots \wedge (z_3 = z_2 + x_2 * y_2) \Rightarrow$
$$(z_3 = z_1 + x_1 * y_1)$$

$(\rightarrow)$ $(z_3 = z_1 + x_1 * y_1) \Rightarrow (z_3 = z_1 + x_1 * y_1)$

$(\rightarrow)$ True

r_3: $\mathrm{pre\text{-}LOOP}(\sigma_1) \wedge \mathrm{to\_end}(\sigma_1, \sigma_2) \Rightarrow \mathrm{post\text{-}LOOP}(\sigma_1, \sigma_2)$

$(\rightarrow)(x_1 \geqslant 0) \wedge (z_1 = 0) \wedge (z_2 = z_1 + x_1 * y_1) \Rightarrow (z_2 = x_1 * y_1)$

$(\rightarrow)$ True

t_1: $\mathrm{pre\text{-}LOOP}(\sigma) \Rightarrow (\mathrm{term}(\sigma) \geqslant 0)$

$(\rightarrow)$ $(z = 0) \wedge (x \geqslant 0) \Rightarrow (x \geqslant 0)$

$(\rightarrow)$ True

t_2: $\mathrm{invar}(\sigma) \wedge (\mathrm{term}(\sigma) > 0) \Rightarrow b(\sigma)$

$(\rightarrow)$ $(x \geqslant 0) \wedge (x > 0) \Rightarrow \neg(x = 0)$

$(\rightarrow)$ True

t_3: $\mathrm{invar}(\sigma) \wedge (\mathrm{term}(\sigma) = 0) \Rightarrow \neg b(\sigma)$

$(\rightarrow)$ $(x \geqslant 0) \wedge (x = 0) \Rightarrow (x = 0)$

$(\rightarrow)$ True

t_4: $\mathrm{pre\text{-}BODY}(\sigma_1) \wedge \mathrm{post\text{-}BODY}(\sigma_1, \sigma_2) \Rightarrow (\mathrm{term}(\sigma_2) < \mathrm{term}(\sigma_1))$

$(\rightarrow)$ $(x_1 > 0) \wedge \ldots \wedge (0 \leqslant x_2 < x_1) \Rightarrow (x_2 < x_1)$

$(\rightarrow)$ True

Hence the realisation is valid. But what a lot of work! Yes, ten separate rules to check does seem rather excessive, but each of the ten was almost trivial. Indeed if we had replaced $(x \geqslant 0)$ by True, they would have been even simpler.

Important factors illustrated by this example are

(i) that despite the identical forms of *LOOP* and *INNER*, pre-*LOOP* and pre-*INNER* (now called *invar*) are not always the same but must be related as in d_3,

(ii) that if we make a wrong choice of *term*, *invar* or *to_end* then all that will happen is that one or more of the rules will not hold. This would indicate lack of comprehension of the underlying computational process and reference back to the relevant flowchart segment should act as a guide to the logical error, and

(iii) that there is an inherent computational link between pre-*LOOP*, post-*BODY*, *to_end*, the test *b*, and post-*LOOP*. The actual state changes are caused by *BODY* and must be in accord with its post-condition. Post-*BODY* is of the form $f(\sigma) = f(\sigma')$, i.e. some combination of the variables in the state is preserved. Put another way, the expression $z + x * y$ is invariant as we pass from σ to $BODY(\sigma)$ – notice that part of σ which changes is indicative of how *term* must be defined, and although the value of $z + x * y$ is constant we cannot indicate this within *invar* since it would require knowledge of two successive 'generations' of σ. Now, using pre-*LOOP* to simplify $z + x * y$ yields $x * y$. Similarly using the exit condition to simplify $z + x * y = z' + x' * y'$ gives $z + x * y = z'$, the *to_end* function, and applying both simplifications gives $z' = x + y$ which is post-*LOOP*.

Example 7.4.4

We know by virtue of Example 7.3.1 that the sequence

$$total \leftarrow total + n$$

$$n \leftarrow n - 1$$

satisfies the post-condition

$$\left(total' + \sum_{i=0}^{n'} i \right) = \left(total + \sum_{i=0}^{n} i \right)$$

where $\sigma \triangleq \langle total, n \rangle \in \mathbb{Z} \times \mathbb{Z}$ and $n > 0$

Hence by a simple substitution, details of which are left as an exercise, we can show that

$$total \leftarrow 0$$

while $n \neq 0$

do $total \leftarrow total + n$

$$n \leftarrow n - 1$$

od

satisfies the specification

> *ADDER*
>
> states: $\mathbb{Z} \times \mathbb{Z}$
>
> pre--$ADDER(\sigma) \triangleq \text{True}$
>
> post-$ADDER(\sigma,\sigma') \triangleq \left(total' = \sum_{i=0}^{n} i \right)$
>
> where $\sigma \triangleq \langle total, n \rangle$ □

Finally, as promised in the previous section, we give the proof of an iterative realisation of the factorial function.

Example 7.4.5

Firstly we need to adjust the specification to remove the type line.

> *FACT*
>
> states: $\mathbb{Z} \times \mathbb{Z}$
>
> pre--$FACT(\langle x,y \rangle) \triangleq x \geqslant 0$
>
> post-$FACT(\langle x,y \rangle,\langle x',y' \rangle) \triangleq y' = x!$

Now for the realisation:

> $FACT \triangleq y \leftarrow 1$
>
> > while $\neg(x=0)$
> >
> > do $\quad y \leftarrow y*x$
> >
> > $\qquad x \leftarrow x-1$
> >
> > od

Regarding this as $y \leftarrow 1$; *LOOP* we can use

> pre-$LOOP(\langle x,y \rangle) \triangleq (x \geqslant 0) \wedge (y=1)$.

Moreover, after a bit of thought and possibly several false starts, the post-*BODY* may be written as

> post-$BODY(\langle x,y \rangle,\langle x',y' \rangle) \triangleq ((x'!*y')=(x!*y)) \wedge (0 \leqslant x' < x)$

and, trivially,

> pre-$BODY(\langle x,y \rangle) \triangleq (x>0)$

Following the chain of argument given after Example 7.4.3 we have

> $to\_end(\sigma,\sigma') \triangleq (y' = x!*y)$
>
> where $\sigma \triangleq \langle x,y \rangle$.

Without justification we shall try

> $term(\sigma) \triangleq x$

and

$$invar(\sigma) \triangleq (x \geqslant 0)$$

The domain rules then reduce to:

d_1: $(x \geqslant 0) \wedge \neg(x=0) \Rightarrow (x>0)$

d_2: $(x_1 > 0) \wedge (x_2! * y_2 = x_1! * y_1) \wedge (0 \leqslant x_2 < x_1) \Rightarrow (x_2 \geqslant 0)$

d_3: $(x \geqslant 0) \wedge (y=1) \Rightarrow (x \geqslant 0)$

which are all true.

Similarly, for the range rules:

r_1: $(x \geqslant 0) \wedge (x=0) \Rightarrow (y = x! * y)$

r_2: $(x_1 > 0) \wedge (x_2! * y_2 = x_1! * y_1) \wedge (0 \leqslant x_2 < x_1) \wedge (y_3 = x_2! * y_2) \Rightarrow$

$$(y_3 = x_1! * y_1)$$

r_3: $(x_1 \geqslant 0) \wedge (y_1 = 1) \wedge (y_2 = x_1! * y_1) \Rightarrow (y_2 = x_1!)$

and for termination:

t_1: $(x \geqslant 0) \Rightarrow (x \geqslant 0)$

t_2: $(x \geqslant 0) \wedge (x > 0) \Rightarrow \neg(x=0)$

t_3: $(x \geqslant 0) \wedge (x=0) \Rightarrow (x=0)$

t_4: $(x_1 > 0) \wedge (x_1! * y_1 = x_2! * y_2) \wedge (0 \leqslant x_2 < x_1) \Rightarrow (x_2 < x_1)$

Here there is virtually nothing to do when the rules are written out with the proper functions in place. $\qquad\square$

Exercises 7.4

1. Consider the effect of the scheme

$$F : \sigma \mapsto \text{if} \qquad b(\sigma)$$
$$\text{then} \quad G_1(F(G_2(\sigma)))$$
$$\text{else} \quad H(\sigma)$$
$$\text{fi}$$

when G_2 is replaced by the identity operation. How might such a scheme be included in a new scheme that would give rise to post-check loops?

2. Prove that the statement

'all prime natural numbers are odd'

is false. Explain your logical argument.

3. Show that the realisation

$$multp(x,y) \triangleq \text{if} \quad x=0$$
$$\text{then} \quad 0$$
$$\text{else} \quad multp(x-1,y)+y$$
$$\text{fi}$$

satisfies the specification

> *multp*
>
> type: $\mathbb{Z} \times \mathbb{Z} \to \mathbb{Z}$
>
> pre--$multp(\langle x,y \rangle) \triangleq x \geqslant 0$
>
> post-$multp(\langle x,y \rangle, z) \triangleq z = x * y$

4. Use *SEG1* of Exercise 7.3.1 to show that

$$ADD \triangleq \text{while} \quad \neg(y=0)$$
$$\text{do} \quad y \leftarrow y+1$$
$$x \leftarrow x-1$$
$$\text{od}$$

satisfies the specification

> ADD
>
> states: $\mathbb{Z} \times \mathbb{Z}$
>
> pre--ADD$(\langle x,y \rangle) \triangleq y \leqslant 0$
>
> post-ADD$(\langle x,y \rangle, \langle x',y' \rangle) \triangleq x' = x+y$

7.5   Conclusion

The main reason for being so particular about writing specifications in a formal manner is so that, when necessary, we can show that an appropriate piece of program (which by virtue of the way it controls a computer alway has a formal description) actually does what it should. As witnessed by the examples in this chapter, even when the computation is comparatively simple, the associated proof can be quite long. Having said this, using sets of rules rather than attempting proofs from first principles makes the proof easier to carry out, providing of course that the code is correct.

In practice the major part of most specifications and programs are very commonplace and need not be formally verified. We can therefore concentrate our time and effort on those parts of the problem (specification or program) which are unfamiliar enough to warrant special attention; the amount of time allowed for formal verification of (part of) a program being indicative of its importance.

The control flow forms considered here are sufficient to cope with classical structured programs. Other forms may be added to PDL and ought to relate properly to code templates for the target language. Such matters take us into the semantics of these languages but this subject is not within the scope of our current study. How some of these other forms **should** correspond to the basic ones is briefly discussed in Chapter 8.

To summarise; what **is** necessary is that formal correctness proofs should be possible. However, use of the standard forms means that only small amounts of code will have to be verified from first principles.

8
Examination of templates and target code

The purpose of this chapter is to caution the reader about straying from the templates given in Chapter 6; to explicitly state the semantic assumptions inherent in our basic PDL, and to highlight factors which must be checked when extending PDL or devising templates for target languages not mentioned in this text.

PDL is a very small language, having relatively few fundamental operations and processes. Moreover the semantics, the meanings, of these components relate directly and simply to corresponding features in implemented languages. Proper definition of programming language semantics is a non-trivial task and definitely far too involved to be adequately discussed here. However, since we want our programs to actually carry out computations, and not be purely static objects represented by symbols on paper or on a screen, we cannot totally avoid semantics; so what do we do?

Recall that an implementation of an operation is correct if all its required external characteristics are described by its specification. It would therefore be true to say that the semantics of the operation can be fully described/ defined by the inter-relationship between input/state and output/state of an appropriate specification. So what is the problem? The problem is that very few implementations of programming languages are defined adequately enough to enable us to use the definition in a formal way. Thus, we use a small subset (which may or may not be reliable but, being smaller than the entire language, is easier to check out) and build more complex constructs using well-defined translations in PDL and avoid the more advanced, but probably less reliable, features directly available in the target code. We should therefore

    (i) try to cater for users who don't read language or implementation descriptions,

   (ii) be aware that implementors may not read or understand language definitions (specifications), and

  (iii) admit that there are language designers who don't draw up proper (i.e., complete and unambiguous) specifications.

How do we check what a language implementation actually does? There are two practical approaches which may yield fruit. The first is to try to force the (high-level) language to 'self-trace'. If allowed by the language/ implementation, this requires that certain functions be allowed to cause side-effects (see below) which can subsequently be examined to give information concerning the order in which the side-effects happened and consequently also the order in which the functions were executed. This method does, however, require that the addition of extra print statements (even just one extra) does not materially affect the running of the program as a whole. As you might perceive from the general tone of this digression, there are horror stories about cases when this has not been so.

The other approach, and the one which we really have to apply when using low-level languages, is to inspect the code to see what checks are included.

What checks do we need? Which checks do we take for granted? Which (PDL) language extensions and facilities are safe and which are decidedly dangerous?

We consider the main features of PDL and the related target code in three broad subdivisions; assignment, control and parameter-passing. Each of these is given a separate section (although of course there is interplay) and these are followed by a summary of concluding remarks.

8.1   Assignment statements

An assignment statement of the form

$$x \leftarrow E$$

is the most fundamental unit of procedural computation and would seem to present no problems. The meaning is familiar, we evaluate the expression E and assign that value to x. The value of x should be the only **value** that changes since that change is the only **effect** required of the statement. More precisely the evaluation of E should not result in any changes in the state. In terms of specification we have

eval_E

states: σ

type: $\rightarrow Res$

pre--$eval\_E(\sigma,) \triangleq \ldots$

post-$eval\_E(\sigma,,\sigma',r) \triangleq$ $(r = \ldots)$

$$\wedge (\sigma' = \sigma)$$

where the result is subsequently passed to x. The value or r in the post-condition obviously depends on E; the pre-condition is a little more difficult to stipulate formally in a general way. The requirements are

(i) that all 'variables' in σ which are used in E should have assigned values (so that each can be evaluated to give a proper value which can then take part in the evaluation of E), and

(ii) that the ensuing calculation does in fact give the correct 'arithmetic' value. (A sufficient, but not necessary, condition that ensures this is that all subcalculations are also arithmetically correct – see [9] for some simple examples). In practice this usually requires that calculations should not overflow, a particularly messy constraint when subrange types are involved.

So the actual assignment is simple but the evaluation of the *right-hand-side* expression is fraught with possible complications.

Similar errors must be avoided when evaluating expressions elsewhere, notably expressions which describe parameters of functions and, as we now see, Boolean expressions used in flow control statements. How the properties of such expressions may be introduced into a computing system is discussed at length in Chapter 10.

8.2   Control statements

In contrast to the previous section where, apart from syntactic considerations, all languages treat assignment in a similar way, here we must draw a distinction between pure PDL and other forms of procedural control.

Initially we took the control primitives of PDL more or less for granted but following the work of Chapter 7 we are able to give proper, rigorous, definitions. The semantics of these constructs can be defined in terms of state changes and so, at the risk of overtaxing pre- and post-conditions, these will be used where thought appropriate so as to avoid the introduction of proper language definition notations which would be out of place in the context.

The three usual syntactic forms are

(i) $p;q$

or

p

q

(ii) if b then p else q fi

and

(iii) while b do p od

Sequencing is simply the procedural form of functional composition and hence can be defined by

$$(p;q)\sigma \triangleq q(p(\sigma))$$

or, using a post-condition

$$\text{post-}(p;q)(\sigma,\sigma') \triangleq \sigma' = q(p(\sigma))$$

Conditional forms like

if b then ... else ... fi

obviously require a logical description such as:

$$b \Rightarrow \ldots$$
$$\neg b \Rightarrow \ldots$$

As usual, b must yield a Boolean (logical) value but we must also have Boolean values after the implications in order for these operators to yield valid results. This is easy but we need to know the context in which the conditional is used. For instance the conditional expansion used in the assignment.

$$x \leftarrow \text{if } b \text{ then } y \text{ else } z \text{ fi}$$

infers (only) the change from x to x' given by

$$(b \Rightarrow x' = y) \wedge (\neg b \Rightarrow x' = z)$$

For a conditional statement we therefore have:

$$\text{post-(if } b \text{ then } p \text{ else } q \text{ fi)}(\sigma,\sigma') \triangleq (b \Rightarrow \sigma' = p(\sigma)) \wedge (\neg b \Rightarrow \sigma' = q(\sigma))$$

In a similar vein, from Section 7.4, we have

$$\text{post-(while } b \text{ do } p \text{ od)}(\sigma,\sigma') \triangleq \quad b \Rightarrow \sigma' = (\text{while } b \text{ do } p \text{ od})p(\sigma)$$
$$\wedge \neg b \Rightarrow \sigma' = \sigma$$

PDL also admits a post-check loop. This may be defined directly as above, or by:

$$(\text{repeat } p \text{ until } b)\sigma \triangleq (p; \text{ while } \neg b \text{ do } p \text{ od})\sigma$$

Adopting this approach means that the semantics of *repeat-until* must be derived from the other forms and therefore should be consistent with them – hence we avoid a possible source of ambiguity.

Before venturing from the familiar PDL constructs we ought to mention procedure calls. Procedure calls (with or without parameters) are generally regarded as control statements. The question of parameters will be dealt with in depth in the next section but, as witnessed by the low-level coding in Chapter 6, parameters in PDL necessitate extra code before and after the actual call in an assembler-level realisation. Hence parameter-less calls are a subproblem of more complex subroutine invocations.

From the specification and logical standpoints a call is just like any other statement. Calls must simply obey their specification; transfer and return of control have no logical significance. Indeed, as exemplified in Chapters 7 and 9, the body of a procedure may be switched in and out of line at will. To be able to do this necessitates that there is no logical interference in the flow of control – i.e., the routine does what it seems to do regardless of whether the code is in-line or not.

Of course there are other possible control statements. These may be viewed as potential extensions to PDL or as existing facilities in a target language. In either case we need to ensure their proper definition in terms of our base language.

Consider a counting loop of the form:

> for i from j to k do p od

The definition of a *for*-loop is **not** obvious. One possibility is:

> $i \leftarrow j$
>
> while $\quad i \neq k$
>
> do $\quad p$
>
> $\qquad i \leftarrow i+1$
>
> od

Here it is presumed that i, j and k are integers (or some other enumerated type). In general p has access to i, j and k but should not change i or k; and what if $j > k$? These possibilities can all be checked for or disallowed by requiring that p has access to a state including i, j and k and that post-p incorporates the clause $i' = i \wedge j' = j \wedge k' = k$.

A variation on the *for*-loop is

> for i from j to k by ℓ do p od

In this version what do we do if $\ell = 0$ or $\ell < 0$? Pascal (see, e.g. [31]) side-steps this issue by making it the users responsibility to ascertain whether $k > j$ or $k < j$ and then use a **to** or **downto** form, thus implying $\ell = 1$ or $\ell = -1$. The Algols (60 and 68) [27] and [33] on the other hand are defined to do a much more comprehensive job – however they are not always implemented as defined.

There are also other, less obvious, areas of diversification. Consider the FORTRAN equivalent of

> for i from j to k by $\ell \dots$

i.e.

> DO...I=J, K, L

The 1966 and 1977 standards ([1], [2]) differ in respect of the restrictions that apply to the forms and values of the three control parameters represented here by J, K and L. It goes without saying (!?) that all implementations should react in the same way and invalid combinations of control parameters should cause the program to be halted. Most users, however, only have need of a single system and hence, without comparisons, presume that their results are correct. So what can go wrong with the DO loop?

It would be remiss of us not to note the fact that the '66 DO loop is post-check (and hence cannot be executed zero times) and the '77 version is pre-check but this, provided you are aware of the discrepancy, is easily programmed around. Our main concern here is more subtle and is another consequence of side-effects.

If J, K and L are expressions which may therefore contain functions (and hence side-effects which in turn may actually alter the values of J, K and L – see [7] for more details) then the order in which they are evaluated can effect the execution of the loop. The basic question is how should the loop be represented as a flowchart? Two of the numerous possibilities are given in Figure 8.1. Which, if any, of these is correct? The answer to this question seems to depend on when and where you ask it.

So, to put it mildly, for-loops are a bit of a semantic minefield. Fortunately adding a few bells and whistles to alternation to yield a *case* construct is straightforward. The case statement of the form

$$\text{case } s \text{ in}$$

$$1: p_1,$$
$$2: p_2,$$
$$\vdots$$
$$\vdots$$
$$n: p_n$$

$$\text{esac}$$

may be defined by

$$\text{pre-}(\text{case } s \text{ in } 1: p_1,\ldots,n: p_n \text{ esac})(\sigma) \triangleq (1 \leqslant s \leqslant n)$$

$$\text{post-}(\text{case } s \text{ in } 1: p_1,\ldots,n: p_n \text{ esac})(\sigma,\sigma') \triangleq$$

$$(s=1) \Rightarrow (\sigma' = p_1(\sigma))$$
$$\wedge (s=2) \Rightarrow (\sigma' = p_2(\sigma))$$
$$\wedge$$
$$\vdots$$
$$\wedge (s=n) \Rightarrow (\sigma' = p_n(\sigma))$$

For correctness purposes we could use the tests $(s=1),\ldots,(s=n-1)$ to nest suitable alternations or, make direct use of the given post-condition and write down rules of the form.

$$d_i: \text{pre-case}(\sigma) \wedge (s=i) \Rightarrow \text{pre-}p_i(\sigma)$$

and

$$r_i: \text{pre-case}(\sigma) \wedge (s=i) \wedge \text{post-*}_i(\sigma,\sigma') \Rightarrow \text{post-case}(\sigma,\sigma')$$

for all values of $i \in 1 .. n$.

Of course a particular realisation may not use tests of the form $(s=i)$ but indexing instead. This is quite acceptable and can be done without causing any logical problems with our specification. As with all operations (including these operations on operations) we don't care **how** the processes are carried out providing that we can rely on their compliance with the specifications.

Fig. 8.1

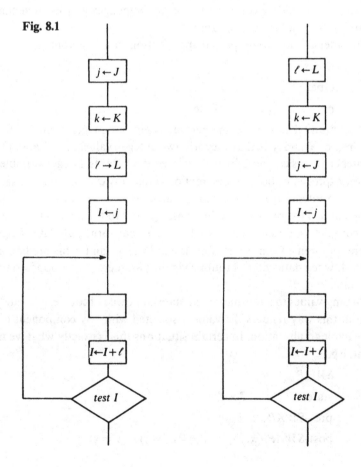

Exercises 8.2

1 By examining compiled segments of simple high-level code determine, in terms of an appropriate flowchart, the actual semantics of a *for*-loop for at least one such language to which you have access.

8.3   Parameter passing

In Section 7.2 we suggested that a programmer could exercise a degree of choice between whether to communicate with subprograms via parameters and results or via states. Ultimately, to allow us to write proofs more easily, we opted to treat all routines as acting entirely on states although the notation looked more like a function. In PDL terms, use of states is always sufficient, however in practical languages the same effect may be achieved by handling parameters in different ways to that adopted by PDL. The purpose of this section is to identify the main parameter mechanisms found in common high-level languages and as such can be regarded as an adjunct to Chapter 6.

Consider the following partial specification of a function:

states:

type: $\mathbb{Z} \times \mathbb{Z} \to \mathbb{Z}$

pre-... $(\langle x, y \rangle) \triangleq \text{True}$

The function takes a pair of integers and yields an integer result. All that is required of x and y is that they are two integer values, e.g. 7 and 13.

Integer values can be delivered by integer constants, integer variables or integer expressions, but the presumption is that any evaluation (necessary to obtain an integer from the actual parameter) is done prior to the values being handed over to the function. Once passed to the function, the values are completely dissociated from their external forms, all knowledge of where they come from is lost. This is *call by value* and is the method used by PDL when data enters a routine via the parameter list as opposed to via the state.

Passing values to a routine via the state is allowed of course, but handling data in this way renders the value associated with any component of the state liable to alteration. In certain situations this is exactly what we must want, e.g.

SWAP

states: $\mathbb{Z} \times \mathbb{Z}$

pre--*SWAP*...

post-*SWAP*$(\langle x, y \rangle, \langle x', y' \rangle) \triangleq (x' = y) \wedge (y' = x)$

This is *call by reference* (or call by location). The value of x must always be referred to by a name (a name which is 'known' outside the routine – it is not local to the specification or code, as is the case with call by value), the name of a location in which the value is held.

There is a further method which is very powerful and in fairly common usage but is not included in our basic PDL (although it could be if we allowed more complex types). This is variously referred to as *call by name*, call by expression or call by procedure. Here the actual parameter is an expression which is carried into the procedure (operation, etc.) and re-evaluated every time it is referenced. Upon evaluation it may be required to yield a value or a location and, since the expression may include state variables which may change, these qualities will in general change during the execution of the procedure.

Why mention non-PDL methods of parameter passing, indeed why elaborate over and above the cases for pure functions (type: $D \rightarrow R$) and pure operations (states: S)? If you don't know how parameters are passed in a particular language then you don't know how the specifications are structured or which templates to use. Most modern languages require the user to be explicit about how he wishes to use parameters but cautionary tales from the recent past may serve as a warning about the follies of ignorance in such matters.

Algol 60 uses call by value and, by default, call by name. Thus, even when call by value would be sufficient, if no method is specified, call by name would be used and the same value worked out (or even just looked up) time and time again. Whilst this may not seem so much of a penalty, it can result, with certain highly recursive functions, in the computer spending over 99% of its time doing no useful work. In such an instance, changing the parameter passing mode accordingly can cause a seemingly miraculous program speed up. But we are not usually concerned about efficiency in this sense so we move on to a more important illustration.

The default method of passing parameters in Fortran (FORTRAN 66 if you wish to be specific) is call by reference. So how do you deal with F(6)? The integer 6 is a value and you want a location name. One way round is to write (in PDL style)

$$x \leftarrow 6$$

$$\ldots f(x)$$

This makes clear what is going on but most implementations hide x from you and, together with other very clever bits of manipulation, can result in the following situation.

Suppose f merely increments its parameter value by 1 – it can since we are using call by reference – and we have the sequence:

$$a \leftarrow 6 + b$$

$$y \leftarrow f(6)$$

$$z \leftarrow g(6)$$

You're right, it shouldn't happen but the way some systems work it is possible for z to be assigned the value $g(7)$ – another horror story!

Exercises 8.3

1 Find out how to simulate call by procedure in Pascal.
2 By referring to a suitable text in Algol 60 programming, find out what ic Jensen's Device. Write a Pascal program to sum the elements of a real array using Jensen's Device.

8.4   Summary

There are lots of gremlins within programming language systems. As you proceed through your career you will doubtless fall foul of such quirks. We suggest that you steer clear of anything which you think is ambiguous, stay with what you know; what you are sure of.

Use simple PDL except where it becomes over verbose and repetitive. Then, define your own extensions and, if warranted by sufficient usage, write a translator from extended PDL into simple PDL, and then to the target language. (See [29] for examples of this.)

Why then, you might ask, don't we actually implement PDL? We could. A translator is easy – being merely mechanised templates – a run-time system is more involved. But PDL is not a language as much as the core of a language. If your personal or local PDL would economically benefit from the undoubtedly costly provision of such a system then OK. A far more attainable objective is just to write a translator; use PDL as an intermediate code from which the target code is generated, and then use the target language's run-time system. Moreover, provided that you translate via simple PDL, the resultant target code will also be simple, using no special features. Such code will be more portable and also more amenable to successful optimisation.

9
Abstract data types

Most programming languages allow programmer defined data structures (e.g. *array... of ...*) and when there is a rich choice available (*array, record, set, pointer,* etc.) there is no doubt that very neat, expressive data models can be built. However there is one major drawback. That is that the syntax used for accessing each type of structure is distinctive and fixed. This has two effects. Firstly, if for example, a *list* structure is altered from an *array* implementation to a *record-with-pointer* implementation then every reference to the *list* in the program must be changed. The distinctive array reference syntax ($a[i]$) has to be changed to *record/pointer* reference syntax ($p\uparrow.field$). Secondly the program becomes more machine-oriented and less problem-oriented because of the intrusion of programming details.

The way of avoiding the problems mentioned above is to think of a data structure not just as a storage area but as a collection of distinctive operations on certain data. This almost establishes the informal definition of an *abstract data type* (ADT)

$$ADT = Data\ Structure + Distinctive\ Operations$$

We have been using one abstract data type (the *list*) without naming it as such. Its distinctive operations are *head* and *tail*, 'concatenate' ($\|$) and 'creation from elements' ($\langle e_1, e_2, \ldots, e_n \rangle$). We have also introduced **realisations** or **implementations** of the abstract data type list in various languages – see Chapter 6. In fact in Section 6.3, Templates for FORTRAN, the implementation of LIST as a **module** shows the clear intention to treat the data space and the operations as an indivisible unit.

Notice that an ADT can be said to be abstract with respect to a particular programming language. An *array* is an abstract data type as far as most assembly languages are concerned but is not for most high-level languages. A *list* that is modelled in assembly language via an array is making use of two levels of abstract data types and we speak of the possibility of several layers of abstraction.

The philosophy of using ADT's is to postulate the existence of the data type which would be ideal to solve the problem at hand. This ADT is then used to write out a solution of the problem. A realisation of the ADT (possibly multilayered) is then produced so that the problem can be solved using data structures that are actually available.

We will show this philosophy in action by considering some well-known problems, feigning ignorance of their solution, and thus re-inventing the standard ADT's called stacks, queues & trees. It is hoped that this style of presentation will encourage a creative approach to ADT's while discussing 'well-known' examples.

9.1   ADT example – a siding

Suppose we wanted to reorder ordinary arithmetic expressions so that instead of the operator coming between its operands (infix notation), it is placed after its operands (postfix notation). This would mean that

$1 + x$

would be written

$1x +$

This can still be done when there is more than one operator of the same type and when the operators are mixed

Infix Form	Postfix Form
$1 + x$	$1x +$
$2*3$	$23*$
$1 + x + y$	$1x + y +$
$1 + 2*3$	$123* +$
$1*2 + 3*4$	$12*34* +$

If we were having to solve this problem for the first time we might have stumbled on the classic solution known as *Dijkstra's Shunting Algorithm*. The operands and operators are thought of as trucks on a railway line which takes the form shown below. It is clear that this layout allows the

Fig. 9.1. A railway siding.

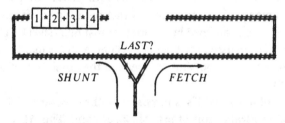

operators to be delayed (shunted into the siding) until both their operands (which may themselves contain operators) have come through (on the main line).

The details of the algorithm are not important here. It is sufficient to notice that three operations will be needed to handle the movement of the trucks containing operators

   SHUNT_ONTO_SIDING

– to shunt a truck from the main line onto the siding

   FETCH_FROM_SIDING

– to retrieve a truck from the siding onto the main line

   LAST_ONTO_SIDING_?

– to discover what is in the truck that was last shunted onto the siding

Thus we have identified an ADT as a place to store trucks which allows the operations *SHUNT_ONTO_SIDING, FETCH_FROM_SIDING* and *LAST_ONTO_SIDING_?* to be performed.

With a different background we may have imagined a 'well' of operators with the associated operations

   DROP_IN

   LIFT_OUT

   LOOK_INTO

but you have no doubt already decided that what is needed is that well-known ADT the *stack* with its distinctive operations *PUSH, POP* and *PEEP*.

We now show one way that the ADT called a *stack* can be specified.

The data structure which forms the basis of the *stack* is the *list*. Rather

Fig. 9.2. A well.

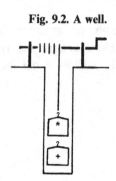

than restrict the presentation to the operator/operand example we will have a *stack* of values of type *Elt* and deliberately not specify here the exact type of *Elt*. Thus we write

Stack::*Elt*-List

PUSH
states:*Stack*
type :*Elt* →
pre--$PUSH(s,e) \triangleq \neg IS\_FULL(s)$
post-$PUSH(s,e,s',) \triangleq s' = \langle e \rangle \parallel s$

POP
states:*Stack*
type : → *Elt*
pre--$POP(s,) \triangleq \neg IS\_EMPTY(s)$
post-$POP(s,,s',e) \triangleq e = head(s) \wedge s' = tail(s)$

PEEP
states:*Stack*
type : → *Elt*
pre--$PEEP(s,) \triangleq \neg IS\_EMPTY(s)$
post-$PEEP(s,,s',e) \triangleq e = head(s) \wedge s = s'$

Note especially the last line of *PEEP*. It would have been all too easy to write

post-$PEEP(s,,s',e) \triangleq e = head(s)$

which would have obtained the correct 'answer' (i.e. result) in e but not specified that the stack was to remain unchanged – hence the addition of $s = s'$.

The auxiliary operation *IS_EMPTY* can easily be specified. The operation *IS_FULL* could be defined to be always False for a truly abstract data type but may be more realistically defined to allow a maximum number of *Elt*'s in the *stack*.

IS_EMPTY
states:*Stack*
type : → $\mathbb{B}$
pre--$IS\_EMPTY(s,) \triangleq$ True
post-$IS\_EMPTY(s,,s',b) \triangleq (b \Leftrightarrow (s = \langle \rangle)) \wedge s' = s$

IS_FULL

states:*Stack*

type :→ $\mathbb{B}$

pre--*IS_FULL(s,)* ≜ True

post-*IS_FULL(s,,s',b)* ≜ $(b \Leftrightarrow (length(s) \geqslant max)) \wedge s' = s$

Since the *stack* is regarded as being part of the *state* of these operations, we
will also need the operation *INIT* to initialise the *stack*.

INIT

states:*Stack*

type :→

pre--*INIT(s,)* ≜ True

post-*INIT(s,,s',)* ≜ $s' = \langle \rangle$

If there is a requirement for more than one *stack* then the operations will
need to be told which *stack* to operate on. This may conveniently be done
by bringing the *stack* out of the 'state' and supplying it as a parameter
(shown on the type line). This changes *PUSH* as follows

PUSH

states:

type :*Stack* × *Elt* → *Stack*

pre--*PUSH(,⟨s,e⟩)* ≜ $\neg IS\_FULL(s)$

post-*PUSH(,⟨s,e⟩,,s')* ≜ $s' = \langle e \rangle \| s$

If it is desired that the *stacks* are to remain in the 'state' then it will be
necessary to name them in some way

Named_Stack::*Name* × *Stack*

where *Name* might be an identifier made up of letters or it might be a
natural number, etc.

The state would then contain a set of *Named_Stacks* This would affect
PUSH as follows

PUSH

states:*Named_Stack*-Set

type :*Name* × *Elt* →

pre--*PUSH(nss,⟨n,e⟩)* ≜

$$\exists s: \langle n,s \rangle \in nss \quad \&$$
$$\neg IS\_EMPTY(s)$$

$$\text{post-}PUSH(nss,\langle n,e\rangle,nss',) \triangleq$$

$$nss' = (nss\backslash\{\langle n,s\rangle\})\cup\{\langle n,s'\rangle\} \quad \&$$

$$s' = \langle e\rangle\|s$$

This may still not be quite what was required but enough has been done to show

(i) Even a well-known ADT (like a *stack*) **should** be specified so as to make the meaning precise in each context.

(ii) The specification notation is capable of displaying all the variations that might be required.

In any case what is required next is a realisation of a particular stack in PDL. A realisation of *PUSH* for each of the first two specifications is given below.

Stack :: *Elt*-List

PUSH

states: *Stack*

type : *Elt* →

pre--$PUSH(s,e) \triangleq \neg IS\_FULL(s)$

post-$PUSH(s,e,s',) \triangleq s' = \langle e\rangle\|s$

is written in PDL as

s: *Stack*

function *push*

e: *Elt* →

$s \leftarrow \langle e\rangle\|s$

whereas

PUSH

states:

type : *Stack* × *Elt* → *Stack*

pre--$PUSH(,\langle s,e\rangle) \triangleq \neg IS\_FULL(s)$

post-$PUSH(,\langle s,e\rangle,,s') \triangleq s' = \langle e\rangle\|s$

is written in PDL as

function *push*

s_in: *Stack* , e: *Elt* → s_out: *Stack*

s_out ← $\langle e\rangle\|$ s_in

9.2   ADT example – an In_Tray

In a document or message passing system a person has an *In_Tray* into which all incoming documents are placed. The intention is that these documents are to be processed in the order that they arrived, i.e. 'First In First Out'.

We can immediately see a possible ADT with a document store and operations *NEW_DOCUMENT*, *PROCESS_DOCUMENT*, *IS_EMPTY_IN_TRAY*.

Once again this ADT has already been invented and it is called a *Queue*, with operations *JOIN*, *SERVE* and *IS_EMPTY*.

The specification for a single queue is given below. It is not the only possible specification. As for the previous example the queue may be in the 'state' or supplied as a parameter and there may be several queues so that each has to have a name.

Queue::*Elt*-List

JOIN

states:*Queue*

type :$Elt \rightarrow$

pre--$JOIN(q,e) \triangleq \neg IS\_FULL(q)$

post-$JOIN(q,e,q',) \triangleq q' = q \| \langle e \rangle$

Fig. 9.3. Operation JOIN.

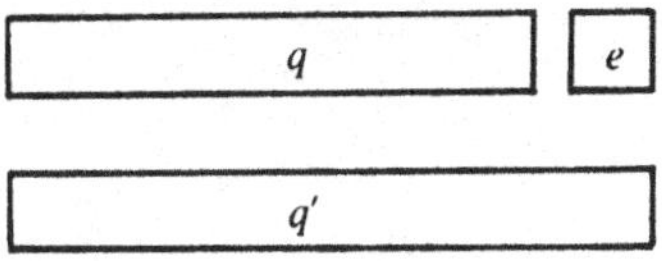

SERVE

states:*Queue*

type :$\rightarrow Elt$

pre--$SERVE(q,) \triangleq \neg IS\_EMPTY(q)$

post-$SERVE(q,,q',e) \triangleq q = \langle e \rangle \| q'$

Fig. 9.4. Operation SERVE.

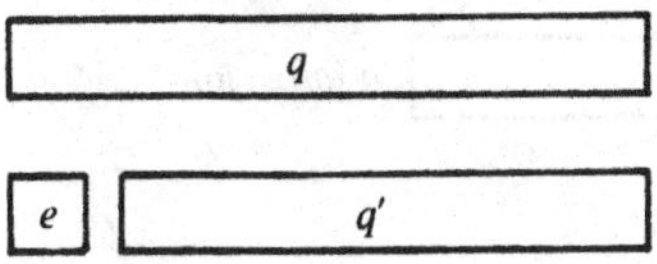

Notice especially the post-condition of *SERVE*. The single element concatenation is on the left rather than the right as for *JOIN*. It would be easy (but wrong) to read the post-condition as a rule for computing the initial state q from the final state q'. This is an implicit specification – it specifies a relation which is to be true but is not intended to be constructive (i.e. point to a particular implementation).

There is a very obvious implementation of a *queue* in PDL which just uses variable length *lists* as follows

$q:Elt^*$

function *join*

$e:Elt \rightarrow$

$q \leftarrow q \| \langle e \rangle$

function *serve*

$\rightarrow e:Elt$

$e \leftarrow head(q)$

$q \leftarrow tail(q)$

If the maximum number of elements that can ever join the queue is known, then an implementation as a **fixed** length list with two position markers is possible

function *join*

$e:Elt \rightarrow$

$q[joinp] \leftarrow e$

$joinp \leftarrow joinp + 1$

Fig. 9.5. Function join.

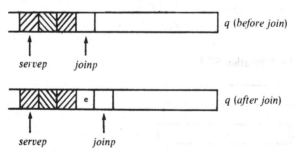

function *serve*

$\rightarrow e:Elt$

$e \leftarrow q[servep]$

$servep \leftarrow servep + 1$

Fig. 9.6. Function serve.

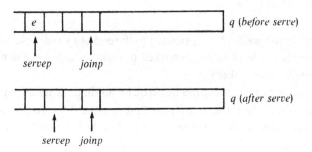

The restriction is clearly that no more elements can join the *queue* when *joinp* exceeds the length of the *list*. A neat extension of this scheme which reduces the restriction to a maximum number of elements in the list **at any one time** is to imagine the fixed length list curved round to form a 'circle'.

Fig. 9.7. A circular queue.

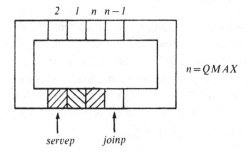

The line *joinp* ← *joinp* + 1 in the PDL function *join* is changed to

if   *joinp* = *QMAX*

then   *joinp* ← 1

else   *joinp* ← *joinp* + 1

fi

and similarly for *servep* ← *servep* + 1 in the function *serve*.

9.3   ADT example – LR Lookup store

Imagine a situation where items are being provided in a sequence and it is required to remember all the distinct items which occur.

For example, if the items were words then on processing

> to be or not to be, that...

the words

> to be or not that...

are stored.

Obviously the items could be appended to the end of a variable length list once each item in the list had been checked to make sure that the new item was not already among them.

No doubt an improvement could be made by holding the items in the list **in ascending order**, then the search to find whether a 'new' item was already present could stop if an item was found in the list which was larger than the new item.

On average we would still expect about half of the list to be searched each time a new item arrived.

Is there any way of improving on this?...

> IDEA!

Suppose we have a data structure of the form

> $L\_Store \times Item \times R\_Store$

so that no item in L_Store is greater than the 'central' item and no item in R_Store is less than the 'central' item. If we can operate L_Store and R_Store in the same way as the overall data structure, then the search should reduce the number of items left to be searched by (approximately) half at each stage. If L_Store and R_Store are to be the same structure, which is the same as the overall structure, we have apparently

> $LR\_Store :: LR\_Store \times Item \times LR\_Store$

Unfortunately there is no way of writing down values of this type since every attempt requires two more values.

> $\ell r\_value = \langle \quad , i, \quad \rangle$

what do we put in here?

We need to extend the LR_Store concept with the value 'empty'.

> $LR\_Store :: (LR\_Store \times Item \times LR\_Store) \cup \{empty\}$

then we can have

$\ell r_value1 = $ empty

$\ell r\_value2 = \langle$empty,i,empty$\rangle$

$\ell r\_value3 = \langle\langle$empty,$i$,empty$\rangle$,$j$,empty$\rangle$

$\ell r\_value4 = \langle\langle$empty,$i$,empty$\rangle$,$j$,$\langle$empty,$k$,empty$\rangle\rangle$, etc.

We will not specify the operation *ENTER_NEW_ITEM* for this data structure. Instead we notice that this is once again a well-known ADT called a (*binary*) *tree*. This is discussed under its usual name in the next section.

9.4 ADT example – a binary tree

A *binary tree* (see Chapter 3) is usually represented by a data structure with three components of which the 'left' component is called a *left branch* and the 'right' component a *right branch*.

$Bin\_Tree::(Bin\_Tree \times Item \times Bin\_Tree) \cup \{\text{empty}\}$

We now specify the operation *ENTER_NEW_ITEM* for this data structure.

ENTER_NEW_ITEM

states:

type :$Bin\_Tree \times Item \rightarrow Bin\_Tree$

pre--$ENTER\_NEW\_ITEM(,\langle t,i\rangle) \triangleq$ True

post-$ENTER\_NEW\_ITEM(,\langle t,i\rangle,,t') \triangleq$

$\quad t = $ empty $\wedge t' = \langle$empty,i,empty$\rangle$

$\quad\quad \vee$

$\quad t = \langle \ell,e,r\rangle \wedge i < e \wedge \ell' = ENTER\_NEW\_ITEM(,\langle \ell,i\rangle) \wedge$
$\quad\quad\quad\quad\quad\quad\quad\quad\quad\quad\quad\quad t' = \langle \ell',e,r\rangle$

$\quad\quad \vee$

$\quad t = \langle \ell,e,r\rangle \wedge i > e \wedge r' = ENTER\_NEW\_ITEM(,\langle r,i\rangle) \wedge$
$\quad\quad\quad\quad\quad\quad\quad\quad\quad\quad\quad\quad t' = \langle \ell,e,r'\rangle$

$\quad\quad \vee$

$\quad t = \langle \ell,e,r\rangle \wedge i = e \wedge t' = t$

This specification says

(i) If the present tree is 'empty', a new tree with empty branches is created for the new item.

(ii) If the present tree is 'not empty', it has a left branch, a central item and a right branch. If the new item is less than the central item then a new tree is created with the same central item and right branch but with a new left branch treated by entering the new item in its proper place.

(iii) Similarly if the new item is greater than the central item, a new tree is created with the same left branch and central item but with a new right branch.

(iv) If the new item is already in the tree it is not entered again.

One of the difficulties arising from this when met for the first time is that following a branch (left or right) does not lead to 'smaller' branches as it would on a 'real' tree but to a *tree*. Thus we speak of a tree as having left and right *subtrees*. The central item in each non-empty tree is said to be at the *root* of the tree. But then this means that each non-empty subtree has its own root!

This specification is recursive and may seem plausible in a superficial way but there may be reservations until it haś been seen 'in action'.

Suppose the sequence of words

> *Mary had a little lamb*

was available and each word in turn was to be processed by the operation *ENTER_NEW_ITEM*, starting from a completely empty tree.

(i) New Word is *Mary*, present tree is 'empty'

The specification yields the new tree ⟨empty,*Mary*,empty⟩

(ii) New word is *had*, present tree is ⟨empty,*Mary*,empty⟩

Since *had* occurs in dictionary order before *Mary* the new item *i* is 'less than' the item *e* at the root so the new tree is

> ⟨*new_left_branch*,*Mary*,empty⟩

where *new_left_branch* is the result of the operation *ENTER_NEW_ITEM* with the new item *had* and tree 'empty' (the old left branch).

Using the specification again we deduce that the new left branch will be

> ⟨empty,*had*,empty⟩

and that finally the full tree resulting from the original operation *ENTER_NEW_ITEM* and the sub-operation required by the recursion is

> ⟨⟨empty,*had*,empty⟩,*Mary*,empty⟩

(iii) New word *a*, present tree that resulting from (ii).

Resulting tree is

> ⟨⟨⟨empty,*a*,empty⟩,*had*,empty⟩,*Mary*,empty⟩

(iv) New word is *little*.

Resulting tree is

> ⟨⟨⟨empty,*a*,empty⟩,*had*,⟨empty,*little*,empty⟩⟩,*Mary*,empty⟩

or

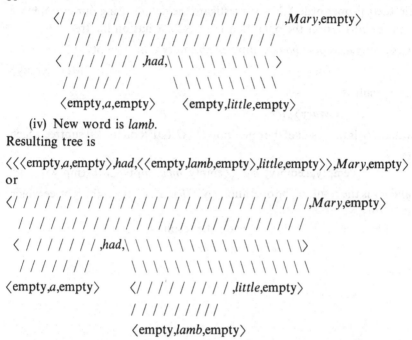

⟨/ ,*Mary*,empty⟩
/ /
⟨ / / / / / / / / ,*had*,\ \ \ \ \ \ \ \ \ \ ⟩
/ / / / / / /   \ \ \ \ \ \ \ \ \ \
⟨empty,*a*,empty⟩   ⟨empty,*little*,empty⟩

(iv) New word is *lamb*.

Resulting tree is

⟨⟨⟨empty,*a*,empty⟩,*had*,⟨⟨empty,*lamb*,empty⟩,*little*,empty⟩⟩,*Mary*,empty⟩

or

⟨/ /,*Mary*,empty⟩
/ /
⟨ / / / / / / / ,*had*,\ \ \ \ \ \ \ \ \ \ \ \ \ \ \⟩
/ / / / / / /   \ \ \ \ \ \ \ \ \ \ \ \ \ \ \
⟨empty,*a*,empty⟩   ⟨/ / / / / / / / / ,*little*,empty⟩
                          / / / / / / / / /
                          ⟨empty,*lamb*,empty⟩

The main idea behind the operation *ENTER_NEW_ITEM* was to record each distinct item that occurred and ignore duplicates. At some stage it will probably be necessary to give a full sorted list of all the items that have been stored. For this we need to specify the operation *IN_ORDER*, which can be done as follows

    IN_ORDER

    states:

    type : *Bin_Tree* → *Item*-List

    pre--*IN_ORDER*(,t) ≜ True

    post-*IN_ORDER*(,t,,iℓ) ≜

        $t = empty$ ∧ $iℓ = \langle \rangle$

        ∨

        $t = \langle ℓ,i,r \rangle$ ∧ $iℓℓ = IN\_ORDER(,ℓ)$

                        ∧ $iℓr = IN\_ORDER(,r)$

                        ∧ $iℓ = iℓℓ \| \langle i \rangle \| iℓr$

This specification is again recursive. The result on a non-empty tree is an item list *iℓ* containing all the items from the left subtree (in their proper order), then the item at the root and then all the items from the right subtree (in their proper order). If we investigate the details using our example we can see what effect the operation *IN_ORDER* has on the tree

$$\langle\langle\langle\text{empty},a,\text{empty}\rangle,had,\langle\langle\text{empty},lamb,\text{empty}\rangle,\ little,\text{empty}\rangle\rangle,$$

$$Mary,\text{empty}\rangle$$

The result is

$$i\ell\ell\,\|\,\langle Mary\rangle\,\|\,i\ell r$$

where $i\ell\ell$ is the result of the operation *IN_ORDER* on the left subtree which is

$$\langle\langle\text{empty},a,\text{empty}\rangle,had,\langle\langle\text{empty},lamb,\text{empty}\rangle,little,\text{empty}\rangle\rangle$$

and $i\ell r$ is the result of the operation *IN_ORDER* on the right subtree which is 'empty'.

After investigating the recursion the result is

$$\langle a,had,lamb,little\rangle\,\|\,\langle Mary\rangle\,\|\,\langle\,\rangle$$

which is finally

$$\langle a,had,lamb,little,Mary\rangle$$

9.4.1   Recursive implementation of tree operations in PDL

First the data structure *Bin_Tree* has to be defined. Because it is a union data type we have the following

$Bin\_Tree\_Node = \langle LEFT{:}Bin\_Tree\ ,\ ITEM{:}Item\ ,\ RIGHT{:}Bin\_Tree\rangle$

$Bin\_Tree = \langle IS\_TREE{:}\mathbb{B}\ ,\ TREE{:}Bin\_Tree\_Node\ ,\ EMPTY{:}(\text{empty})\rangle$

The *Bin_Tree* record is to be used in such a way that True in the *IS_TREE* field implies that there is a *Bin_Tree_Node* value stored in the *TREE* field and that False in the *IS_TREE* field implies that there is a value from the enumerated type '(empty)' stored in the *EMPTY* field. As there is only one possible value for the *EMPTY* field, this field can be omitted entirely as the information it contains can be deduced from the value in the *IS_TREE* field. Thus we have a simplified form of *Bin_Tree*

$$Bin\_Tree = \langle IS\_TREE{:}\mathbb{B}\ ,\ TREE{:}Bin\_Tree\_Node\rangle$$

Notice that an empty tree will now be written as

$$\langle\text{False},\rangle$$

while non-empty trees will be written as

$$\langle\text{True},\langle\ldots,\ldots,\ldots\rangle\rangle$$

In converting the rest of the specification to a recursive PDL program the following translations are used

$p \wedge x$	becomes	if	p
$\vee$		then	x
$\neg p \wedge y$		else	y
		fi	

$t = \langle \ell,i,r \rangle$	becomes	
$\dots \ell \dots$		$\dots LEFT(t) \dots$
$\dots i \dots$		$\dots ITEM(t) \dots$
$\dots r \dots$		$\dots RIGHT(t) \dots$

Using these translations the function declarations become

```
        function enter_new_item
        bt1:Bin_Tree , i:Item → bt2:Bin_Tree
        if      ⌐IS_TREE(bt1)
        then    bt2 ← ⟨True,⟨⟨False,⟩,i,⟨False,⟩⟩⟩
        else

                t ← TREE(bt1)
                if      i<ITEM(t)
                then    bt2 ← ⟨True,⟨enter_new_item(LEFT(t),i),
                                           ITEM(t),RIGHT(t)⟩⟩
                else

                        if      i>ITEM(t)
                        then    bt2 ← ⟨True,⟨LEFT(t),ITEM(t),
                                            enter_new_item(RIGHT(t),i)⟩⟩
                        else    bt2 ← bt1
                        fi

                fi

        fi

        function in_order
        bt:Bin_Tree → iℓ:Item-List
        if      ⌐IS_TREE(bt)
        then    iℓ ← ⟨⟩
```

else $t \leftarrow TREE(bt)$

$i\ell \leftarrow in\_order(LEFT(t)) \| \langle ITEM(t) \rangle \| in\_order(RIGHT(t))$

fi

These functions are easy to convert via coding templates into a language which has recursion. If in addition the language has pointer variables then the 'empty' tree can be shown by a 'nil' pointer making the code much neater by avoiding the union data type.

For those languages that do not have recursion, alternative versions are developed below.

9.4.2   Non-recursive implementation of tree operations

Non-recursive implementation of ENTER_NEW_ITEM

In order to use the results on recursion removal presented in Appendix D, we need to separate the non-recursive and recursive parts of our specification to produce a post-condition with an overall structure

post-$f(,x,,y) \triangleq$

$y = $ if $p(x)$

then $g(x)$

else $\ldots f(\ldots) \ldots$

where the 'then' branch involves no recursion, all the recursion being confined to the 'else' branch. The form of the 'else' branch will dictate which, if any, of the recursion removal schemes of Appendix D can be used. Rewriting the specification using an 'if'-structure gives

post-$ENTER\_NEW\_ITEM(,x,,y) \triangleq$

$y = $ if $x = \langle t,i \rangle \wedge t = $ empty

$\vee$ $x = \langle t,i \rangle \wedge t = \langle \ell,e,r \rangle \wedge i = e$

then   if $x = \langle t,i \rangle \wedge t = $ empty

then $\langle empty,i,empty \rangle$

else t

else   if $x = \langle t,i \rangle \wedge t = \langle \ell,e,r \rangle \wedge i < e$

then $\langle ENTER\_NEW\_ITEM(\langle \ell,i \rangle),e,r \rangle$

else $\langle \ell,e,ENTER\_NEW\_ITEM(\langle r,i \rangle) \rangle$

In order to match this against a template of the form

$$\text{if} \quad p(x)$$
$$\text{then} \quad g(x)$$
$$\text{else} \quad \dots f(\dots) \dots$$

we need to see that

$$f \equiv ENTER\_NEW\_ITEM$$
$$p(x) \equiv$$

$$\qquad x = \langle t,i \rangle \wedge t = \text{empty}$$

$$\qquad \vee$$

$$\qquad x = \langle t,i \rangle \wedge t = \langle \ell,e,r \rangle \wedge i = e$$

$$g(x) \equiv$$

$$\qquad \text{if} \quad x = \langle t,i \rangle \wedge t = \text{empty}$$
$$\qquad \text{then} \quad \langle \text{empty},i,\text{empty} \rangle$$
$$\qquad \text{else} \quad t$$

$$\dots f(\dots) \dots \equiv$$

$$\qquad \text{if} \quad x = \langle t,i \rangle \wedge t = \langle \ell,e,r \rangle \wedge i < e$$
$$\qquad \text{then} \quad \langle \; ENTER\_NEW\_ITEM(\langle \ell,i \rangle),e,r \; \rangle$$
$$\qquad \text{else} \quad \langle \; \ell,e,ENTER\_NEW\_ITEM(\langle r,i \rangle) \; \rangle$$

Let us try to match the recursive branch $(\dots \text{else} \dots f(\dots) \dots)$ against each of the forms given in Appendix D. There are eight forms as follows

T1 – Tail Recursion

$$\dots \text{else} \; f(h(x))$$

T2 – Invertible Recursion

$$\dots \text{else} \; h(f(k(x)),x)$$

T3 – Right-Permutative Recursion

$$\dots \text{else} \; g(f(h(x)),k(x))$$

T4 – Double Recursion

$$\dots \text{else} \; h(f(k(x)),f(u(x)))$$

T5 – Associative Recursion

$$\dots \text{else} \; h(f(k(x)),u(x))$$

T6 – Linear Recursion

$$\dots \text{else} \; h(f(k(x)),x)$$

T7 – Embedded Single Recursion

$$\ldots \text{else } k(f(h(x)))$$

T8 – Multiple or Extended Recursion

$$\ldots \text{else } K1(x)@K2(x)@\ldots@Kn(x)$$

(Note that in T4, T5 a u has been substituted in place of the ℓ which appears in Appendix D. This has been done to avoid a clash with the ℓ of this chapter meaning 'left' as in $t = \langle \ell, e, r \rangle$.)

T1 – Tail recursion

> if $p(x)$
>
> then $g(x)$
>
> else $f(h(x))$

This does not match because the result is not the plain result of the recursion $f(\ldots)$ but a structure **containing** the result of the recursion $\langle f(\ldots), \ldots, \ldots \rangle$ or $\langle \ldots, \ldots, f(\ldots) \rangle$.

So we cannot use this style of recursion removal.

T2 – Invertible recursion

> if $x = a$
>
> then $g(x)$
>
> else $h(f(k(x)), x)$

To use this method of recursion removal we need to find an inverse for function k. In our present situation the argument of the recursive call is either $\langle \ell, i \rangle$ or $\langle r, i \rangle$, so

> $k(x) = \text{if}$ $x = \langle t, i \rangle \wedge t = \langle \ell, e, r \rangle \wedge i < e$
>
>   then $\langle \ell, i \rangle$
>
>   else $\langle r, i \rangle$

There is no way of reconstructing $t = \langle \ell, e, r \rangle$ given only ℓ or r so $x = \langle \langle \ell, e, r \rangle, i \rangle$ cannot be reconstructed from $\langle \ell, i \rangle$ or $\langle r, i \rangle$. So there is no inverse function and we cannot use this style of recursion removal.

T3 – Right-permutative recursion

> if $p(x)$
>
> then a
>
> else $g(f(h(x)), k(x))$

In order to use this method a function u must be found such that

$$g(u(x,y),z) = u(g(x,z),y)$$

and

$$g(a,x) = u(a,x)$$

so that the parameters y and z can be permuted.

This means that the types of the two functions must be the same and in this case they must both be

$$Bin\_Tree \times (Bin\_Tree \times Item) \rightarrow Bin\_Tree$$

We have to look for a function u such that

$$g(\, u(bt1,\langle bt2,i \rangle) \, , \, \langle bt3,i \rangle \,) = u(\, g(bt1,\langle bt3,i \rangle) \, , \, \langle bt2,i \rangle \,)$$

Looking at the specification of *ENTER_NEW_ITEM* we could say that roughly speaking g would have to be a function which puts its first argument as the left or right subtree of its second argument. So on the left-hand side of the above expression we have a tree built by the function u out of $bt1$ and $bt2$ being placed as a subtree of $bt3$. On the right-hand side we have a tree built by the function g out of $bt1$ and $bt3$ being offered as a parameter to u.

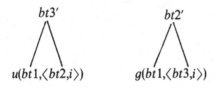

Since it seems that these will not produce the same result we will try another style of recursion removal.

T4 – *Double recursion*

$$\begin{aligned} &\text{if} \quad p(x). \\ &\text{then} \quad g(x) \\ &\text{else} \quad h(\,f(k(x)),f(u(x))) \end{aligned}$$

If we were to try to use this method we would require

$$h(\, f(\langle \ell,i \rangle) \, , \, f(\langle r,i \rangle) \,)$$

to construct either

$$\langle f(\langle \ell,i \rangle),e,r \rangle$$

or

$$\langle \ell, e, f(\langle r, i \rangle) \rangle$$

which is impossible since e is not provided. So we cannot use this style of recursion removal.

T5 –Associative recursion

if $p(x)$

then $g(x)$

else $h(f(k(x)), u(x))$

where the function h is associative, i.e.

$$h(x, h(y, z)) = h(h(x, y), z)$$

For h to associate in this way its arguments must be of the same type and its result must be of the same type as each of its arguments, i.e.

type: $T \times T \to T$

for some T. But following a similar argument to that used for case T3, h has to be

type: $Bin\_Tree \times (Bin\_Tree \times Item) \to Bin\_Tree$

so we cannot use this style of recursion removal.

T6 –Linear recursion

if $p(x)$

then $g(x)$

else $h(f(k(x)), x)$

with no restrictions on h (or k).

   This can be made to match if

$$k(x) = k(\langle \langle \langle \ell, e, r \rangle, i \rangle)$$

$= $ if $i < e$

then $\langle \ell, i \rangle$

else $\langle r, i \rangle$

and

$$h(bt1, \langle bt2, i \rangle) = h(bt1, \langle \langle \ell, e, r \rangle, i \rangle)$$

$= $ if $i < e$

then $\langle bt1, e, r \rangle$

else $\langle \ell, e, bt1 \rangle$

So we shall be able to use the PDL realisation given in Appendix D which is

$(y1,s) \leftarrow (x,\langle \rangle)$

while $\neg p(y1)$

do $\quad (y1,s) \leftarrow (k(y1),\langle y1 \rangle \parallel s)$

od

$y \leftarrow g(y1)$

while $s \neq \langle \rangle$

do $\quad (y,s) \leftarrow (h(y,head(s)),tail(s))$

od

where the result of the function is the final value of the variable y. This is not quite identical to the form given in Appendix D. The presentation in Appendix D assumes for simplicity that the recursive function f has an output type which is the same as the input type, i.e.

type: $\quad T \to T$

for some T. However we are dealing with the case of a function with type

type: $\quad Bin\_Tree \times Item \to Bin\_Tree$

hence the small adjustment.

If we substitute the forms of the functions p,g,h,k and use the notation of the stack treated as an abstract data type, i.e. operations $PUSH$, POP, IS_EMPTY_STACK, etc. with the stack in the 'state' we obtain

$Rec = \langle \ TREE\_OF\_PAIR:Bin\_Tree \ , \ ITEM\_OF\_PAIR:Item \ \rangle$

$Stack = Rec*$

$s:Stack$

$bt\_y1:Bin\_Tree$

$i\_y1:Item$

        -- $y1$ is being handled as two variables bt_y1, i_y1

        -- rather than a single Rec $y1 = \langle bt\_y1,i\_y1 \rangle$

$v:Rec$

$t:Bin\_Tree$

function $init\_stack \dots$

function $is\_empty\_stack \dots$

function $push \dots$

function $pop \dots$

function *is_empty_tree*
      -- auxiliary function for clarity

$t:Bin\_Tree \rightarrow b:\mathbb{B}$

$b \leftarrow \neg IS\_TREE(t)$

function *contains_item*
      -- auxiliary function for clarity

$t:Bin\_Tree\ ,\ i:Item \rightarrow b:\mathbb{B}$

if $IS\_TREE(t)$
then $b \leftarrow ITEM(TREE(t)) = i$
else $b \leftarrow$ False
fi

function *enter_new_item*
      -- non-recursive version

$bt1:Bin\_Tree\ ,\ i:Item \rightarrow bt2:Bin\_Tree$

$bt\_y1 \leftarrow bt1$

$i\_y1 \leftarrow i$

init_stack

while $\neg ($ *is_empty_tree*(bt_y1)

                  $\vee$

               contains_item(bt_y1, i_y1)

      $)$

do

      push$(\ \langle bt\_y1, i\_y1 \rangle\ )$
      if $i\_y1 < ITEM(TREE(bt\_y1))$
      then $bt\_y1 \leftarrow LEFT(TREE(bt\_y1))$
      else $bt\_y1 \leftarrow RIGHT(TREE(bt\_y1))$
      fi

od

if   *ic_empty_tree*(bt_y1)
then $bt2 \leftarrow \langle \text{True}, \langle \langle \text{False}, \rangle, i\_y1, \langle \text{False}, \rangle \rangle \rangle$
else $bt2\ bt\_y1$
fi

while $\neg$*is_empty_stack*

do

      $v \leftarrow pop$

$$t \leftarrow TREE\_OF\_PAIR(v)$$

if $ITEM\_OF\_PAIR(v) < ITEM(TREE(t))$

then

$$bt2 \leftarrow \langle \text{True}, \langle bt2, ITEM(TREE(t)), RIGHT(TREE(t)) \rangle \rangle$$

else

$$bt2 \leftarrow \langle \text{True}, \langle LEFT(TREE(t)), ITEM(TREE(t)), bt2 \rangle \rangle$$

fi

od

It can be seen that i_y1 is never altered in this program so that the assignment

$$i\_y1 \leftarrow i$$

can be removed, with corresponding changes elsewhere

$contains\_item(bt\_y1, i\_y1)$	becomes	$contains\_item(bt\_y1, i)$
if $i\_y1 < ITEM(TREE(bt\_y1))$	becomes	if $i < ITEM(TREE(bt\_y1)) \ldots$
$push(\langle bt\_y1, i\_y1 \rangle)$	becomes	$push(\langle bt\_y1, i \rangle) \ldots$
$\langle\langle \text{False},\rangle, i\_y1, \langle \text{False},\rangle\rangle$	becomes	$\langle\langle \text{False},\rangle, i, \langle \text{False},\rangle\rangle$

Since the second field of each record on the stack is going to be the same, there is no need to stack the whole record, just the first field. So the stack becomes a stack of *Bin_Tree* and

$push(\langle bt\_y1, i \rangle)$	becomes	$push(bt\_y1)$
$v \leftarrow pop$		
$t \leftarrow TREE\_OF\_PAIR$	becomes	$t \leftarrow pop$
$i \leftarrow ITEM\_OF\_PAIR$	becomes	i

Rewriting the function declaration using these simplifications and changing bt_y1 to t gives

$$Stack = Bin\_Tree*$$

$$s : Stack$$

$$t : Bin\_Tree$$

function *enter_new_item*

        -- non-recursive version 2

$bt1 : Bin\_Tree , \ i : Item \rightarrow bt2 : Bin\_Tree$

$$t \leftarrow bd1$$

init_stack

while $\neg ($ $is\_empty\_tree(t)$

        $\lor$ $contains\_item(t, i)$

       $)$

do

       push(t)

       if $i < ITEM(TREE(t))$

       then $t \leftarrow LEFT(TREE(t))$

       else $t \leftarrow RIGHT(TREE(t))$

       fi

od

if   *is_empty_tree(t)*

then $bt2 \leftarrow \langle \text{True},\langle\langle \text{False},\rangle,i,\langle \text{False},\rangle\rangle\rangle$

else $bt2 \leftarrow t$

fi

while $\neg is\_empty\_stack$

do

       $t \leftarrow pop$

       if $i < ITEM(TREE(t))$

       then $bt2 \leftarrow \langle \textit{True},\langle bt2,ITEM(TREE(t)),$

                               $RIGHT(TREE(t))\rangle\rangle$

       else $bt2 \leftarrow \langle \text{True},\langle LEFT(TREE(t)),$

                               $ITEM(TREE(t)),bt2\rangle\rangle$

       fi

od

If the operation *ENTER_NEW_ITEM2* were defined as follows

    ENTER_NEW_ITEM2

    states: *Bin_Tree*

    type: *Item* →

    pre--*ENTER_NEW_ITEM2(s,i)* ≙ True

    post-*ENTER_NEW_ITEM2(s,i,s',)* ≙

        $s' = ENTER\_NEW\_ITEM(\langle s,i\rangle)$

then we would know that the tree supplied in the initial state *s* was no longer required after the operation. This would allow the new tree in the final state to be built out of the tree in the initial state in the same way that concatenation avoided rebuilding both lists in Section 6.2. If we use a construction like

    $p \leftarrow address(LEFT(bt1))$

    $p\uparrow \leftarrow bt2$

we can **alter** tree *bt1* so that it has a new left branch (*bt2*) while leaving the *ITEM* and *RIGHT* branch unchanged. A declaration of *enter_new_item2* incorporating this idea is given below. It is much shorter as it does the absolute minimum of tree building.

> function *enter_new_item2*
>
> $i:Item \rightarrow$
>
> $p \leftarrow address(t)$
>
> while $\neg($ *is_empty_tree*$(p\uparrow)$
>
> $\vee$
>
>   *contains_item*$(p\uparrow,i)$
>
> $)$
>
> do
>
>   if $i < ITEM(p\uparrow)$
>   then $p \leftarrow address(LEFT(p\uparrow))$
>   else $p \leftarrow address(RIGHT(p\uparrow))$
>   fi
>
> od
>
> if   *is_empty_tree*$(p\uparrow)$
>
> then $p\uparrow \leftarrow \langle \text{True}, \langle \langle \text{False},\rangle, i, \langle \text{False},\rangle \rangle \rangle$
>
> fi

This version captures the idea of walking down the tree from the root turning *LEFT* or *RIGHT* as required until the site for the entry of the new item is found. If the new item is not already in the tree a new subtree is grafted on at that site otherwise the tree is left unchanged.

Non-recursive version of IN_ORDER

The non-recursive version of *IN_ORDER* is developed in the same way as for *ENTER_NEW_ITEM* using transformation T8 – 'Multiple or Extended Recursion' from Appendix D. The specification is

> *IN_ORDER*
>
> states:
>
> type :*Bin_Tree* → *Item*-List
>
> pre--*IN_ORDER*$(,t) \triangleq$ True
>
> post-*IN_ORDER*$(,t,,i\ell) \triangleq$
>
> $t = $ empty $\wedge i\ell = \langle \rangle$
>
> $\vee$

$$t = \langle \ell,i,r \rangle \wedge i\ell\ell = IN\_ORDER(,\ell)$$
$$\wedge\; i\ell r = IN\_ORDER(,r)$$
$$\wedge\; i\ell = i\ell\ell \,\|\, \langle i \rangle \,\|\, i\ell r$$

Writing this out using an 'if'-structure, we obtain

post-$IN\_ORDER(,t,,i\ell) \triangleq$

$i\ell =$ if $t = empty$

then $\langle\,\rangle$

else $IN\_ORDER(LEFT(t)) \,\|\, ITEM(t) \,\|$

$IN\_ORDER(RIGHT(t))$

The form of the recursive function from Appendix D (for the case $n = 3$) is

$f(,x,,y) \triangleq$

$y =$ if $p(x)$

then $g(x)$

else $K1(x) @ K2(x) @ K3(x)$

so in this case

$f \equiv$ IN_ORDER

$p(x) \equiv$ $x = empty$

$g(x) \equiv$ $y = \langle\,\rangle$

$@ \equiv$ $\|$

$K1(x) \equiv f(k1(x))$,	$k1(x) \equiv$	$LEFT(x)$
$K2(x) \equiv k2(x)$,	$k2(x) \equiv$	$ITEM(x)$
$K3(x) \equiv f(k3(x))$,	$k3(x) \equiv$	$RIGHT(x)$

The realisation given in Appendix D is

$Rec = \langle MARK: \mathbb{B}, VALUE : \text{Value} \rangle$

$Stack = Rec*$

$(y,s) \leftarrow (a, \langle \langle \text{True}, x \rangle \rangle)$

while $s \neq \langle\,\rangle$

do

$(v,s) \leftarrow (head(s), tail(s))$

$m \leftarrow MARK(v)$

$w \leftarrow VALUE(v)$

if $p(w)$

                        then $y \leftarrow y @ g(w)$
                        else   if $\neg m$
                                then $y \leftarrow y @ w$
                                else
                                        $s \leftarrow \langle \text{True},k1(x) \rangle \parallel$
                                                $\langle \text{False},k2(x) \rangle \parallel$
                                                $\langle \text{True},k3(x) \rangle \parallel s$
                                fi
                        fi
                od

Once again the 'stack' is recognised as being an abstract data type and the operations *PUSH*, *POP*, *IS_EMPTY_STACK*, etc. are used. After substituting the forms of the functions *p,g,k1,k2,k3*, and noting that *k1* and *k3* have type

   $Bin\_Tree \rightarrow Bin\_Tree$

whereas *k2* has type

   $Bin\_Tree \rightarrow Item$

we obtain

   $Rec :: \langle\ MARK : \mathbb{B}\ ,\ TVAL : Bin\_Tree\ ,\ IVAL : Item\ \rangle$

   $Stack :: Rec*$

   $s : Stack$
   $v : Rec$

   function *init_stack* ...
   function *is_empty_stack* ...
   function *push* ...
   function *pop* ...
   function *is_empty_tree* ...

   function *in_order*
               -- non-recursive version
   $t : Bin\_Tree \rightarrow i\ell : Item\text{-List}$
   $i\ell \leftarrow \langle \rangle$
   init_stack

$push(\langle \text{True},t,\rangle)$

while $\neg is\_empty\_stack$

do

    $v \leftarrow pop$

    if $MARK(v)$

    then $v\_is\_empty\_tree \leftarrow is\_empty\_tree(TVAL(v))$

    else $v\_is\_empty\_tree \leftarrow \text{False}$

    fi

    if $v\_is\_empty\_tree$

    then $i\ell \leftarrow i\ell \,\|\, \langle\,\rangle$

    else

        if $\neg MARK(v)$

        then $i\ell \leftarrow i\ell \,\|\, IVAL(v)$

        else $push(\langle \text{True},RIGHT(TVAL(v)),\rangle)$

                $push(\langle \text{False},ITEM(TVAL(v))\rangle)$

                $push(\langle \text{True},LEFT(TVAL(v)),\rangle)$

        fi

    fi

od

Since $i\ell \,\|\, \langle\,\rangle = i\ell$ this can be simplified a little.

9.5   On preserving ADT discipline
9.5.1   What is ADT discipline?

The methodology encouraged throughout this text is one of strict adherence to rules which relate successive stages of refinement from PDL to a target language. Within the context of ADTs we can extend this rationale to include more intermediate stages by regarding PDL plus appropriate ADTs as a higher level PDL. This extended PDL must also follow the refinement rules and it is the discipline dictated by these rules to which we now refer.

To some extent we already have ADTs within 'standard' PDL in that there are *vectors* (one dimensional *arrays*), *records* and *lists*. Indeed, to illustrate how different refinement strategies might proceed, it will be useful to consider two variants of PDL, PDLa which does not have *lists* and PDL b which does. Thus we may view a general situation (Figure 9.8(*a*)) and the more particular PDLa/b case (Figure 9.8(*b*)) as being synonymous. Of course if our target code supports the required ADTs then there is little to be gained by removing them; if these structures are not supported by the final language then we have a choice as to whether we remove them before or during the move from PDL to target code – cases (1) or (2) in Figure 9.8(*b*). Either route, or indeed the direct translation ((3) in Figure 9.8(*b*)) is acceptable providing that each translation stage is template-driven and self-contained, no information being available except along the chosen translation path.

If this discipline of self-contained translation phases is strictly adhered to then the composition of translations follows predictably, rendering the intermediate forms of a program invisible in the final code. One observable consequence, particularly noticeable in cases amenable to clever low level coding, is that PDL-derived programs may be wasteful in their usage of space and time (but they **should** be right!). It is at this stage when purpose-built optimisers could be brought into use. Of course, optimisers are just programs and as such are open to correctness proofs like other programs. Unfortunately optimisers seem not to have attracted the care and effort that such important programs warrant. Maybe the recognition of programming as a scientific/engineering/mathematical discipline will rectify this shortfall but, although this is a worthwhile and interesting topic, it is outside the scope of our current study. We shall therefore presume that either optimisers are not used or, that the code they yield is sufficiently good so that the user does not feel the need to 'tweak' the resultant code.

Fig. 9.8

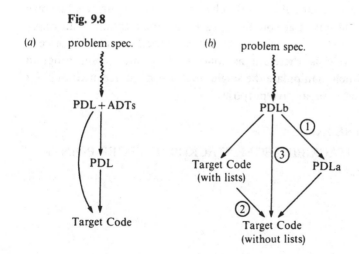

Where a user does feel tempted to indulge in modifying code without due regard to how the original code was obtained, he runs the risk of invalidating what we hope was hitherto a correct program. Moreover, whilst such manual 'transformation' might be valid the likelihood of this is so small as to encourage the use of mechanisms within (high-level) target languages to prevent the user from being able to even attempt any modification.

The purpose of the following subsection is not to furnish the reader with specific details of certain languages in which these security features are present (though we will have to mention some via examples) but to illustrate how these devices may be used.

To set the scene in which these features will be used consider the following example. Suppose an extended PDL included stacks as an abstract data type, and that these were realised in a FORTRAN implementation directly as arrays of size 10. As detailed elsewhere, a *stack* is a collection of store locations which are accessed by a set of related operations (*push, pop, peep, is_empty* and *is_full*). In order to highlight how these operations interact with the FORTRAN operations and restrict unnecessary detail we shall only consider *push* and *pop*. Once the general principles are grasped the other operations/functions can be easily incorporated.

Instead of translating **PDL** *stacks* to FORTRAN *arrays* via PDL *lists*, we shall go directly to FORTRAN so that the *stack*-to-*array* correspondence can be more clearly seen.

Within FORTRAN, *arrays* are the only structures and hence provide the only means by which a single identifier can be used to access multiple locations. This language also has the characteristic of requiring all storage areas to be determined at compile time. Hence the creation of an *empty stack* is reduced at run time to an initialisation process. A suitable piece of FORTRAN code is therefore as follows. The three main program statements which manipulate the single *stack* are, of course, used only for illustrative and comparative purposes.

```
SUBROUTINE INIT
COMMON/STACKS/INTEGER STACK(10), INTEGER POINTR
POINTR = 0
RETURN
END
```

```
SUBROUTINE PUSH(IX)
COMMON/STACKS/INTEGER STACK(10), INTEGER POINTR
POINTR = POINTR + 1
IF (POINTER .GT. 10) CALL ERROR1
STACK(POINTR) = IX
RETURN
END

INTEGER FUNCTION POP
COMMON/STACKS/INTEGER STACK(10), INTEGER POINTR
IF(POINTR .EQ. 0) CALL ERROR2
POP = STACK(POINTR)
POINTR = POINTR - 1
RETURN
END
    ⋮
    ⋮
CALL INIT
CALL PUSH(1)
PRINT *, POP
```

Now STACK and POINTR are accessible to all subprograms that use the relevant COMMON block. Within these subprograms it is quite legal, according to the rules of FORTRAN, to include such expressions as STACK(1), STACK(POINTR − 1) and STACK(POINTR + 1) – assuming the value of POINTR is between 2 and 9. In terms of the stack ADT these are **not** allowed; they correspond to accessing the bottom of the stack, the next to top item of the stack and, worst of all, the location just above the top – conceptually this does not even exist.

To prevent what we might regard as improper use of this array we need to encapsulate it so that it may only be accessed by way of the stack operations. FORTRAN, particularly those variants which support multiple-entry subroutines (see [29]), goes some way to achieving this aim but some newer languages tackle the problem more directly.

9.5.2   Data type encapsulation

Of course it is always possible for the informed user to purposely corrupt the code defining, say, the PUSH operation. In an attempt to avoid such possibilities one could deny him access to the source code and hold the routines in a self-contained library or undertake more elaborate security measures. Protection of the code (of PUSH, etc.) is only one aspect of the problem and that which is unlikely to fall foul of **accidental** interference; what is more important, and likely to lead to corruption in programs that use many data structures, is protection of store areas (arrays in situations similar to our simple example) from manipulation by rogue operations.

We shall look at how this is done in two specific languages. In neither case will we fully explain all the intricacies of the language extracts (it will be sufficient for our purposes to infer the general idea from the earlier FORTRAN version), nor should it be construed that we are necessarily using these languages in the 'best' possible way.

Our first excerpt is from ADA (see [35]) which employs a construct called a package.

The code is as follows:

```
package   STACK_ORGANISER is
        procedure   PUSH(I: in INTEGER);
        procedure   POP(J: out INTEGER);
        ERROR1,ERROR2: exceptions;
end     STACK_ORGANISER;

package body   STACK_ORGANISER is
        STACK:       array (1..10) of INTEGER;
        POINTER:   INTEGER:= 0;
        procedure   PUSH(I: in INTEGER) is
        begin
                POINTER:= POINTER + 1;
                if   POINTER > 10 then raise ERROR1;
                end   if;
                STACK(POINTER):= I
        end     PUSH;

        procedure   POP(J: out INTEGER) is
        begin
                if   POINTER = 0 then raise ERROR2;
```

```
            end   if
            J := STACK(POINTER);
            POINTER := POINTER − 1;
        end   POP;
    end   STACK_ORGANISER;

    use   STACK_ORGANISER
    begin
        ⋮

        I := 1
        PUSH(I);
        POP(J);
        PUT(J,FIELD_WIDTH);
        ⋮

    end
```

The package used here, called STACK_ORGANISER, defines an interface between the *stack* and the (main) program. Explicitly it introduces the two routines PUSH and POP and also indicates that the packge will refer, in exceptional circumstances, to procedures ERROR1 and ERROR2 defined elsewhere. The body of the package, which can be separately compiled and recompiled as necessary, is where the *stack* space is actually allocated and initialised. Also included are the predictable code segments for PUSH and POP.

The **use** clause effectively causes initialisation of the *stack* by setting POINTER to zero. Subsequently, within the *begin-end* block following this clause, the *stack* can be indirectly accessed by means of the PUSH and POP routines. However, direct reference to STACK or POINTER within the block is forbidden and gives rise to a syntax error.

This seems to work OK. Now, any use of the identifiers outside of this package is either syntactically illegal or refers to other quantities having different scopes; in any case the *stack* in this package is **not** corrupted.

A consequence of this mechanism is that different sets of routines (with different names) are required for each data structure – even if the structures are all of the same type. Obviously this can become unwieldy if a large (possibly unknown) number of structures is required.

An alternative strategy, which deals with a class of structures rather than individual instances, is adopted by the Flex version of Algol68 [11] implemented by the Royal Signals and Radar Establishment, RSRE.

Let's see how our example works in Flex.

MODE STACK = STRUCT(PROC(INT)VOID *push*,

PROC INT *pop*);

PROC *make* =   STACK:

([*1*:*10*]INT *store*;

INT *pointer*:= *0*;

((INT *i*)VOID:

(*pointer* PLUSAB *1*;

IF *pointer* > *10* THEN *error*(*1*) FI;

store[*pointer*] := *i*),

INT:(INT *j*;

IF *pointer* = *0* THEN *error*(*2*) FI;

j := *store*[*pointer*];

pointer MINUSAB *1*;

j)));

⋮
⋮

STACK *x* = *make*;

(*push* OF *x*)(*1*);

print(*pop* OF *x*)

Here a STACK is a structure, rather like a record, in which the components are the routines *push* and *pop*. The ADA package is replaced by a procedure which allocates space, initialises it and defines the procedures which are allowed to act upon it. STACK is defined as any other new type and henceforth can be used in exactly the same way as INTEGER, etc. The procedure *make*, when called, allocates a 10-element array called *store* and a *pointer* which subsequently can only be accessed by the two routines (*push* and *pop*) which make up the STACK which it delivers.

Within the program a new STACK, for which we must have a name, is introduced just like any other constant, e.g.,

REAL *pi* = *3.141*

Following the declaration

$$STACK \ x = make$$

a private array *store* exists but
can only be referenced by the routines *push* OF *x* and *pop* OF *x*. The
declaration

$$STACK \ y = make$$

would introduces another
private *array* only accessible via **its** component operations. We can
therefore have as many STACKs as required. Moreover, the routine *make*
can be parameterised, for example:

PROC *make* (INT *size*)STACK:

([*1* :*size*]INT *store*;

...

This way of introducing safe ADTs takes some getting used to. It is very
powerful and seems to solve many of the security problems associated with
user defined data types. However, like all dynamic store manipulation
schemes, it is expensive in terms of the operational overheads required to
perform *garbage collection* – tidying up areas of store no longer accessible.
To this end special purpose-built processors are being developed [15] so as
to capitalise on the advantages to be had from this software construction
method.

Exercises 9

1 Choose an implementation language from the five discussed in
Chapter 6 and code the abstract data types *Stack*, *Queue* and
Bin_Tree into that language.

2 In Section 5.6 a data type *Expression* was discussed which has
similarities with the *Bin_Tree* discussed in this chapter.

Write a specification for the equivalent of *IN_ORDER* for an
Expression.

What simple modifications to your specification could be made
to print the binary expressions in prefix form where

$1+2$ is written $+12$

and in postfix (reverse Polish) form where

$1+2$ is written $12+$

3 A particular graph called a network was introduced in Chapter 3.
Design an ADT called *Network* which represents an network and
has the operations *INIT_NETWORK*,
IS_EMPTY_NETWORK, *ADD_EDGE*, *REMOVE_EDGE*.

10

The mathematical basis of abstract data types

In Chapter 7 we discussed the desired logical relationships between segments of program and their specifications. In that discussion it was sufficient to take for granted all the common properties of integers, etc., and to concentrate on the more important (deductive) issues. However, in order to make our arguments mathematically sound we must explain how these 'facts' are introduced into a programming system. The method, outlined below, not only gives a foundation for the mathematical manipulations that are central to our methodology, but also provides a set of requirements against which implementations can be checked, and can also be applied to (abstract) data types which may not be native to the target computer system.

We begin, in Section 10.1, with a look at probably the most fundamental data type, *Boolean*. Objects and expressions of type Boolean are required in one form or another in all programming languages to control the flow of a computation. They are also used to manipulate tests associated with other, more explicitly data-related, types and since the type has only two data values we can defer consideration of problems associated with large, potentially infinite, sets of data values.

Next, in Section 10.2, we look at lists. Constructing a list-of-something is one of the more familiar ways of building a new type from an existing one. Although a set of lists may be infinite, lists provide a vehicle for the introduction of more facilities of our definition system before going on to discussing problems associated with numeric types in Section 10.3. Before bringing the chapter to a close we take a predictable diversion to consider sets and then finally, in Section 10.5, we discuss the inter-relationship between *pre-* and *post*-conditions and the equational systems which we introduce shortly.

10.1   Booleans

Naively we might initially regard the Boolean type simply as the set of *values* {True, False}, or {1,0}, or any set of two *distinct* values. But of course we need more than this. There are certain operations which we expect to be 'automatically' available and by implication these operations should relate to each other in characteristic ways. These operations should then permit manipulation and evaluation of Boolean expressions, including the trivial and often overlooked expressions True and False.

Let us see what we can do using the set of values, $BOOL \triangleq \{True, False\}$, and defining operators on $BOOL$ by suitable functions specified by *pre-* and *post*-conditions. Explicitly we consider the functions *not*, *and* and *or*. In the familiar notation we have:

not

type: $BOOL \rightarrow BOOL$

pre--$not(,b) \triangleq$ True

post-$not(,b,,b') \triangleq b' \Leftrightarrow$ if b then False

else True fi

and

type: $BOOL \times BOOL \rightarrow BOOL$

pre--$and(,\langle b_1,b_2 \rangle) \triangleq$ True

post-$and(,\langle b_1,b_2 \rangle,,b') \triangleq b' \Leftrightarrow$ if b_1 then b_2

else False fi

or

type: $BOOL \times BOOL \rightarrow BOOL$

pre--$or(,\langle b_1,b_2 \rangle) \triangleq$ True

post-$or(,\langle b_1,b_2 \rangle,,b') \triangleq b' \Leftrightarrow$ if b_1 then True

else b_2 fi

If these specifications were acceptable then we could reintroduce the usual operator notation by the definitions

$\neg b \triangleq not(b)$

$b_1 \wedge b_2 \triangleq and(b_1,b_2)$

$b_1 \vee b_2 \triangleq or(b_1,b_2)$

This reduces *and-or-not* expressions to expressions involving *if-then-else-fi* and equivalence, but how do we evaluate such expressions? Do we regard these conditional expressions as part of our base language or do they need to be further specified and, if they do, then how can this be done? – we cannot use conditional expressions!

Before describing a way out of this impasse consider for a moment the kind of manipulation/evaluation/simplification we want to perform on logical expressions. Suppose we have:

$(\neg(\text{True})) \vee \text{False}$

which becomes

$\text{False} \vee \text{False}$

and hence

False.

Here we are merely replacing one subexpression by another one with the same value (e.g. $\neg(\text{True})$ by False) and so on until we have removed all the operators and we are left with an expression which directly represents the answer. This is known as *substitution of equals for equals* and makes explicit the notion of changing the form, but not the value, of an expression by replacing a subexpression α by β when we know that $\alpha = \beta$. Giving an appropriate set of expression equations therefore provides the basis of a system for manipulating Boolean expressions including *if...* forms and equivalence.

Without further ado we give a formal definition of *BOOLEAN* and then discuss its various segments.

type *BOOLEAN*

sorts *BOOL*

ops

$$\text{True} \rightarrow BOOL$$
$$\text{False} \rightarrow BOOL$$
$$\neg(BOOL) \rightarrow BOOL$$
$$(BOOL \Leftrightarrow BOOL) \rightarrow BOOL$$
$$(BOOL \vee BOOL) \rightarrow BOOL$$
$$(BOOL \wedge BOOL) \rightarrow BOOL$$
$$(\text{if } BOOL \text{ then } BOOL \text{ else } BOOL \text{ fi}) \rightarrow BOOL$$

eqns

$$\neg(b) = (\text{if } b \text{ then False else True fi})$$
$$(b_1 \Leftrightarrow b_2) = (\text{if } b_1 \text{ then if } b_2 \text{ then True}$$
$$\text{else False fi}$$
$$\text{else if } b_2 \text{ then False else True fi fi})$$
$$(b_1 \vee b_2) = (\text{if } b_1 \text{ then True else } b_2 \text{ fi})$$
$$(b_1 \wedge b_2) = (\text{if } b_1 \text{ then } b_2 \text{ else False fi})$$

(if True then b_1 else b_2 fi) = b_1

(if False then b_1 else b_2 fi) = b_2

The definition begins by making the distinction between the **type**, *BOOLEAN*, and the *set*, *BOOL*, of values technically known as a **sort**. (The names are **not** important, the distinction **is**.) To work in the expected way *BOOL* must have two elements. We will generally regard this set as {True, False} and presume, arbitrarily but in accordance with prejudice, that the value of the *BOOLEAN* expression True is True, and the expression False has the value False. Now the **ops** part of the definition introduces the syntax of *BOOLEAN* expressions and the kind of result which can be derived. The brackets may be omitted when no ambiguity arises. Here all the results are in the set *BOOL* – later examples will be more complex – but notice the number of occurrences of *BOOL* before the arrow '→', these tell us that True and False are constants†, ⌐ is a prefix monadic operator, ⇔, ∨ and ∧ (*equivalence*, *or* and *and*) are infix diadic operators and *if-then-else-fi* is a triadic operator.

Finally, the **eqns** part of the definition is a set of equations which must be satisfied by any implementation of the type.‡ They are genuine equations, no direction is intended or implied and the fact that one side of an equation might be 'simpler' than the other has no mathematical significance. With a suitable set of equations it should be possible to take two expressions and test for equality between them by checking that they have the same value. Consequently, we can also check whether an expression is true by testing for equality with the expression True. Special care must be taken when ' = ' also appears as an operator associated with the type being specified; all we are doing is listing pairs of expressions which we stipulate should have the same value.

The equations given may not be the ones you expected. Is this important? If not, why not? If it does matter, who is right? Several factors need to be

---

† Constants are merely operators with no arguments and hence always give the same value. In more complicated types the distinction between a constant and its value will be easier to see.

‡ It is common to refer to these equational definitions as specifying the *initial algebra* semantics of the type under consideration. Technically this term arises from a branch of mathematics called *category theory*, however the following observation indicates the underlying concept in less mathematical terms:
  Note that there are very many implementations which satisfy these equations and most of these do far more than we require, more than we are permitted to assume. Such implementations are partially ordered by virtue of possessing more facilities and at the bottom of this ordering is a minimal implementation which obeys the equations and does nothing else.

considered. Firstly, is the set *complete*? Are there relations between the operators and constants which we wish to be true but which cannot be derived from the given equations? If there are such relations which can neither be proved nor disproved then extra equations can be added to the **eqn** set provided that we do not violate *consistency*. This is our second consideration; a set of equations is consistent provided that there is no expression that can give rise to two different answers when reduced by the set.

Finally, we might consider minimality. Is the set of equations as small as possible but still complete? Provided that the set is consistent this does not matter. However a small **eqn** set is easier to check for consistency and it is often a good idea, when possible, to introduce new operators by a single equation (such as with ¬, ⇔, ∨ and ∧ in our *BOOLEAN* example) and allow their properties to be deduced implicitly from the other operators via that one equation. Once such properties have been deduced their equational form (if one exists) can be added to the set without violating consistency. One might even subsequently disregard some of the more fundamental equations in favour of adequate higher-level ones which give more implementation freedom. To investigate this issue fully would cause an untimely distraction but nevertheless we can briefly look at four deductions from our equational axioms. We shall then write down a more familiar set of axioms and proceed without recourse to the more fundamental definition given above.

Our first two results allow simplification of certain *if-then-else-fi* expressions in the sequel.

Lemma 1: (if b then True else False fi) $= b$

Proof: $b \in BOOL$ so $b =$ True or $b =$ False.

$b =$ True $\Rightarrow$ (if b then True else False fi)

$=$ (if True then True else False fi)	by assumption
$=$ True	by eqn
$= b$	by assumption

$b =$ False $\Rightarrow$ (if b then True else False fi)

$=$ (if False then True else False fi)	by assumption
$=$ False	by eqn
$= b\cdot$	by assumption

Hence in all cases when $b \in BOOL$, (if b then True else False fi) $= b$ ☐

Lemma 2: (if b_1 then b_2 else b_2 fi) $= b_2$

Proof: $b_1 =$ True or $b_1 =$ False

$b_1 =$ True $\Rightarrow$ (if b_1 then b_2 else b_2 fi)

$\quad\quad = $ (if True then b_2 else b_2 fi)   by assumption

$\quad\quad = b_2$ by eqn

$b_1 =$ False $\Rightarrow$ (if b_1 then b_2 else b_2 fi)   etc.

$\quad\quad = $ (if False then b_2 else b_2 fi)

$\quad\quad = b_2$

Hence the result holds.   □

Theorem: $b_1 \vee b_2 = b_2 \vee b_1$

Proof:$b_1 =$ True or $b_1 =$ False

$b_1 =$ True $\Rightarrow b_1 \vee b_2 = $ (if b_1 then True else b_2 fi)

$\quad\quad = $ (if True then True else b_2 fi)

$\quad\quad = $ True

$b_1 =$ False $\Rightarrow b_1 \vee b_2 = $ (if b_1 then True else b_2 fi)

$\quad\quad = $ (if False then True else b_2 fi)

$\quad\quad = b_2$

Similarly,

$b_1 =$ True $\Rightarrow b_2 \vee b_1 = $ (if b_2 then True else b_1 fi)

$\quad\quad = $ (if b_2 then True else True fi)

$\quad\quad = $ True   by Lemma 2

$b_1 =$ False $\Rightarrow b_2 \vee b_1 = $ (if b_2 then True else b_1 fi)

$\quad\quad = $ (if b_2 then True else False fi)

$\quad\quad = b_2$ by Lemma 1

Hence we have

$b_1 \vee b_2 = b_2 \vee b_1$ □

Theorem: $(b \Leftrightarrow b) =$ True

Proof: Again $b \in$ BOOL so consider the two cases, $b =$ True and $b =$ False

$b =$ True $\Rightarrow$ (if b then if b then True else False fi

$\quad\quad\quad$ else if b then False else True fi fi)

$= ($if True then if True then True else False fi

else if True then False else True fi fi)

$= ($if True then True else False fi)

$= $True

$b = $False $\Rightarrow ($if b then if b then True else False fi

else if b then False else True fi fi)

$= ($if False then if False then True else False fi

else if False then False else True fi fi)

$= ($if False then False else True fi)

$= $True

So the result holds for all (i.e. both) possible values of b.   □

Using these and other similar results we can achieve an alternative set of equations. These resemble the more familiar logic axioms but notice that the equation '$a \Leftrightarrow a = $True' is insufficient to define '$\Leftrightarrow$' since it can never give rise to the value False. Obviously, not all expressions are equivalent and it is desirable that our equation scheme allows us to determine that this is so. The equation 'True $\Leftrightarrow$ False = False' generates these negative results.

We shall have reason to consider similar 'non-results' later but for the present will state a second version of the Boolean type definition which can be used in more substantial data type specifications.

type   *BOOLEAN2*

sorts   *BOOL*

ops   True $\rightarrow BOOL$

False $\rightarrow BOOL$

$\neg(BOOL) \rightarrow BOOL$

$(BOOL \Leftrightarrow BOOL) \rightarrow BOOL$

$(BOOL \wedge BOOL) \rightarrow BOOL$

$(BOOL \vee BOOL) \rightarrow BOOL$

(if $BOOL$ then $BOOL$ else $BOOL$ fi) $\rightarrow BOOL$

eqns $\neg($True$) = $False

$\neg($False$) = $True

$b_1 \vee (b_2 \vee b_3) = (b_1 \vee b_2) \vee b_3$

$b_1 \vee b_2 = b_2 \vee b_1$

$b \vee $False$ = b$

$$b \vee (\neg b) = \text{True}$$
$$b_1 \wedge (b_2 \wedge b_3) = (b_1 \wedge b_2) \wedge b_3$$
$$b_1 \wedge b_2 = b_2 \wedge b_1$$
$$b \wedge \text{True} = b$$
$$b \wedge (\neg b) = \text{False}$$
$$b_1 \wedge (b_2 \vee b_3) = (b_1 \wedge b_2) \vee (b_1 \wedge b_3)$$
$$b_1 \vee (b_2 \wedge b_3) = (b_1 \vee b_2) \wedge (b_1 \vee b_3)$$
$$b \Leftrightarrow b = \text{True}$$
$$b_1 \Leftrightarrow b_2 = b_2 \Leftrightarrow b_1$$
$$\text{True} \Leftrightarrow \text{False} = \text{False}$$
$$(\text{if True then } b_1 \text{ else } b_2 \text{ fi}) = b_1$$
$$(\text{if False then } b_1 \text{ else } b_2 \text{ fi}) = b_2$$

This set of equations provides all the necessary replacement rules required for the manipulation of Boolean expressions over the appropriate set of operators. But was all this absolutely necessary, could we have just taken the definition of the primitive logical connectives for granted and reverted to using pre- and post-conditions? Well pre- and post-conditions are fine for defining new functions and operators in terms of more fundamental functions, but there are problems when it comes to 'defining something from nothing'. A way out of this stalemate is to use equations to specify the inter-related properties of the operators. Lists provide a suitable illustration of how this works, but first some exercises.

Exercises 10.1

1. Devise an equational scheme for specifying the properties of logic operations $\wedge$, $\vee$, $\neg$ and $\Rightarrow$ over the extended set of truth values, $\mathbb{E}$, introduced in Exercise 7.1.

2. Using appropriate equations from the definition of the type *BOOLEAN* (not *BOOLEAN2*) show that

   (a) $b_1 \vee b_2 = b_2 \vee b_1$, and

   (b) $\neg(b_1 \wedge b_2) = (\neg b_1) \vee (\neg b_2)$

10.2   Lists

Suppose that our lists are 'flat', with elements from some sort *ELEM* on which equality has been defined.

If we denote the set of such lists by *LIST* then we need (i) an *empty list*, $\langle \rangle \in LIST$, (ii) the ability to take $e \in ELEM$ and create a single-element list $\langle e \rangle \in LIST$, (iii) a *concatenation operator*, $\|$, which merges two lists end to end, so

$$\langle a,b,c \rangle \| \langle d,e,f,g \rangle = \langle a,b,c,d,e,f,g \rangle,$$

(iv) a function *head* (or *hd*) which delivers the leftmost ELEM of a non-empty list, and (v) a function *tail* (or *tℓ*) which when applied to a non-empty list returns that list with the left-most *ELEM* omitted. To facilitate proper use of *hd* and *tℓ* we also need (vi) a test for an empty list, call this *is_empty* and finally, for completeness, let us have (vii) an equality test between two lists.

Hence we may define *LISTS* by

type *LISTS*

sorts *LIST* (with *BOOL, ELEM*)

ops
$$\langle \rangle \rightarrow LIST$$
$$\langle ELEM \rangle \rightarrow LIST$$
$$LIST \| LIST \rightarrow LIST$$
$$is\_empty(LIST) \rightarrow BOOL$$
$$head(LIST) \rightarrow ELEM$$
$$tail(LIST) \rightarrow LIST$$
$$LIST = LIST \rightarrow BOOL$$

eqns
$$(\ell_1 \| \ell_2) \| \ell_3 = \ell_1 \| (\ell_2 \| \ell_3)$$
$$\ell \| \langle \rangle = \ell$$
$$\langle \rangle \| \ell = \ell$$
$$is\_empty(\langle \rangle) = \text{True}$$
$$is\_empty(\langle e \rangle) = \text{False}$$
$$is\_empty(\ell_1 \| \ell_2) = (is\_empty(\ell_1) \wedge is\_empty(\ell_2))$$
$$head(\langle e \rangle \| \ell) = e$$
$$tail(\langle e \rangle \| \ell) = \ell$$
$$(\langle \rangle = \langle \rangle) = \text{True}$$
$$((\langle e_1 \rangle \| \ell_1) = (\langle e_2 \rangle \| \ell_2)) = ((e_1 = e_2) \wedge (\ell_1 = \ell_2))$$
$$(\langle e \rangle \| \ell = \langle \rangle) = \text{False}$$
$$(\ell_1 = \ell_2) = (\ell_2 = \ell_1)$$

err eqns $head(\langle \rangle) = $ error

$tail(\langle \rangle) = $ error

Notice that this specification includes a component not present in *BOOLEAN* or *BOOLEAN2*, namely *error equations* (**err eqns**). There is no way that attempting to compute the *head* or *tail* of the empty list can give rise to a valid answer; moreover if either of the subexpressions $head(\langle \rangle)$ or $tail(\langle \rangle)$ occur within a list expression then there is no way that they can be changed and should therefore, sooner or later, generate *error*. Adopting the convention that any list expression that includes *error* is itself in error it is clear that occurrence of any error indicates the ultimate abortion of the current evaluation and hence it is more efficient to treat any such situation as indicative of an immediate error termination.

Regarding the rest of the type specification you will notice that the definitions of some of the operators are inter-dependent; equality of lists is defined in terms of equality of elements (of *ELEM*) and *concatenation, head* and *tail* are defined so as to generate partial inverses of the combination $\langle e \rangle \parallel \ell$, and the predicate *is_empty* is defined in terms of the list construction operator $\langle \ldots \rangle$ and $\parallel$. At first sight this looks rather awkward and does not indicate how these operations might be implemented. Put the other way round, we can use this phenomenon to advantage. Recall that our aim is to be able to perform proofs/manipulations/calculations by referring only to these equations and consequently *any* set of routines is admissible if it can be shown to satisfy the equations.

How equation systems fit with pre- and post-conditions will become clearer later. For the base types something equivalent to our equational system is essential.

10.3   Some numeric types

Now let us see how we can progress in the same way with a type based on a suitably sophisticated set of integer operations. Integer arithmetic is derived from the notion of counting using the numbers 1,2,3, etc. and for convenience 0 and, eventually, $^-1$, $^-2$, etc. Even if we start by restricting consideration to the positive integers we must address the problem of having infinitely many values. However, we do not wish to get embroiled in philosophical issues of exactly what numbers are or other interesting but, for our immediate purposes, irrelevant issues such as number representation. What we require is the usual set of numerals 0,1,2, etc. (for ever) related in the traditional way so that from this mathematical base we can justify the properties that we have come to expect of integer expressions. If you are worried about the gaps that must inevitably occur in a definition of this form, remember that all it amounts to is trusting that, provided that overflow bounds are not encountered, computers (driven by suitable languages) can count.

type   *POSINT1*

sorts   *POS*

ops $0 \rightarrow POS$

$1 \rightarrow POS$

$2 \rightarrow POS$ etc.

$succ(POS) \rightarrow POS$

$POS + POS \rightarrow POS$

eqns1 $succ(0) = 1$

$succ(1) = 2$

$succ(2) = 3$ etc.

$(P + 0) = P$

$(P_1 + succ(P_2)) = succ(P_1 + P_2)$

The successor function, *succ*, simply returns a value *1* greater than its operand. The integer 7 is achieved by incrementing *0* by *1* seven times, i.e. it is merely (and only!!) a shorthand for

$$succ(succ(succ(succ(succ(succ(succ(0)))))))$$

or, using an invalid but obvious abbreviation,

$$succ^7(0)$$

Using arguments like this we can explain where all positive integers come from and then refer back all arithmetic questions to this basis. Of course this explanation is recursive, 7 cannot be defined by $succ^7(0)$ because $succ^7(0)$ itself requires us to know what 7 means, we must use the longhand version. Such philosophical matters are important for pure mathematicians but irrelevant for our purposes; we take on trust the existence of the set of integers, related by *succ* as indicated above.

From the definition of *POSINT1* we can proceed to more adventurous types by a process of enrichment achieved by adding further operations and equations.

type   *POSINT2*

sorts   *POS*

ops2 (= **ops1** augmented by)

$$pred(POS) \to POS$$

$$(POS \dotminus POS) \to POS$$

eqns2 (= **eqns1** augmented by)

$$pred(0) = 0$$

$$pred(succ(P)) = P$$

$$(P \dotminus 0) = P$$

$$(P_1 \dotminus succ(P_2)) = pred(P_1 \dotminus P_2)$$

Here *pred* is the predecessor function, the inverse of *succ* with suitable modification to cope with the fact that there are no negative values in *POS*, and $\dotminus$ is the *truncated subtraction* operator which has to be restricted in a similar fashion.

Without undue formality we can avoid explicit mention of implied operations and equations within an *enrichment* by saying that *POSINT2* is an enrichment of *POSINT1* since

ops1 $\subseteq$ **ops2**

eqns1 $\subseteq$ **eqns2**

(and **sorts** of *POSINT1* $\subseteq$ **sorts** of *POSINT2*; in fact both are equal to *POS*). Symbolically we can denote this enrichment by

$$POSINT1 \subseteq POSINT2$$

With this extra notation we can progress to more familiar, fuller, type definitions.

type   *POSINT3 (POSINT2 $\subseteq$ POSINT3)*

sorts   *POS*

ops $(POS * POS) \to POS$

eqns $(P * 0) = 0$

$$(P_1 * succ(P_2)) = P_1 + (P_1 * P_2)$$

type   *POSINT4 (POSINT3 $\subseteq$ POSINT4)*

             (BOOLEAN $\subseteq$ POSINT4)

sorts   *POS, BOOL*

ops $(POS \leqslant POS) \to BOOL$

eqns $(0 \leqslant P) = \text{True}$

$$(succ(P) \leqslant 0) = \text{False}$$

$$(succ(P_1) \leqslant succ(P_2)) = (P_1 \leqslant P_2)$$

type   *POSINT5 (POSINT4 ⊆ POSINT5)*

sorts *POS, BOOL*

ops $(POS = POS) \rightarrow BOOL$

eqns $(P_1 = P_2) = ((P_1 \leqslant P_2) \wedge (P_2 \leqslant P_1))$

So *POSINT5* now gives us, as far as possible within the limitations of *POS*, the arithmetic operations of $+$, $\div$ (almost $-$) and $*$, together with the familiar predicates $\leqslant$ and $=$. *POSINT5*, when written out in full, is quite an extensive example but is uncharacteristic in that, given operands of the correct type, any expression can be reduced by the equations to an answer – True, False or a positive integer. Turning to integer division we immediatley encounter a case where success cannot be guaranteed and hence we again need an error equation. Moreover, since real division of integers does in general not give an integer result, even when a valid result is obtainable, the specification is not trivial. In fact we have:

type   *POSINT6 (POSINT5 ⊆ POSINT6)*
sorts *POS, BOOL*

ops $(POS \div POS) \rightarrow POS$

eqns $((P_1 \div succ(P_2)) = P_3) = ((P_1 = (succ(P_2)) * P_3) + P_4)$
$$\wedge (P_4 \leqslant P_2))$$

err eqn $(P \div 0) = error$

So much for types based on positive integers but what about more common types such as *INTEGER*s and *REAL*s?

The integers can be constructed in much the same way as positive integers but working in both positive and negative directions from zero. The relational operators cause more than a little trouble but, as with *POSINT*s, we shall layer the definition and dispose of the more straightforward operators first.

type   *INTEGER1*

sorts *INT*

ops $0 \rightarrow INT$

$1 \rightarrow INT$ etc.

$^{-}1 \rightarrow INT$ etc.

$succ(INT) \rightarrow INT$

$pred(INT) \rightarrow INT$

eqns $succ(0) = 1$

$succ(1) = 2$ etc.

$$pred(0) = {}^-1$$
$$pred({}^-1) = {}^-2 \text{ etc.}$$
$$pred(succ(i)) = i$$
$$succ(pred(i)) = i$$

All this amounts to is a system for generating the integers. Notice however, that in this type *succ* and *pred* are proper inverses. Hence the combinations *succ(pred(...))* and *pred(succ(...))* can be introduced or deleted, without changing the value of an expression, to facilitate application of equations. Notice also that a change in the representation scheme (binary, octal, etc.) would only alter the constants – the value (i.e. the numbers) would stay the same!!

Now for the proper operations.

type *INTEGER2 (INTEGER1 ⊆ INTEGER2)*

sorts *INT*

ops $INT + INT \rightarrow INT$
$INT - INT \rightarrow INT$
$INT * INT \rightarrow INT$

eqns $(i + 0) = i$
$(i_1 + succ(i_2)) = succ(i_1 + i_2)$
$(i_1 + pred(i_2)) = pred(i_1 + i_2)$
$(i - 0) = i$
$(i_1 - succ(i_2)) = pred(i_1 - i_2)$
$(i_1 - pred(i_2)) = succ(i_1 - i_2)$
$(i * 0) = 0$
$(i_1 * succ(i_2)) = (i_1 * i_2) + i_1$
$(i_1 * pred(i_2)) = (i_1 * i_2) - i_1$

Notice that integer division, ÷, is not yet included because, as in the *POSINT* case, we need to ensure the correct magnitude of the remainder and this requires use of relational operators. These are not so simple to define because of the need to generate the value False in certain situations. To see how the various equations fit together we give the specification and then discuss the numbered equations.

type *INTEGER3 (INTEGER2 ⊆ INTEGER3)*
(BOOLEAN2 ⊆ INTEGER3)

sorts $INT, BOOL$

ops $INT < INT \rightarrow BOOL$

$INT \leqslant INT \rightarrow BOOL$

$INT = INT \rightarrow BOOL$

$INT \div INT \rightarrow INT$

eqns

$$\left.\begin{array}{l} (0 < 1) = \text{True} \\ (0 \leqslant 1) = \text{True} \\ (0 < 0) = \text{False} \\ (0 \leqslant 0) = \text{True} \end{array}\right\} \text{(i)}$$

$$\left.\begin{array}{l} (succ(i_1) \leqslant succ(i_2)) = (i_1 \leqslant i_2) \\ (succ(i_1) < succ(i_2)) = (i_1 < i_2) \end{array}\right\} \text{(ii)}$$

$$\left.\begin{array}{l} (i_1 \leqslant i_2) = \text{if } (i_1 \leqslant i_3) \wedge (i_3 \leqslant i_2) \\ \qquad\qquad \text{then True else } (i_1 \leqslant i_2) \text{ fi} \\ (i_1 < i_2) = \text{if } (i_1 < i_3) \wedge (i_3 < i_2) \\ \qquad\qquad \text{then True else } (i_1 < i_2) \text{ fi} \end{array}\right\} \text{(iii)}$$

$$(i_1 < i_2) = \neg(i_2 \leqslant i_1) \qquad\qquad\qquad \text{(iv)}$$

$$(i_1 = i_2) = ((i_1 \leqslant i_2) \wedge (i_2 \leqslant i_1)) \qquad\qquad \text{(v)}$$

$$\left.\begin{array}{l} ((i_1 \div i_2) = i_3) = (i_1 = (i_2 * i_3) + i_4) \\ \qquad \wedge (((0 \leqslant i_4) \wedge (i_4 < i_2)) \\ \qquad \vee ((i_2 < i_4) \wedge (i_4 \leqslant 0))) \end{array}\right\} \text{(vi)}$$

Equations (i) give the base cases with operand values being equal or differing by 1 and using (ii) we can shift these values up or down to evaluate cases such as $x < x$ or $x \leqslant x + 1$, etc. In order to widen the gap between the two values we use the *transitive* property. This is usually written as an implication

$$\text{if } (a \leqslant b) \wedge (b \leqslant c) \text{ then } (a \leqslant c) \text{ fi,}$$

but we require an answer even when the condition is false, and we require an equation. The first of the pair of equations (iii) provides the link. Notice that all it says is that provided that we can find a value i_3 such that $i_1 \leqslant i_3$ and $i_3 \leqslant i_2$ then $i_1 \leqslant i_2$; if no such i_3 can be found it tells us nothing new.

So far, apart from being able to deduce that $x < x$ is False, our equations only give rise to True results. However, since we have partial definitions of both the operators $<$ and $\leqslant$, we can link the two and, using the property that for any two integers x and y either $x < y$ or $y \leqslant x$, stipulate that

$$(x < y) = \neg(y \leqslant x).$$

This gives equation (iv) which, by virtue of the *not* operator, yields False in the appropriate situations.

Equality can then be introduced (v) in a manner which yields True or False as required. Finally, (vi), integer division is specified by using all three relational operators.

As with the definition of *BOOLEAN* we use *INTEGER3* to investigate the truth of statements about integers, but the arguments are very long. An alternative to using *INTEGER3* directly is to use it as the basis of a more approachable type definition. For example, suppose $0<a$ and $b<0$ and consider the expression $a+b$. So

$$a = succ^n(0) \quad \text{for some } n \in \mathbb{N}$$

and

$$b = pred^m(0) \quad \text{for some } m \in \mathbb{N}$$

Presuming the true, but as yet unjustified, facts that

$$(x=y) = (succ(x) = succ(y)) = (pred(x) = pred(y))$$

we also have

$$pred^n(a) = 0$$

and

$$succ^m(b) = 0$$

Hence

$$
\begin{aligned}
a+b &= a + pred^m(0) \\
&= a + pred(pred^{m-1}(0)) \\
&= pred(a + pred^{m-1}(0)) \\
&= pred^2(a + pred^{m-2}(0)) \\
&= \ldots \qquad \text{etc. by induction} \\
&= pred^m(a + pred^{m-m}(0)) \\
&= pred^m(a + 0) \\
&= pred^m(a) \\
&= pred^m(succ^n(0)) \\
&= \begin{cases} pred^{m-n}(0) & \text{if } n<m \\ 0 & \text{if } m=n \\ succ^{n-m}(0) & \text{if } m<n \end{cases}
\end{aligned}
$$

Continuing the case when $n < m$

$$pred^{m-n}(0) = succ^n(pred^n(pred^{m-n}(0)))$$
$$= succ^n(pred^m(0))$$
$$= succ^n(b)$$
$$= succ^n(b+0)$$
$$= succ^{n-1}(b+succ(0))$$
$$= \ldots \qquad \text{etc.}$$
$$= succ(b+succ^{n-1}(0))$$
$$= b+succ^n(0)$$
$$= b+a$$

and similarly when $m = n$ and $m < n$.

With this and other results (consequences) we can assemble a large set of equations which allow shorter, and hence much more powerful, logical arguments to be put together.

type $INTEGER\ (INTEGER3 \subseteq INTEGER)$

sorts $INT, BOOL$

ops
$$0 \to INT$$
$$1 \to INT$$
$$2 \to INT \quad \text{etc.}$$
$$^{-}1 \to INT$$
$$^{-}2 \to INT \quad \text{etc.}$$
$$(INT + INT) \to INT$$
$$(INT - INT) \to INT$$
$$(INT * INT) \to INT$$
$$(INT \div INT) \to INT$$
$$(INT \leqslant INT) \to BOOL$$
$$(INT = INT) \to BOOL$$
$$(INT < INT) \to BOOL$$

eqns
$$0 + 1 = 1$$
$$1 + 1 = 2$$
$$2 + 1 = 3 \quad \text{etc.}$$
$$0 + {}^{-}1 = {}^{-}1$$
$$^{-}1 + {}^{-}1 = {}^{-}2$$
$$^{-}2 + {}^{-}1 = {}^{-}3 \quad \text{etc.}$$

(1) $\qquad (i_1 + i_2) = (i_2 + i_1)$

(2) $\qquad (i_1 + i_2) + i_3 = i_1 + (i_2 + i_3)$

(3) $\qquad i + 0 = i$

(4) $\qquad ((i_1 - i_2) = i_3) = ((i_1 + i_4) = i_3 \wedge (i_2 + i_4) = 0)$

(5) $\qquad i_1 * i_2 = i_2 * i_1$

(6) $\qquad (i_1 * i_2) * i_3 = i_1 * (i_2 * i_3)$

(7) $\qquad i * 1 = i$

(8) $\qquad (i_1 * (i_2 + i_3)) = ((i_1 * i_2) + (i_1 * i_3))$

(9) $\qquad (i < (i+1)) = \text{True}$

(10) $\qquad (i \leqslant (i+1)) = \text{True}$

(11) $\qquad (i < i) = \text{False}$

(12) $\qquad (i \leqslant i) = \text{True}$

(13) $\qquad ((i_1 + i_3) < (i_2 + i_3)) = (i_1 < i_2)$

(14) $\qquad ((i_1 + i_3) \leqslant (i_2 + i_3)) = (i_1 \leqslant i_2)$

(15) $\qquad (i_1 < i_2) = \neg(i_2 \leqslant i_1)$

(16) $\qquad (i_1 < i_2) = \text{if } (i_1 < i_3) \wedge (i_3 < i_2) \quad \text{then True}$
$\qquad\qquad\qquad\qquad\qquad\qquad\qquad\qquad \text{else } (i_1 < i_2) \text{ fi}$

(17) $\qquad (i_1 \leqslant i_2) = \text{if } (i_1 \leqslant i_3) \wedge (i_3 \leqslant i_2) \quad \text{then True}$
$\qquad\qquad\qquad\qquad\qquad\qquad\qquad\qquad \text{else } (i_1 \leqslant i_2) \text{ fi}$

(18) $\qquad (i_1 < i_2) = (0 < (i_2 - i_1))$

(19) $\qquad (i_1 \leqslant i_2) = (0 \leqslant (i_2 - i_1))$

(20) $\qquad (0 \leqslant (i_1 + i_2)) = \text{if } (0 \leqslant i_1) \wedge (0 \leqslant i_2) \quad \text{then True}$
$\qquad\qquad\qquad\qquad\qquad\qquad\qquad\qquad \text{else } 0 \leqslant (i_1 + i_2) \text{ fi}$

(21) $\qquad (0 < (i_1 + i_2)) = \text{if } (0 < i_1) \wedge (0 < i_2) \quad \text{then True}$
$\qquad\qquad\qquad\qquad\qquad\qquad\qquad\qquad \text{else } 0 < (i_1 + i_2) \text{ fi}$

(22) $\qquad (0 \leqslant (i_1 * i_2)) = \text{if } (0 \leqslant i_1) \wedge (0 \leqslant i_2) \quad \text{then True}$
$\qquad\qquad\qquad\qquad\qquad\qquad\qquad\qquad \text{else } 0 \leqslant (i_1 * i_2) \text{ fi}$

(23) $\qquad (0 < (i_1 * i_2)) = \text{if } (0 < i_1) \wedge (0 < i_2) \quad \text{then True}$
$\qquad\qquad\qquad\qquad\qquad\qquad\qquad\qquad \text{else } 0 < (i_1 * i_2) \text{ fi}$

(24) $\qquad (i_1 = i_2) = (i_1 \leqslant i_2) \wedge (i_2 \leqslant i_1)$

(25) $\qquad ((i_1 \div i_2) = i_3) = (i_1 = (i_2 * i_3) + i_4)$
$\qquad\qquad\qquad\qquad \wedge ((0 \leqslant i_4 \wedge i_4 < i_2)$
$\qquad\qquad\qquad\qquad\qquad \vee (i_2 < i_4 \wedge i_4 \leqslant 0))$

Not all these equations are needed. There is much redundancy in this definition and although this enables us to take short cuts in normal proofs and evaluations it may cause problems for a theorem-prover by making it more difficult to detect logical loops.

The un-numbered equations are illustrative of the inter-relationship between the elements of the sort INT; (1–3) define addition and (4) introduces subtraction as the inverse of addition; (5–8) and (25) bring in multiplication and integer division. All the other equations connect the relational operators ($<$, $\leqslant$, $=$). Some of these are new and deserve further comment.

Equations (9–12) result from the combination of equations (i) and (ii) in the specification of $INTEGER3$; (13) and (14) relate addition of constants to inequalities, and (18) and (19) connect inequalities to subtraction in the usual way. Finally, (20–23) stipulate that the sum and product of (strictly) positive integers are also (strictly) positive.

So much for $BOOLEAN$s and $INTEGER$s. As already noted, such basic types are almost always provided as inbuilt operations of the target system and their properties assumed. Properly these properties relate to the semantics of the target language about which we have no specific knowledge and therefore we are not in a position to verify this relationship. However, compilers of high-level languages are amongst the most widely used programs and their basic data manipulation has, over the years, been subjected to what must amount to exhaustive testing. Errors are still detected in the more elaborate areas of compilers but these basic routines are probably as reliable as they can be. We do not therefore need such equational specifications from which to construct implementations; we do need them in program verification.

$REAL$s can be specified in the same way. Indeed, if you regard the $REAL$ type as a (given) set of values on which operations act then the properties of the common functions **must** be defined axiomatically. (It is possible to equate real numbers with limits of sequences of rational numbers, i.e. fractions, and to derive the properties of real operations from similar operations on rationals – but again that is for the pure mathematicians.) Of course any actual implementation of $REAL$s will use finite representations and will therefore inevitably involve overflow and/or approximations. Proper treatment of such issues lies within realms of numerical analysis and outside the scope of our course but, as a compromise, we give a semi-formal definition of the rational type. The definition is semi-formal because we shall not attempt to define the sort $QUOT$, of *quotients*, and we shall represent the rational r_i as the quotient of integers p_i/q_i (with $q_i \neq 0$) whenever convenient.

type $RATIONAL\ (INTEGER,\ BOOLEAN2 \subseteq RATIONAL)$

sort $QUOT$

ops

$$0 \to QUOT$$
$$1 \to QUOT\ \text{etc.}$$
$$INT/INT \to QUOT$$
$$QUOT + QUOT \to QUOT$$
$$QUOT - QUOT \to QUOT$$
$$QUOT * QUOT \to QUOT$$
$$QUOT/QUOT \to QUOT$$
$$QUOT < QUOT \to BOOL$$
$$QUOT \leqslant QUOT \to BOOL$$
$$QUOT = QUOT \to BOOL$$

eqns

$$(r_1 + r_2) + r_3 = r_1 + (r_2 + r_3)$$
$$r_1 + r_2 = r_2 + r_1$$
$$r + 0 = r$$
$$((r_1 - r_2) = r_3) = ((r_1 + r_4) = r_3 \land (r_2 + r_4) = 0)$$
$$(r_1 * r_2) * r_3 = r_1 * (r_2 * r_3)$$
$$r_1 * r_2 = r_2 * r_1$$
$$r * 1 = r$$
$$((r_1/r_2) = r_3) = ((r_1 * r_4) = r_3 \land (r_2 * r_4) = 1)$$
$$((p_1/q_1) = (p_2/q_2)) = (p_1 * q_2 = q_1 * p_2)$$
$$((p_1/q_1) \leqslant (p_2/q_2)) = (p_1 * q_2 \leqslant q_1 * p_2)$$
$$((p_1/q_1) < (p_2/q_2)) = (p_1 * q_2 < q_1 * p_2)$$

err eqns $p/0 = \text{error}$

Exercises 10.3

1. Using the full set of equations for the type $INTEGER3$, prove that
$$(x = y) = (pred(x) = pred(y))$$

2. Deduce, using the equations for the type $INTEGER$ that
   (a) $(5 < 3) = \text{False}$
   (b) $((3 + 2) = 5) = \text{True}$

282 The mathematical basis of abstract data types

3. Devise an extension to the type *INTEGER* which incorporates the operator *SIGMA* where

$$SIGMA(a,b) = \sum_{i=a}^{b} i$$

as introduced in Example 7.3.1.   □

10.4 Sets

An ADT much used in our specifications is sets. As with our various progressively more powerful definitions of integers we shall begin with a compact definition based on very primitive operations and then move, rapidly, to a formulation involving more familiar operators. The type *SETS1* (defined over some fixed bounded set of integers, just to keep things relatively straightforward, and also using *BOOLEAN*s) is similar to *POSINT* in that we have the empty set $\emptyset$, the operations *insert* and *delete* which are very similar to *0*, and the operations *succ* and *pred*.

type   *SETS1 (INTEGER, BOOLEAN2 ⊆ SETS1)*

sorts   *SET* (the sets are all subsets of some given set of *INT*s)

ops $\emptyset \rightarrow SET$

            insert(INT,SET) $\rightarrow$ *SET*

            delete(INT,SET) $\rightarrow$ *SET*

              (SET is_empty) $\rightarrow$ *BOOL*

              (INT is_in SET) $\rightarrow$ *BOOL*

eqns   *($\emptyset$ is_empty)* = *True*

        ((insert(i,S)) is_empty) = *False*

            (i is_in $\emptyset$) = *False*

   $(i_1$ *is_in(insert(i_2,S)))* = if $(i_1 = i_2)$ then True

                              else $(i_1$ *is_in S)* fi

          delete(i,$\emptyset$) = $\emptyset$

  delete(i_1,insert(i_2,S)) = if $(i_1 = i_2)$ then *S*

                    else   *insert(i_2,delete(i_1,S))* fi

SETS1 can now be enriched by adding new operators and associated equations. Proceeding in this way we may add

ops   *(SET ∪ SET)* $\rightarrow$ *SET*

            (SET ∩ SET) $\rightarrow$ *SET*

$$(SET \setminus SET) \rightarrow SET$$
$$|SET| \rightarrow INT$$

eqns
$$(i\ is\_in(S_1 \cup S_2)) = ((i\ is\_in\ S_1) \vee (i\ is\_in\ S_2))$$
$$(i\ is\_in(S_1 \cap S_2)) = ((i\ is\_in\ S_1) \wedge (i\ is\_in\ S_2))$$
$$(i\ is\_in(S_1 \setminus S_2)) = ((i\ is\_in\ S_1) \wedge \neg(i\ is\_in\ S_2))$$
$$|\varnothing| = 0$$
$$|insert(i,S)| = \text{if } (i\ is\_in\ S)\text{ then } |S|$$
$$\text{else } |S| + 1 \text{ fi}$$

We can also introduce the subset operator, $\subseteq$, with **ops** declaration

$$(SET \subseteq SET) \rightarrow BOOL$$

and satisfying the equations:

$$(\varnothing \subseteq S) = \text{True}$$
$$(S \subseteq \varnothing) = (S\ is\_empty)$$
$$(S_1 \subseteq S_2) = \text{if } x\ is\_in\ S_1$$
$$\text{then if } x\ is\_in\ S_2$$
$$\text{then } S_1 \setminus \{x\} \subseteq S_2 \setminus \{x\}$$
$$\text{else False fi}$$
$$\text{else } S_1 \subseteq S_2 \setminus \{x\} \text{ fi}$$

$$\text{where } \{x\} = insert(x, \varnothing).$$

Notice that although the ordering, $\subseteq$, is not total, we do not have the problems associated with the *INTEGER* ordering $\leqslant$ because $0 \leqslant |S|$ for all sets S.

We could therefore glue these operators onto *SETS1* but this would produce unfamiliar rules which, although correct, would lead to long verification proofs. Alternatively we give a more familiar collection of operators and equations which are derivable from *SETS1*.

type   *SETS2 (INTEGER, BOOLEAN2 $\subseteq$ SETS2)*

sorts   *SET (SETs are subsets of the finite integer set X)*

ops
$$\varnothing \rightarrow SET$$
$$\{INT\} \rightarrow SET$$
$$(SET \cup SET) \rightarrow SET$$
$$(SET \cap SET) \rightarrow SET$$

$$(SET \backslash SET) \rightarrow SET$$
$$(SET \ is\_empty) \rightarrow BOOL$$
$$(INT \ is\_in \ SET) \rightarrow BOOL$$
$$|SET| \rightarrow INT$$
$$(SET = SET) \rightarrow BOOL$$
$$(SET \subseteq SET) \rightarrow BOOL$$

eqns $\quad (S_1 \cup S_2) = (S_2 \cup S_1)$
$$(S_1 \cup S_2) \cup S_3 = S_1 \cup (S_2 \cup S_3)$$
$$S \cup \emptyset = S$$
$$S \cup (X \backslash S) = X$$
$$(S_1 \cap S_2) = (S_2 \cap S_1)$$
$$(S_1 \cap S_2) \cap S_3 = S_1 \cap (S_2 \cap S_3)$$
$$S \cap X = S$$
$$S \cap (X \backslash S) = \emptyset$$
$$(S_1 \cap (S_2 \cup S_3)) = (S_1 \cap S_2) \cup (S_1 \cap S_3)$$
$$(S_1 \cup (S_2 \cap S_3)) = (S_1 \cup S_2) \cap (S_1 \cup S_3)$$
$$S_1 \backslash S_2 = S_1 \cap (X \backslash S_2)$$
$$(x \ is\_in \ S) = \neg (x \ is\_in (X \backslash S))$$
$$x \ is\_in \ \emptyset = \text{False}$$
$$(x \ is\_in \ S) = (S = S \cup \{x\})$$
$$(\emptyset = \emptyset) = \text{True}$$
$$(S_1 = S_2) = \text{ if } x \ is\_in \ S_1 \quad \text{then}$$
$$(\text{if } x \ is\_in \ S_2 \quad \text{then } (S_1 \backslash \{x\}) = (S_2 \backslash \{x\})$$
$$\text{else} \quad \text{False fi})$$
$$\text{else (if } x \ is\_in \ S_2 \text{ then False}$$
$$\text{else } S_1 = S_2 \text{ fi) fi}$$
$$(S_1 \subseteq S_2) = ((S_1 \cup S_2) = S_2)$$
$$|\emptyset| = 0$$
$$|S \cup \{x\}| = \text{if } x \ is\_in \ S \text{ then } |S|$$
$$\text{else } |S| + 1 \text{ fi}$$

Of course there is nothing very special about the elements of these sets, we could just as easily have had sets of *strings*, or sets of *lists*, etc. Definition of such sets would be essentially identical and give rise to so-called parameterized specifications, but we will not have cause to go further into that topic.

Exercises 10.4

1. Extend *SETS2* to include equational definitions of *for_all* and *there_exists* as introduced in Section 7.4.2.

   (You may assume the existence of objects of type $INT \to BOOL$ which can be used as operands of *for_all* and *there_exists* but which cannot be introduced as variables within the system.)

2. Within the framework of Question 1, define specific '$INT \to BOOL$' functions *is_even* and *is_odd*. Using the style of the quantifiers in Question 1, derive set versions of these functions.

$$all\_even: SET \to BOOL$$
$$some\_even: SET \to BOOL$$
$$all\_odd: SET \to BOOL$$
$$some\_odd: SET \to BOOL$$

10.5 Equations versus conditions

So, we have two ways of specifying types; *pre-* and *post-* conditions, or equations. If the type is one which cannot be defined in terms of more fundamental objects then we are obliged to use an axiomatic system such as equations. On the other hand, if the type is genuinely 'constructed' then we could use either scheme. Which should we use and how do they relate to each other?

To make the discussion more specific let us consider the definition of *INTSTACKS*, *stacks* of integers, implemented by (defined in terms of) *lists*. First look at a possible equational definition.

type $INTSTACKS\ (INTEGERS \subseteq INTSTACKS)$

sorts *STACK*

ops $is\_empty(STACK) \to BOOL$

$$\langle \rangle \to STACK$$
$$push(INT, STACK) \to STACK$$
$$pop(STACK) \to (INT, STACK)$$
$$peep(STACK) \to (INT, STACK)$$

eqns
$$is\_empty(\langle\,\rangle) = \text{True}$$
$$(is\_empty(\,push(i,s))) = \text{False}$$
$$pop(\,push(i,s)) = (i,s)$$
$$(\,push(i,s_1) = s_2) = (\,pop(s_2) = (i,s_1))$$
$$(\,push(i,s_1) = s_2) = (\,peep(s_2) = (i,s_2))$$

err eqns
$$pop(\langle\,\rangle) = \text{error}$$
$$peep(\langle\,\rangle) = \text{error}$$

This definition tells us how the various operations interact with each other and, using substitution of *equals for equals*, provides the information required to perform evaluations, proofs, etc. and to reduce predicates to True, False or *error*. It does not however, and it is purposely not intended to, give any guide to implementation.

An alternative approach, which may help with implementation but is less useful in proofs, is to use pre- and post- conditions associated with all the proper operations for the type (i.e. all except those that generate constants). In an implementation we need a facility for introducing, *INIT*ialising, new objects. Such a routine is not included within the equational system but the rest of the specification follows in a fairly obvious way. Without undue formality we give specifications of a stack (of integers).

$Stack::Int^*$

$INIT$

states:$Stack$

pre--$INIT(s,) \triangleq \text{True}$

post-$INIT(s,,s',) \triangleq s' = \langle\,\rangle$

$PUSH$

states:$Stack$

type :$Int \rightarrow$

pre--$PUSH(s,i) \triangleq \text{True}$

post-$PUSH(s,i,s',) \triangleq s' = \langle i\rangle \,\|\, s$

$PEEP$

states:$Stack$

type :$\rightarrow Int$

pre--$PEEP(s,) \triangleq s \neq \langle\,\rangle$

post-$PEEP(s,,s',i) \triangleq s' = s \wedge i = hd(s)$

POP

states: *Stack*

type : $\rightarrow Int$

pre--$POP(s,) \triangleq s \neq \langle \rangle$

post-$POP(s,,s',i) \triangleq s' = t\ell(s) \wedge i = hd(s)$

IS_EMPTY

states: *Stack*

type : $\rightarrow Bool$

pre--$IS\_EMPTY(s,) \triangleq$ True

post-$IS\_EMPTY(s,,s',b) \triangleq s' = s \wedge (b \Leftrightarrow s = \langle \rangle)$

Alternatively we may change the functionality of *push* to give

PUSH

states:

type : $Int \times Stack \rightarrow Stack$

pre--$PUSH(,\langle i,s \rangle) \triangleq$ True

post-$PUSH(,\langle i,s \rangle,,s') \triangleq s' = \langle i \rangle \| s$

This version of *push* fits more closely with the equational form in that it has a blank states line and therefore its meaning is defined in terms of *effects* rather than the *side-effects* possible when routines are allowed to update state variables.

As noted in Chapter 7, proofs about segments of program are much easier to perform when all inputs and outputs are identified explicitly. To improve efficiency, it is possible in many procedural languages to gain access to non-local variables and this facility is modelled by using states. As we have often remarked, run-time efficiency considerations are secondary to the correctness of the resultant code. Consequently any juggling of input and output quantities between *state* and *type* lines within a pre-post specification can be regarded as pertaining to the syntax and style of the target language; all matters of logic requiring a unified *type/state* line explicitly encompassing all interface values.

How does this relate to type definitions in general and *INTSTACKS* in particular? The answer can be inferred from Figure 10.1.

Although possible, it is quite difficult to prove properties of a data type directly from its definition in terms of *pre-* and *post-* conditions. It is therefore desirable to split into two the logical link between such a specification and its use in proofs; first deducing properties that follow from the specification to form an adequate set of equational axioms which it

Fig. 10.1

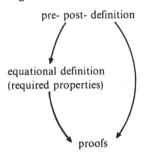

pre- post- definition

equational definition
(required properties)

proofs

satisfies and then use these equations in proofs and not refer back to the original specification. Failure to satisfy the equations indicates inadequacies in the *pre- post-* specification (and hence, presumably, the implementation?!) of the data type, failure to deduce consequences from the equations indicates lack of facility in proofs or the incorrect choice of data type.

The aim of providing proper definitions of abstract data types is to facilitate proofs about programs and their specifications. We ought to know **how** these proofs work and we have already encountered simple examples of such proofs and no more will be given here. It is however a useful and non-trivial task to devise proper specifications of some constructed data types.

Exercises 10.5

1. Give pre- post- style definitions of *is_empty*, *push* and *pop* which have the same characteristics as stipulated in the *ops* section of *INTSTACKS*. Show that these operations satisfy the relevant *eqns* of *INTSTACKS*. (Some information will be lost, e.g., s' in *IS_EMPTY*.

2. Similarly, take the given pre- post- definitions of *pop*, *is_empty* and (the second version of) *push* and write down an appropriate set of equations which they satisfy.

   No information should be lost and hence the *ops* and *eqns* will be more complicated than those in *INTSTACKS*.

11
Utilisation of existing programs

So far we have only considered the construction of new programs, but of course there are very many programs which are already in existence and which we may need to use. Like much old electronics equipment they may or may not have been well-designed but in any case there is a great tendency to 'leave well alone' just in case they stop working.

When a program exists only in its object form (i.e. translated into machine code) little can be usefully done – decompilers, which translate a program back into a high-level language form, do exist but the resulting program is usually pretty unintelligible. Such (object only) programs should be candidates for rewriting as soon as time is available since in their current form they cannot be safely and quickly amended and this, in practice, is an ever-likely requirement.

Programs which exist in source form present a more approachable problem. Because of their age and the rapid development of programming methodology, it is likely that these programs will not have formal specifications from which their correctness could have been demonstrated. Also, in view of their preoccupation with making best use of slow and expensive hardware, it is very probable that the early programmers were not permitted the luxury of programming style. These economic factors served to encourage the production of unintelligible 'spaghetti' code which was very difficult to analyse and/or modify. These days such programs are generally recognised as unsafe and potentially very expensive, any gain in run-time efficiency being of negligible benefit when compared with the cost of locating and correcting errors if a fault does occur. Never-the-less such programs do exist† and there may not be time or manpower available to

---

† We accept this as an unfortunate but irrefutable fact. Certain eminent academics argue that **all** programs should be systematically derived from specifications and the development at each stage proved to be correct. In an ideal world we agree that this is how it **should** be and hence the material in the current chapter would not be required. In recognition of this utopian objective the style of the chapter is markedly less formal than the others.

produce replacements which are provably more reliable, so what can we do?

Working from a flowchart representation of the program we can first attempt to divide it up into logically self-contained modules. This can be done without detailed knowledge of the non-control instructions in the program (the manipulations are *syntactic*). It may be possible, by duplication but without adding any new instructions, to manipulate the program into a structured form. In other cases a structured form can only be achieved by the introduction of extra variables to control looping, but in either case the analysis of the program is greatly assisted by the logical dissection of the program. The program could then be rewritten piecemeal by replacing one, logically self-contained, section at a time. Where the actual effect of a module is not clear we need to investigate the *semantics*. This is a difficult task but we shall briefly look at how this may be achieved by using inductive assertions. Some of these operations (on complete programs!) are hard but any progress that can be made using these methods will (retrospectively) improve the assurance of the product.

11.1   Testing for good structure

Allowing only the possible duplication of code, can an arbitrary *flowchart program* be structured? Unfortunately the answer is 'No.' However such a transformation is well worth attempting because success will produce a program with proper structure but without extraneous variables (see Section 11.2) which might introduce difficulties in any subsequent semantic analysis (Section 11.3).

The method described is based on our own work and will be presented as an informal algorithm for which no justification will be included. Briefly, we

(i) take the flowchart and produce a *linked tree*, then

(ii) transform, by duplicating code if required, into a *simply linked tree* in which we can only branch back up the tree but not jump across branches, then

(iii) migrate labels 'up' the tree – away from the start – to the highest allowable fork (this may involve further code duplication), and finally

(iv) attempt to realise the structured forms from the 'inside out' by reducing (collapsing) structured subprograms to a single process box.

We shall proceed by giving examples and include definitions at the appropriate points in the discussion.

Example 11.1.1 An 'unstructured' program
Consider the flowchart scheme given in Figure 11.1 (based on [3]). In this program ⓢ and ⓧ are entry/start and exit/stop nodes, a, b, etc., are processes and p, q, etc., are tests. (For simplicity only two-way tests will be considered.) A flowchart scheme, like the one in Figure 11.1, devoid of computational detail and indicating only how the various processes are connected, will henceforth be called a *flowgraph*. Within a flowgraph it will also be convenient for all tests and processes to have distinct names.

We now transform the flowgraph into a tree. Traverse the flowgraph from S taking, arbitrarily, *true* branches, until we are required to repeat a segment of the graph. Instead of doing that, insert a label, ℓ_n, at the appropriate point and name the leaf with the integer n. Then return to the branch emanating from the last test encountered whose *false* branch has

Fig. 11.1

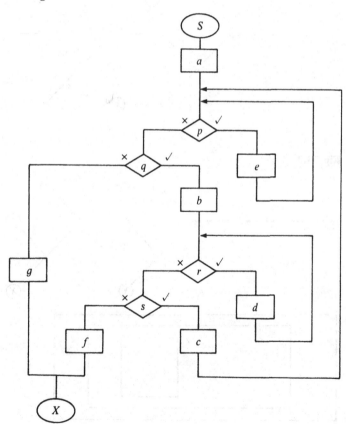

not yet been considered and process this in the same way. Continue until the entire flowgraph has been processed. In Figure 11.1 the graph segments would be considered in the order (p true, p false, q true, r true, r false, s true, s false, q false) giving the tree in Figure 11.2 where the leaves, reading down the right of the diagram, correspond to (p true), (p false, q true, r true), (r false, s true), (s false) and (q false).

In this example the tree is already *simply linked* in that for each leaf, $⑩$, $\ell_n < n$, where $j < k$ if k is in the subtree whose root is j. (So starting at j and moving away from $Ⓢ$ we can, by taking the appropriate branches, reach k.) For instance ℓ_1 occurs between a and p so $\ell_1 < p < e < ①$. Similarly for ℓ_2 and $②$, and ℓ_3 and $③$. Trivially we always have $Ⓢ < Ⓧ$.

Fig. 11.2

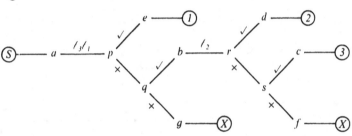

Fig. 11.3

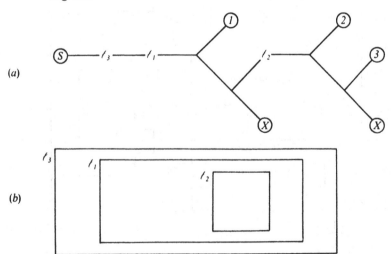

(a)

(b)

Another feature of the example is that no labels can migrate; moving ℓ_1 back over a would change the meaning of the program, moving ℓ_1 over p would require the label ℓ_1 to be present on the 'p-is-false' branch and hence would violate the simple linking. Labels ℓ_2 and ℓ_3 are similarly at their limit.

Concentrating attention only on the labels and implied links we have, in Figures 11.3(a) and (b), the natural 'blocking structure' of the program.

We now attempt to extract a structured version of the program. Sequencing is directly inferred by the graph structure. With respect to alternation and looping we use the templates:

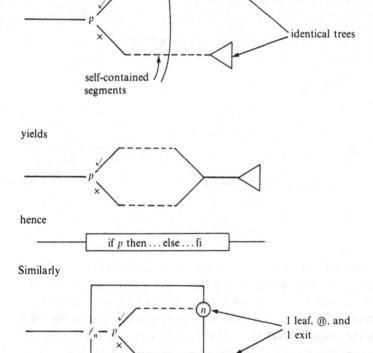

yields

hence

Similarly

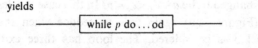

yields

Applying these rules, from the inside, we see that ℓ_2 gives rise to '*while r do d od*' and ℓ_1 yields '*while p do e od*'. However, the flowgraph associated with ③ and ℓ_3 cannot be simplified in an obvious way. Hence we have the situation depicted in Figure 11.4 where the blocks labelled *1* and *2* represent the loops generated from ℓ_1 and ℓ_2 respectively. This cannot be structured since, although ℓ_3 can be migrated past block *1*, to give Figure 11.5, we still have two exits from the '*3*' loop and they cannot be merged by the *if then else fi* template.

Fig. 11.4

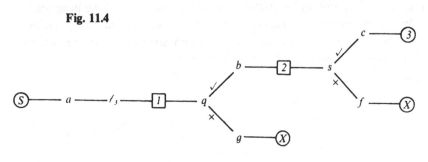

Fig. 11.5

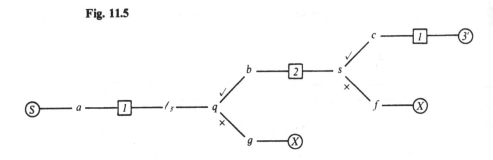

Before the next example we refer the reader back to Figure 11.2. Since the order in which we traversed the original flowgraph (and consequently assigned labels and leaf numbers in the linked tree) was somewhat arbitrary, have we failed to find a valid structured form simply because we did things in the wrong order? No. Label ℓ_2 obviously causes no worry. It may be argued that ℓ_1 and ℓ_3 are equal and hence we might change ③ to ① and remove ℓ_3. Such modifications are possible in a properly structured program and more will be said about this later but what if the (random?) order of ℓ_1 and ℓ_3 is changed to be $a \prec \ell_1 \prec \ell_3 \prec p$? In this case the desirable blocking structure (Figure 11.6) again fails to reduce when the loop associated with label *3* is considered. The loop has three exits, one controlled by p, the others being stops. In other words, we have the **same** structure violation, it has just been detected at a different stage in the analysis.

Fig. 11.6

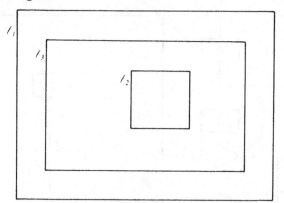

The next example is of a program, which although **not** structured in the classical sense, can be made into a structured program by 'redrawing'. We shall say that it is **essentially** structured, the main point being that no new flowgraph elements will be added, though some may have to be duplicated.

Example 11.1.2 A 'structured' program

Consider the flowgraph in Figure 11.7 and its unfoldment to the tree in Figure 11.8. Notice that ℓ_2, ℓ_3 and ℓ_4 are really all equivalent in that they each precede the process called B. However, provided the topology of the flowgraph is preserved, any variability in how these labels are treated is unimportant; any apparent discrepancies will disappear at the next stage of analysis.

Fig. 11.7

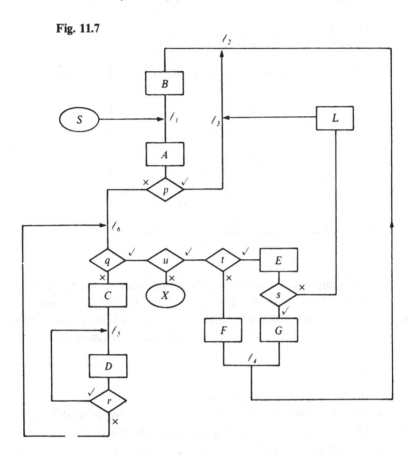

Now, ℓ_2 and ② are on different branches so ② is removed and replaced by the segment of tree following ℓ_2. Similarly for ③ and ④. (Since the tree is finite this process must terminate. At worst the height of the tree cannot exceed the total number of arcs in the original flowgraph because in any one complete branch (from Ⓢ to a leaf) there are no duplicated tests.)

Fig. 11.8

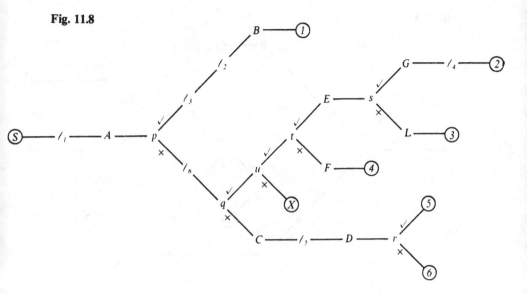

Hence we obtain Figure 11.9. Also, in this example, labels *1* and *5* will migrate. This requires changes both at the label position and at goto leaves. Graphically the transformation for label *1* is:

$$B———①$$

and

$$Ⓢ—\ell_1———A———p$$

become

$$B———A———①$$

and

$$Ⓢ———A———\ell_{1'}———p$$

That is, insert $\ell_{1'}$ so $A \prec \ell_{1'} \prec p$ and replace

$$———① \quad \text{by} \quad A———①$$

and

$$\ell_1———A \quad \text{by} \quad A———\ell_{1'}$$

We can do this only because A is a process and not a test.

Fig. 11.9

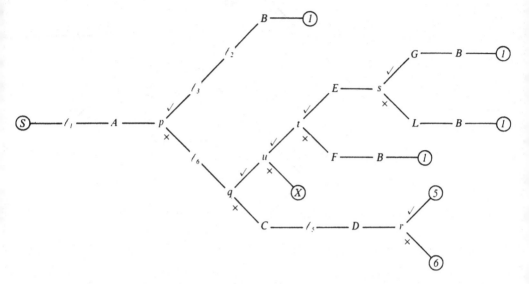

Applying a similar migration to label 5 yields Figure 11.10. Notice that, since a label is only meaningful when the tree has an associated leaf, any processing which results in the deletion of a leaf may also permit removal of a label. To keep our representation simple and devoid of superfluous detail, labels will be removed as soon as possible.

Fig. 11.10

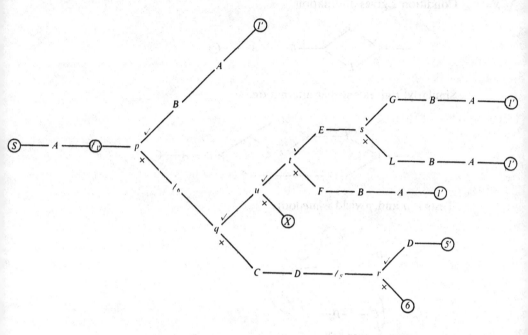

We can now set about simplifying and collecting the branches together. Condition s gives alternation.

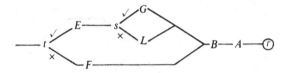

Similarly, t gives another alternation.

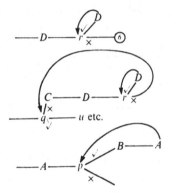

Tests r, q and p yield *while* loops.

To indicate this reduction we can utilise an abbreviated form of our PDL by giving the local identities;

> $\text{ITE}_s = \text{if } s \text{ then } G \text{ else } L \text{ fi}$
>
> $\text{ITE}_t = \text{if } t \text{ then } E; \text{ITE}_s \text{ else } F \text{ fi}$
>
> $\text{WD}_r = \text{while } r \text{ do } D \text{ od}$
>
> $\text{WD}_{\neg q} = \text{while } \neg q \text{ do } C; D; \text{WD}_r \text{ od}$
>
> $\text{WD}_p = \text{while } p \text{ do } B; A \text{ od}$

Of course these abbreviations apply only to this example; since all the tests are different, the predicate r only controls the execution of D so there is no need to specify D, etc. Notice also that the exit from the loop controlled by q is when q is true rather than false. Thus we have '*while q is false do* ...' or '*until q do* ...' as spoken versions of $\text{WD}_{\neg q}$.

Using these abbreviated forms we have Figure 11.11 which, after migration of ℓ_{γ} yields Figures 11.12 and 11.13. Realisation of the resultant code form is left as an exercise. □

Fig. 11.11

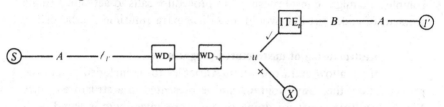

Fig. 11.12

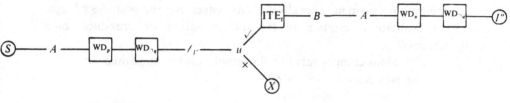

Fig. 11.13

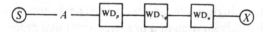

Notice that in the technique used, by migrating labels to the loop control test, we always derive *while* loops. Indeed processing a *repeat...until* construct would result in the duplication of the loop body and conversion of the post-check loop into pre-check form. Explicitly,

> repeat *a* until *p*

would become

> *a*; while ⌐*p* do *a* od

The method of the next section, for application to programs which are not inherently structured, has the characteristic of always yielding post-check loops. Hence it may therefore be appropriate to replace

> if *p* then repeat *a* until ⌐*p* fi

by

> while *p* do *a* od

However, changing the form of iterative constructs is not of fundamental interest to us. We are primarily concerned with the extraction of a structured form. In any case it is not trivial to assess which form is the simplest or most desirable. For instance, in the preceding expansions of *repeat-until* and *while-do*, the process *a* was duplicated. If this process was complex we might consider using two procedure calls to activate a single segment of code; but that would introduce extra run-time overheads!!

11.2   Restructuring of unstructured programs

If we allow extra operations/variables to be included within the program flow then **any** program can be presented in a structured form. Many algorithms exist for doing this; the one given here is based on a formulation by Tausworthe [30] of a method due to Mills [25]. The resultant program includes alternations, sequencing and post-check loops. To facilitate description of the transformation we introduce some terminology.

The various components of a flowgraph will be categorised as:
(i) p-nodes (process nodes)
(ii) ℓ-nodes (label nodes)
(iii) d-nodes (decisions).

A process node has a single entry arc and a single exit arc. It therefore represents a primitive computation or a properly structured process which has been assembled during an earlier phase of the restructuring algorithm. Label nodes are the only ones which have multiple entry arcs (and a single exit arc) and are associated with no process or test. They simply facilitate description of the flowgraph. Finally, d-nodes are binary test boxes. We assume that more complex switches have been replaced by suitable combinations of these nodes each of which has a single entry arc and two exit arcs; the choice of which arc to follow being made by evaluation of the test to yield the value 'True' ($\sqrt{}$) or 'False' ($\times$).

Various segments of program will be dealt with separately; those not under immediate consideration will be saved in a stack which can be regarded informally, but correctly, as an ordered pile of sheets of paper on which the graphs are drawn. Segments of flowgraph/flowchart will be identified by fc_0, fc_1, fc_2, etc.

The main algorithm is couched in terms of four subprocesses. These are as follows:

(A) The partitioning of the flowgraph following a d-node
Given a portion of a graph headed by a test, split it into three sections as follows:

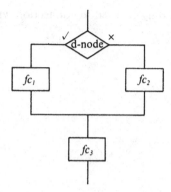

(B) *The merging of labels*

Adjacent labels will be ultimately associated with the same loop and hence, to ensure the desired *repeat-until* structure with a single loop arc, the label discrepancy is moved into the body of the loop. Hence

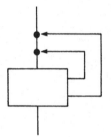

becomes

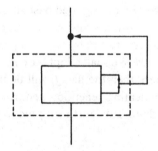

(C) *Label migration*

Whenever a p-node follows a label we can migrate the label past the process and duplicate the process on the 'loop' arc so that it now appears logically before the label (once on the entry arc and once on the loop arc) rather than after the label. This transformation will only be used in connection with loops so that:

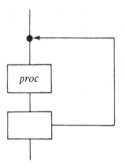

can be replaced by

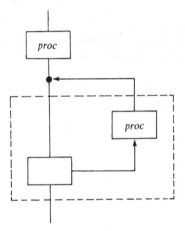

In this way each label is either erased (by (B)) or migrated past all p-nodes until a d-node is reached. All the original d-nodes give rise to alternation constructs, new tests being introduced together with appropriate assignment statements to control the loops. We shall adopt the convention that if t is a test that gives rise to a loop, then the flag f_t will be used to control looping back to t; '$f_t =$ True' indicating repetition and '$f_t =$ False' indicating exit from the loop. This leads to our fourth subprocess.

(D) Loop construction

Suppose we have a loop configuration in which the first node is a d-node utilising the test t. Flowgraph paths out of the subgraph under consideration either loop back to the test or exit by other means. To these paths we add assignment statements of the form '$f_t \leftarrow$ True' and '$f_t \leftarrow$ False' respectively and then merge the paths into a loop decision with test f_t, the *true* branch going back to the original d-node. Hence

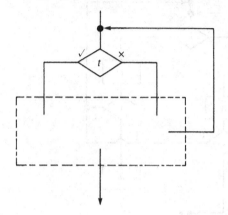

becomes

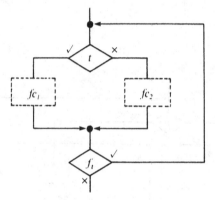

where each path through fc_1 and fc_2 ends in the process

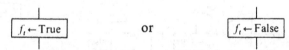

The subprocess D is the most involved so, before giving the complete algorithm, we give an instance of this transformation.

Example 11.2.1
The flowgraph given in Figure 11.14 contains three logical arcs which transfer flow of control back to the test p. These give rise to three assignments of the value 'True' to the flag f_p. All other paths through the body of the resulting loop include assignments '$f_p \leftarrow$ False'. The

Fig. 11.14

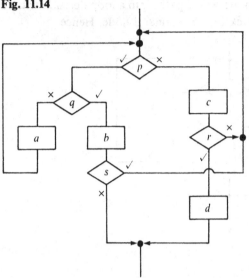

Fig. 11.15

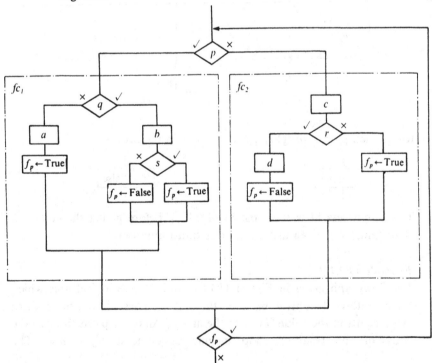

transformation D thus reduces the current flowgraph to a loop controlled by f_p surrounding an alternation controlled by p and two subgraphs (fc_1 and fc_2 in the general form of the rule) which in this case are already structured (Figure 11.15). Notice that the segments fc_1 and fc_2 must be independent and hence in general it will be necessary to duplicate any portion of the graph which they have in common (see exercises at the end of this section). □

Now for the algorithm proper. The original flowchart/flowgraph and subsequent unprocessed subgraphs will be held on a stack. When segments have been processed they are placed in the appropriate position on the 'output' flowchart. It is presumed that each stacked segment is given a unique name or number so as to facilitate insertion into the output. The algorithm is given as a structured flowchart in Figure 11.16.

Example 11.2.2
Applying this algorithm to the unstructured program of example 11.1.1 we obtain the flowgraph in Figure 11.17 (drawn in two parts so as to allow inclusion of all the detail; a benefit not generally afforded by unstructured flowgraphs). □

As stated previously this algorithm always gives post-check loops. The segment FC in Figure 11.17(*b*) illustrates how the *while r do d od* is transformed into

> *repeat if r then d*; $f_b \leftarrow$ True
>
> > *else* ...; $f_r \leftarrow$ False
>
> *until* $\neg f_r$

In contrast with Figure 11.15, here there is a direct correspondence between the original tests and the new flags; explicitly when $r =$ True then (after following the appropriate arcs in the flowgraph) $f_r =$ True, and similarly when $r =$ False it follows that $f_r =$ False. Hence it would seem reasonable that we should be able to remove one of these variables. The equivalence noted above justifies such a removal and hence we may take the opportunity to dispose of f_r, which in general has no obvious semantic content.

Fig. 11.16

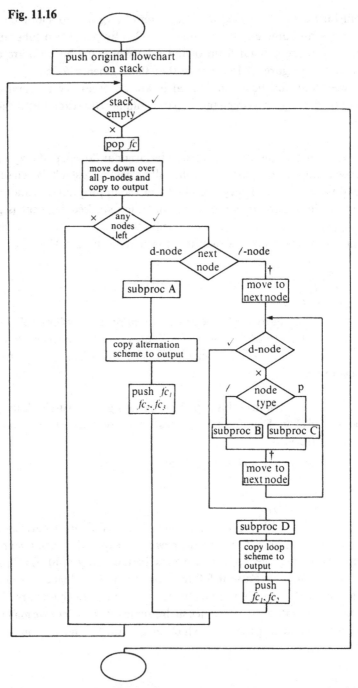

† Notice that any label not followed by another (non-label) node can only give rise to
the construct '*while* True *do od*' which can never exit. Such reasoning may not be
applicable in certain real-time/process-control programs where program control is
partially determined by interrupt mechanisms which are outside the scope of the
current text.

Fig. 11.17

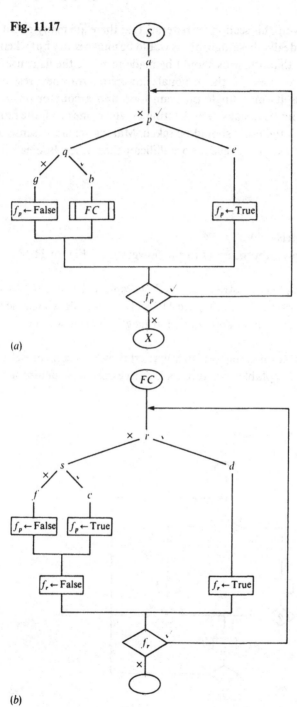

(a)

(b)

Before leaving this section we reiterate that there are many restructuring algorithms. Ideally these algorithms would be unnecessary but when used it is imperative that attempts should be made to relate the flags used to the tests and processes of the original flowchart. Another restructuring algorithm results in a single program loop and a counter (instead of a collection of Boolean flags) that determines which one of a finite number of paths through the body should be taken. Making semantic sense out of a program of this form is even more difficult than when Boolean flags are used.

Exercises 11.2

1. Apply subprocess D to the flowgraph in Figure 11.18.

2. Completely restructure the flowgraph in Figure 11.19 using the algorithm given in Figure 11.16. (This example is a classic one due to John Flynn and studied at length by Tausworthe [30].)

3. Take a small (but nasty) flowchart drawn by someone else. Test it for acceptable structure and, if necessary, restructure it.

Fig. 11.18

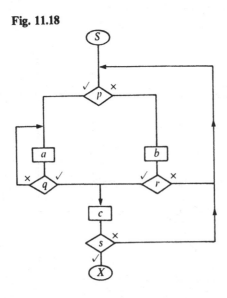

Fig. 11.19

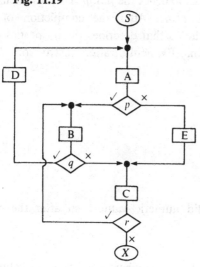

11.3   Analysis of programs

Consider the execution of a program on a specific piece of data and assume that it halts after execution of n, not necessarily distinct, instructions. This may be regarded as a path through nodes of a flowchart and is depicted as in Figure 11.20. Note that for analysis we need to know

Fig. 11.20

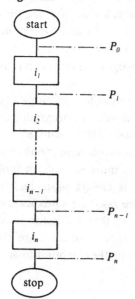

details of the various instructions and hence the *flowgraph* is insufficient, we must have access to the *flowchart*. After the completion of each intermediate stage a predicate holds that describes the properties of the program-accessible information. Explicitly, after instruction i_j the predicate P_j is True.

Example 11.3.1
Provided that Y holds a valid numeric value then after the correct termination of the instruction

$$X \leftarrow Y + 1$$

we know, amongst other things, that $x > y$ where x and y are the values held in locations X and Y. □

In direct contrast to a sequence of deductions about a static object where after completion of the jth stage all the predicates P_0 to P_j are known to be true, when considering a dynamic system (such as the changing states of a machine during a computation) the only facts known after the jth stage are those contained in P_j. If P_0 is true when we start and the action of each instruction i_j causes P_{j-1} to be changed into P_j then, if P_n includes the conditions required of the program, the program is correct relative to the input under consideration.

To verify the program we need to be able to guarantee this for all legitimate inputs. The number of different inputs to a program may well be unbounded as might the number of instructions required to process (correctly process) a given input and hence, rather than trying to verify the program by using selected test data, it is more sensible to look at the program itself, the flowchart of which is always finite and bounded. Explicitly, with each arc of the flowchart we associate a predicate which we assert must give the value 'True' whenever that arc is traversed during execution of the program. Consequently these predicates are also called *assertions*. They must obviously be related by the computational processes specified by the program (although the relationship is not always obvious!) and can be used, by resorting to mathematical induction on the length of the computation sequence (Figure 11.20), to prove the correctness of an appropriate program. The technique, due largely to Floyd [14] is generally known as the method of inductive assertions. Referring back to Chapter 7 these assertions are predicates of one variable, one state. P_0 can be the pre-condition of the specification. Linking P_0 and P_n together so as to conform to the post-condition will require the introduction of some ghost variables which can be referred to globally in the assertions but do not occur explicitly in the code of the program. This requirement arises naturally in the analysis and causes no conceptual problem but must be explicitly mentioned so as to emphasise the discrepancy with the logical methods used in the program synthesis work presented earlier. Again we defer involvement with programming languages and stay with the flowchart representation of a program and regard all flow decisions as strictly binary. However, since we are concerned with how the values associated with program identifiers change as the computation proceeds we shall adopt the convention, as in Example 11.3.1, of denoting identifiers by upper case letters and their **current** values by the corresponding lower case letters. Hence it follows that an assertion is meaningless without reference to a specific position within a program or an associated computation.

We now set about assigning predicates to the portions of the flowchart between instructions. Consider the features illustrated in Figure 11.21. As already noted in Chapter 7, these are essentially the only primitive forms that can occur in a flowchart and correspond to the ℓ-nodes, d-nodes and p-nodes of the previous section, however here we are concerned not with the manipulation of such features but with how the predicates (assertions) associated with them must be related. In Figure 11.21, P, Q and R represent assertions.

At the flow join (Figure 11.21(*a*)) since there is no computation R must be a consequence of P and R must also be a consequence of Q. Logically $P \Rightarrow R$ and $Q \Rightarrow R$ and the strongest possible value of R is

$$R \Leftrightarrow P \vee Q$$

Similarly for the conditional control transfer (Figure 11.21(*b*)) $P \Rightarrow Q$ and $P \Rightarrow R$. However, on the two exit arcs we know that either $B = \text{True}$ or $B = \text{False}$. It therefore follows that

$$Q \Leftrightarrow P \wedge B$$
$$R \Leftrightarrow P \wedge (\neg B)$$

Fig. 11.21

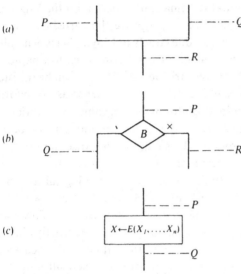

The only way in which (data) values can be changed by a program is by (implicit or explicit) assignments. In Figure 11.21(c) we represent the computation of some expression E from the values of $x_1, \ldots, x_n$ and the assignment of this value to the identifier X. Within P there is information which will be changed or even destroyed by the instruction; turning this round, P is obtained from Q by substituting all (free) occurrences of x in Q by $E(x_1,,,,, x_n)$.

The examples we shall consider will be simple and not involve quantified predicates. Nevertheless situations commonly arise in which quantifiers are used and in such cases the identifiers which are bound to the quantifiers are 'internal' to the predicate and are independent of like identifiers external to the predicate.

For instance $(\forall x : 1 \leqslant x \leqslant n)(f(x) < y)$ describes a relationship between n, f and y. To avoid confusion with any other usage of x it may be convenient to replace x by another variable (name) but such a change can clearly not involve n, f or y without altering the meaning of the predicate.

Examples 11.3.2
The three flowchart segments (Figure 11.22) with predicates appended illustrate the situations alluded to above. In parts (a) and (b) we have applied some logical simplification; explicitly

$$(x > 0) \vee (x < 0) = (x \neq 0)$$

Fig. 11.22

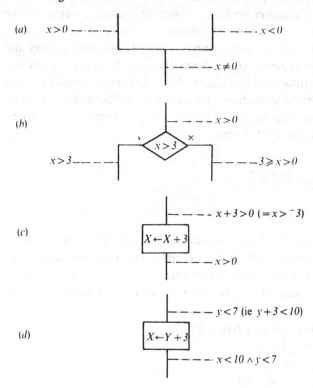

(a) $x>0$ —·—·—   — ·—·· $x<0$

—·—·— $x \neq 0$

(b)   —·— $x>0$

$x>3$ —·—·—   —·—·— $3 \geqslant x > 0$

—·—·- $x+3>0 \; (=x> ^-3)$

(c) $X \leftarrow X + 3$

—·—·— $x>0$

—·—·— $y<7 \; (\text{ie } y+3<10)$

(d) $X \leftarrow Y + 3$

—·—·- $x<10 \wedge y<7$

and

$$(x>0) \wedge (x>3) = (x>3)$$

by absorption since $(x>3) \Rightarrow (x>0)$.

In part (c) the entire predicate is changed by virtue of X occurring on both sides of the assignment whereas part (d) loses a factor when arguing **backwards** through the program. This is reasonable since any previous value of X is lost and hence meaningless and irrelevant in the logical argument.

All that is required now is to assemble sections of flowchart into full programs. We have already dealt with the flow joins and branches, all we need is sequencing. This is easily done; if P and Q are predicates before and after instruction I_1 and when Q is valid before I_2 then R is True after it, we trivially have the situation in Figure 11.23. In principle this is alright and there is no blatantly obvious reason why we could not work back from the end of a program, generating all intermediate assertions until we reach the start. (We work backwards because of the way that assertions filter through assignments, and remember we are analysing an existing program rather than synthesising a new one so the direction is unimportant.) However, matters get rather tedious when unscrambling loops, and anyway the flowchart notation is rather cumbersome. We can, however, restrict our considerations to structured flowcharts which result from transformations such as that described in Section 11.2. Moreover we need only have one kind of loop (again we arbitrarily choose to use pre-check loops). Thus we have the now familiar PDL forms:

$$I_1; I_2,$$

if B then I_1 else I_2 fi

and

while B do I od

Now, following principles first enunciated by Hoare in 1969 [18] but using a notation synonymous with Pascal we can extend PDL with assertions. Explicitly, using $\{P\}I\{Q\}$ to denote that when the antecedent of instruction I is P then the consequent is Q, the rules associating the assertions to the basic forms are:

(a) if $\{P\}I_1\{Q\}$ and $\{Q\}I_2\{R\}$
   then $\{P\}I_1; I_2\{R\}$

(b) if $\{P \wedge B\}I_1\{Q\}$
   and $\{P \wedge \neg B\}I_2\{Q\}$
   then $\{P\}$ if B then I_1 else I_2 fi $\{Q\}$

(c) if $\{P \wedge B\}I\{P\}$
   then $\{P\}$ while B do I od $\{P \wedge \neg B\}$

Fig. 11.23

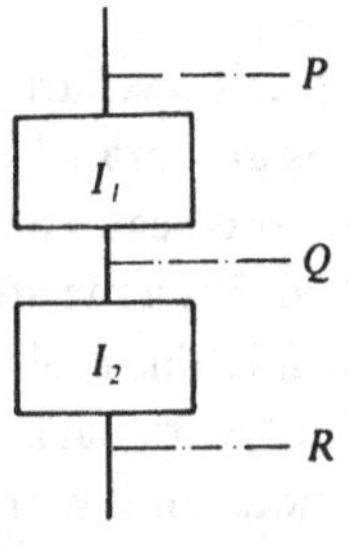

Example 11.3.3

Suppose we are given two compound instructions I_1 and I_2 with associated predicates

$$\{x=\alpha, y=\beta, z=\gamma\}I_1\{x=4-\alpha, y=\alpha*\beta, z=\beta+\gamma\}$$

and

$$\{x=\alpha, y=\beta, z=\gamma\}I_2\{x=\alpha, y=\beta-2, z=\gamma+2*\beta\}$$

and we are asked to find P, such that

$$\{P\}I_1; I_2\{x=b, z=a, y>0\}$$

Firstly we rewrite the assertions for I_2 so as to simplify the consequent. Let it be of the form

$$\{x=\rho, y=\sigma, z=\tau\}$$

So

$$\rho=\alpha, \ \sigma=\beta-2 \ \text{and} \ \tau=\gamma+2*\beta$$

and therefore $\alpha=\rho$, $\beta=\sigma+2$ and $\gamma=\tau-2*(\sigma+2)$ giving

$$\{x=\rho, y=\sigma+2, z=\tau-2*(\sigma+2)\}I_2\{x=\rho, y=\sigma, z=\tau\}$$

Next we equate the antecedent of I_2 with the consequent of I_1, since in the combination $I_1; I_2$ there is no intervening computation, to give:

$$\rho=4-\alpha, \sigma+2=\alpha*\beta \ \text{and} \ \tau-2*(\sigma+2)=\beta+\gamma$$

from which we can obtain relationships for the values of x, y and z before I_1 and after I_2. Thus from the semantic properties of I_1 and I_2 we have:

$$\left.\begin{cases} x=4-\rho, \\ x*y=\sigma+2, \\ y+z=\tau-2*(\sigma+2) \end{cases}\right\} I_1; I_2\{x=\rho, y=\sigma, z=\tau\}$$

Notice that we may not be able to express the resulting antecedent explicitly, for if $\rho=4$ then $x=0$ and the product $x*y$ yields 0 which is independent of y so no initial value of y can be found.

Referring to the required consequent of $I_1; I_2$, we know that $\rho=b, \tau=a$ and $\sigma>0$ and so

$$P=(x=4-b, y*(4-b)>2, 2*x*y=a-y-z) \qquad \square$$

Example 11.3.4

Similar algebraic reorganisation within pairs of assertions surrounding an instruction is required when dealing with alternation. From the general form we are usually forced into a conditional consequent with two parts, one for each side of the flowchart. For suppose that

$$\{P \wedge B\}I_1\{Q_1\}$$

and

$$\{P \wedge \neg B\}I_2\{Q_2\},$$

then we can achieve

$$\{P\} \text{ if } B \text{ then } I_1 \text{ else } I_2 \text{ fi } \{Q\}$$

where Q is of the form

$$((B \text{ was True}) \wedge Q_1) \vee ((B \text{ was False}) \wedge Q_2)$$

and the validity of B at the beginning of the construct is 'remembered' by using a ghost variable (see note (i) after Example 11.3.5).

Of course the alternation should have been used for some sensible programming objective and hence the conditional nature of the assertion Q will often coincide with a conditional definition or specification. Consider the familiar case depicted in Figure 11.24.

Here

$$Q = ((x < 0) \wedge (y = -a) \wedge (x = a)) \vee ((x \geqslant 0) \wedge (y = a) \wedge (x = a))$$

$$\equiv (x = a) \wedge (((a < 0) \wedge (y = -a)) \vee ((a \geqslant 0) \wedge (y = a)))$$

$$\equiv (x = a) \wedge (y = (\text{if } a < 0 \text{ then } -a \text{ else } a))$$

$$\equiv (x = a) \wedge (y = |a|) \qquad \qquad \Box$$

Fig. 11.24

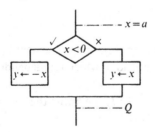

Example 11.3.5
Using the primitive functions $s: x \mapsto x + 1$ and $p: x \mapsto x - 1$, we can derive the following segment of flowchart program (in Figure 11.25) to compute the sum of two non-negative integers.

The sum of the values of x and y, held in X and Y and both assumed non-negative, is given by the final value assigned to B. The predicates P_0 to P_5

Fig. 11.25

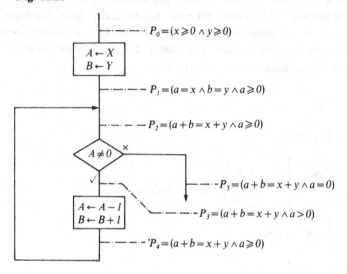

have been appended to distinct arcs of the flowchart and can easily be seen to justify the claim that the program does give the desired answer. P_0 reflects the assumptions made about the data. P_1 follows naturally from P_0 as do P_3 and P_5 from P_2, P_4 from P_3 and P_2 from P_4. The validity of the program is then immediate from P_5 since $P_5 \Rightarrow (b = x + y)$.

A little more effort is required when deriving the predicates in the loop: P_2, P_3 and P_4. These are all called *loop invariants*. We shall primarily be concerned with the one immediately before the test; in this case P_2. However, notice that since

$$(P_2 \wedge (a \neq 0)) \Rightarrow P_3,$$
$$\{P_3\}A \leftarrow A - 1; B \leftarrow B + 1\{P_4\}$$

and

$$P_4 \Rightarrow P_2$$

all three predicates are interrelated and hence when one has been found the rest follow easily. (Notice that when using structured programming constructs the *logic* never gets more complicated than this.)

One way to establish the loop invariant is as follows: break the flowchart at the point where the flow joins a previously travelled path (this is called a *cutpoint*) and open out to form a linear sequence of repeated instructions. This will in general be an infinite process, but we only need to consider the equivalent of a 'few' iterations of the loop (see Figure 11.26). We then write down the would-be loop invariant on the nth iteration in terms of n (this is done by inspection) n is then removed, algebraically, from this expression and the resultant predicate is a loop invariant. Let us examine how this works in the example. Denoting the value of P_m on the nth iteration by P_m^n we have the predicates as in Figure 11.26.

Fig. 11.26

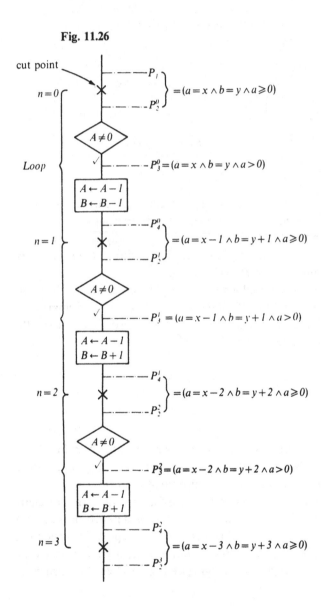

From this it is evident that

$$P_2^n \equiv (a = x - n \wedge b = y + n \wedge a \geqslant 0)$$
$$\equiv (x - a = n = b - y \wedge a \geqslant 0)$$

Eliminating the loop counter, n, we have

$$P_2 \equiv (x - a = b - y \wedge a \geqslant 0)$$
$$\equiv (x + y = a + b \wedge a \geqslant 0)$$

The other predicates then follow immediately. □

This technique is conceptually straightforward and provided we process the program from the inside (analysing the most deeply nested loops first) will, usually, suffice. However there are practical difficulties.

(i) Since the predicates assert relationships valid at a specific point in the program there is no explicit mechanism by which we can refer back to earlier values associated with the identifiers. Using post-conditions of two variables, as in the program synthesis methods described earlier, circumvents this problem; using assertions we do not automatically have such a facility. To achieve the same effect we introduce 'ghost' variables to remember important data values so they can be tested later even though they are no longer associated with any program identifier. In Example 11.3.5 P_1 included $a = x$ and $b = y$, i.e. $x =$ initial value of A and $y =$ initial value of B. However the similar programs for the computation of $X \leftarrow X + Y$, over non-negative integers, given by the schemes

> while $Y \neq 0$ do $X \leftarrow X + 1$; $Y \leftarrow Y - 1$ od

or

> $A \leftarrow Y$;
> while $A \neq 0$ do $X \leftarrow X + 1$; $A \leftarrow A - 1$ od

do not have explicit identifiers which retain the initial value of X and hence cannot be analysed without the introduction of 'ghosts'. This observation leads directly to the next point:

(ii) We do not always know what factors are relevant in the predicates. It is not feasible to include everything so some choice has to be made; for example we could have taken

$$P_1 = (a = x \wedge b = y \wedge a \geqslant 0 \wedge b \geqslant 0)$$

but we knew that the last fact was irrelevant because of the way in which the program was constructed. Carrying unnecessary terms increases the manipulation required; discarding relevant terms would prevent the deduction of sufficiently strong logical conclusions about the program (compare with the proof of synthesised programs in Chapter 7).

(iii) The general form of the invariant as a function of n may not be clear.

(iv) The algebraic elimination of the loop counter may be difficult (or even impossible – the program may be wrong, it may not do **anything**).

(v) When dealing with real numbers in a program the effects of rounding errors need to be taken into account. For example it does not make sense to compare two real numbers for equality; instead of testing for $a = b$, one ought to ask whether $|a - b|$ is less than some tolerance value.

(vi) Apart from the effects related to the accuracy to which reals are stored within the computer used, other *machine dependent* factors may be called into play – such as *overflow* of real or integer values.

(vii) The techniques set out above cannot properly be said to relate to the *correctness* of programs. All they guarantee is that, provided the program reaches proper termination (i.e. execution is curtailed by a *STOP* instruction in the user's program and arithmetic and other computational errors cause the program to be halted by 'the system'), the final state satisfies the predicate associated with the *STOP*. It does **not** guarantee that the program will ever stop. Hence what we have described should more properly be called *partial correctness*. The proof of termination of a program involves the investigation of finite strictly ordered sequences of the type associated with the termination count *term* in Chapter 7. Referring once more to Example 11.3.5, it is clear that the value of A decreases in integer steps and is zero exactly when exit from the loop occurs. Recall that we need a *well-ordering* which is, in effect, a non-negative integer quantity that indicates an upper bound on the number of loop iterations still to be performed (this may not be an integer program variable but an implicit quantity such as the length of a list or string, or the height of a tree); it must decrease strictly though not necessarily uniformly or in steps of one, and it must attain the value zero indicative of loop exit. To emphasise the distinction between *total* and *partial* correctness you are invited to consider Exercise 11.3.1 and study the similarities and discrepancies between the program given there and that given in Example 11.3.5.

(For a fuller treatment of program analysis and its relationship to formal descriptions of programming language semantics, the reader is referred to the texts by Manna [23] and de Bakker [4].)

We also note that assertions can be used directly within the program itself. Certain dialects of Pascal allow predicates to be written as comments in the form of Boolean expressions; these are re-evaluated every time the program passes through the relevant code segment and cause the program to halt if and when the value 'False' is returned. In other languages the user will have to insert code of the form

if not (*P*) then error(*n*) fi

causing entry to a routine which will then indicate the occurrence of a logical error detected by the predicate *P* at position *n*. When predicates are used in this way ghost variables must be declared and maintained (by explicit assignment statements) in order that the Boolean expressions should be valid and give the appropriate values.

Finally, with particular regard to the preceeding list of potential difficulties that might be encountered when analysing a program, notice that when no guidance is available from external sources the search for suitably strong assertions can be a very long process. This only goes to reinforce the premise that synthesis of a program from a specification is in general significantly easier than analysing a (correct) program from scratch.

Exercises 11.3

1. Analyse the flowchart program corresponding to the following PDL segment

$$A, B : \mathbb{P}$$

$$\vdots$$

$$\vdots$$

while $A \neq 0$

do $A \leftarrow A + 1$

   $B \leftarrow B - 1$

od

Under the presumption that this program segment is intended to realise the same specification as the program given in Example 11.3.5, show that both are partially correct. Why is **this** version not totally correct?

2. Similarly, analyse the following PDL segment.

$$W, X, Y, Z : \mathbb{P}$$

$$\vdots$$

$$\vdots$$

$$Y \leftarrow 0$$

while $X \neq 0$

```
do X ← X − 1
   W ← Z
   while W ≠ 0
   do W ← W − 1
      Y ← Y + 1
   od
od
```

(Hint: Analyse the inner loop first, presuming that the variables W and Y have values α and β on entry to that loop.)

3. How would the analysis of the code in Question 2 be effected if the type declaration were changed to $W, X, Y, Z : \mathbb{N}$?

4. Analyse the following PDL segment. (Note, as with the other questions, the identifiers used have been chosen intentionally so as not to be helpful.)

$$X, Y : \mathbb{P}$$
$$\vdots$$
$$\vdots$$

```
X ← 0
while Y ≠ 0
do X ← X + Y
   Y ← Y − 1
od
```

5. Although we have not used quantifiers within our examples of program analysis, the reader should be aware of cases when their use greatly simplifies description of computing processes.

Try your hand at analysing this familiar sorting process.

$$I, J, N, M : 0 .. 10$$
$$Y : \mathbb{N}$$
$$X : \mathbb{N}^{10}$$
$$\vdots$$
$$\vdots$$

```
if N ≠ 0 ∧ N ≠ 1
then M ← N − 1
     while M ≠ 1
```

```
do    I ← 1
      J ← 2
      repeat if X[I] > X[J]
            then Y ← X[I]
                  X[I] ← X[J]
                  X[J] ← Y
            fi
            I ← J
            J ← J + 1

      until J > M
            M ← M - 1
      od
fi
```

(Hint: Begin the formal analysis – from the inside, working out – and then use the universal quantifier 'informally' to describe what is happening. You should reach a conclusion of the form $(\forall i \in 1 .. N - 1)(x_i \leqslant x_{i+1})$.)

12
A small case study – topological sorting

Topological sorting is a classical example in the study of data structures and is often included within introductory programming courses in Computer Science at tertiary level. We shall use the problem to illustrate how a well-defined (and hence **mathematical** but not necessarily **numerical**) problem can yield a specification which, after appropriate transformation, gives rise to non-recursive PDL code and subsequently to a procedural program in a high-level language.

Although programs in procedural language are in effect algorithms, recall that the aim of this text is not the development of algorithms **per se**; and hence the algorithm which emerges at the end of the chapter is a consequence of the way in which we transform the problem specification. Other transformations would imply different algorithms. No value judgements are offered as to the quality of the resultant algorithm but it must be said that many years of programming experience will have had some effect on the way that the specification has been interpreted and subsequently transformed.

12.1   Problem formulation

In mathematical terminology the problem may be stated as: 'To find a linear ordering which is consistent with a given (necessarily acyclic) binary relation on a finite set'. Now whilst this may be fine for a (modern) Mathematician and should also be intelligible to any Computer Scientist who has attended a discrete mathematics course as part of his studies, it does not immediately suggest how we might formulate a proper specification of the process in terms of the fundamental entities at our disposal. A more descriptive approach, with the assistance of a few pictures, is helpful.

As seen in Section 3.4, a finite set can be represented by points and the relation by arrows joining pairs of points that are related (see Figure 12.1). Topological sorting of this system then requires us to put the points in a straight line in such a way that the corresponding arrows in the linear

version all point the same way (from left to right, say). Generally, the result
of this process is not unique. Two acceptable ways of ordering the system in
Figure 12.1 are shown in Figures 12.2(a) and 12.2(b).

Now all that is required as a result of a topological sort is the ordered list
of points (more properly called nodes), the arrows are not part of the
answer. However, remembering where the arrows should be gives us exactly
the characteristics of the resultant list in terms of the arrows in the original
system.

Moreover, since the arrows all point in the same direction we can have no
cycles. A cycle is a sequence of linked arrows which start at a node and
eventually return to the same node, i.e.

$$a_1 \rightarrow a_2 \rightarrow \dots a_{n-1} \rightarrow a_n \rightarrow a_1$$

Fig. 12.1

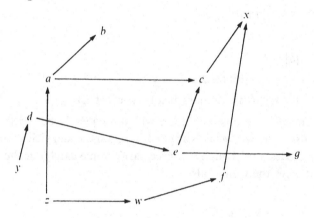

Fig. 12.2

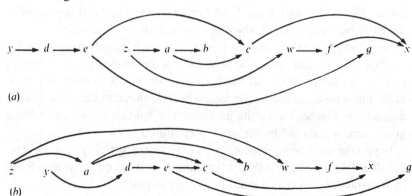

(a)

(b)

The kind of system we have here is called a *directed graph* or *digraph* (as introduced in Chapter 3) and it is a necessary and sufficient condition for a digraph to be topologically sortable that it be *acyclic*, that it has no cycles. We shall return to this condition later but let us have an initial attempt at the specification.

$Node ::$ a finite set (a subset $1 .. n$ of $\mathbb{N}$?)

$Arrow ::$ $Node \times Node$

$Digraph ::$ $\mathscr{P}(Node) \times \mathscr{P}(Arrow)$

$TSORT1$

states:

type: $Digraph \to Node*$

pre--$TSORT1(,D) \triangleq (D$ acyclic?$)$

post-$TSORT1(,D,,L) \triangleq$

$\qquad D = \langle N,A \rangle$

$\qquad \wedge |L| = |N|$

$\qquad \wedge N = \{x : x\ IS\_IN\ L\}$

$\qquad \wedge (\forall \langle x,y \rangle \in A)(`x$ comes_before $y$ in_list $L`)$

The last phrase of the post-condition will subsequently be written as a function *in_list_order* which takes arguments x, y and L and yields the value True if x precedes y (although not necessarily immediately) in the list L, otherwise it gives the value False.

Formally:

$in\_list\_order(x,y,L) \triangleq$

$\qquad (\exists L_x, L_y \in Node*)(x\ IS\_IN\ L_x \wedge y\ IS\_IN\ L_y \wedge L = L_x \| L_y)$

(Note: IS_IN, as used here, is of type $Element \times List \to \mathbb{B}$ and cannot therefore be replaced by $\in$ which is of type $Element \times Set \to \mathbb{B}$.)

So, if the sort works, L has no repeats and contains only items from the original node set and, as argued above, any arrow in the digraph coincides with the ordering in L. But (here is the crunch) the existence of an L satisfying these conditions is precisely what is required to ascertain that the diagraph is acyclic. Hence the pre-condition holds if the post-condition guaranteed – it should be the other way round.

In practice we determine whether D can be sorted by trying to sort it, if we can then OK, if we cannot then it is cyclic. No, it is not quite a case of 'back to the drawing board', we modify the type to give:

TSORT2

States:

type: $Digraph \rightarrow \mathbb{B} \times Node*$

pre--$TSORT2(,D) \triangleq$ 'D is well-formed'

post-$TSORT2(,D,,\langle sortable,L \rangle) \triangleq$

$\quad D = \langle N,A \rangle$

$\quad \wedge Lset = \{\ell : |\ell| = |N|$

$\qquad\qquad \wedge N = \{x : x \; IS\_IN \; \ell\}$

$\qquad\qquad \wedge (\forall \langle x,y \rangle \in A)(in\_list\_order(x,y,\ell))\}$

$\quad \wedge \quad$ if $\quad Lset = \varnothing$

$\qquad\quad$ then $\quad L = \langle \rangle$

$\qquad\qquad \wedge \quad \neg sortable$

$\qquad\quad$ else $\quad L \in Lset$

$\qquad\qquad \wedge \quad sortable$

Therefore,

$\qquad D$ is **not** *sortable* and the empty list is returned.

or

$\qquad D$ **is** *sortable* and the sorted version is L

The words 'well-formed' in the pre-condition are intended to guarantee that for any Digraph D, the nodes mentioned in the arrow set A actually appear in the node set N, i.e.

$\qquad D = \langle N,A \rangle \wedge A \subseteq N \times N$

The precise form of the condition will change as we transform the data structure but the sense will be the same.

So far the recursion is implicit within the quantifier, $\forall \langle x,y \rangle \in A$. We need to bring it out into the open. To do this we take the lead from the clause $L = L_x \parallel L_y$ in the function *in_list_order* and invoke a similar split in D. Since D is a more complex structure this split should be more difficult. Indeed there is more to write down because D is a composite object but it is not too bad. We give the transformed specification and discuss its features afterwards. Only the post-condition is of interest.

$\qquad$ post-$TSORT3(,D,,\langle sortable,L \rangle) \triangleq$

$\qquad\quad D = \langle N,A \rangle$

$\qquad\quad \wedge$ if $\quad N = \varnothing$

$\qquad\quad$ then $\quad L = \langle \rangle \wedge sortable$

$$\text{else} \quad \text{if} \quad |N| = 1$$
$$\text{then} \quad N = \{x\}$$
$$\wedge L = \langle x \rangle$$
$$\wedge \ sortable$$
$$\text{else} \quad Lset = \{\ell : \ell = L_1 \| L_2$$
$$\wedge \langle True, L_1 \rangle = TSORT3(D_1)$$
$$\wedge \langle True, L_2 \rangle = TSORT3(D_2)$$
$$\wedge D_1 = \langle N_1, A_1 \rangle$$
$$\wedge D_2 = \langle N_2, A_2 \rangle$$
$$\wedge N = N_1 \cup N_2$$
$$\wedge \quad N_1 \cap N_2 = \emptyset$$
$$\wedge A_1 \subseteq A$$
$$\wedge A_2 \subseteq A$$
$$\wedge (\forall \langle x, y \rangle \in A)(\quad \langle x, y \rangle \in A_1$$
$$\vee \langle x, y \rangle \in A_2$$
$$\vee (x \in N_1 \wedge y \in N_2))\}$$
$$\wedge \text{if} \quad Lset = \emptyset$$
$$\text{then} \quad L = \langle \rangle$$
$$\wedge \neg \ sortable$$
$$\text{else} \quad L \in Lset$$
$$\wedge \ sortable$$

Notice that the clause adopted if $Lset = \emptyset$ is equivalent to

$$L = \langle \rangle \wedge sortable = \text{False}$$

This may also be written as

$$\langle sortable, L \rangle = \langle \text{False}, \langle \rangle \rangle$$

(n-tuples are equal if they are the same length and corresponding components are equal), a form that will be useful later.

To see how this works refer to Figure 12.3. Clearly D is indivisible if it contains no nodes or just a single node. Otherwise, if it is not cyclic, it can be split into two parts D_1 and D_2 which give rise to sorted lists L_1 and L_2 respectively. D_1 and D_2 comprise sets of nodes and arrows. All nodes in N must be contained in exactly one of the constituent sets N_1 and N_2 and nothing must be omitted. On the other hand, arrows in D must fall entirely within D_1 or entirely within D_2 or can be legally discarded because they link

Fig. 12.3

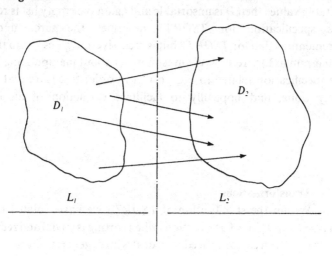

L_1 L_2

Fig. 12.4

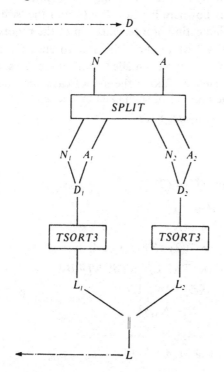

a node in D_1 to a node in D_2 (in that order). If these conditions cannot be met by suitable values then D is unsortable and again the empty list is returned.

The specification for *TSORT3* describes the same underlying requirements as that for *TSORT2* but is recursive and gives rise to the data-flow diagram in Figure 12.4. We must now set about manipulating the part of the specification related to Figure 12.4 in order to ensure that work is actually done, and hopefully to facilitate extraction of an iterative realisation.

12.2   Transformations

Within the specification of *TSORT3* we have isolated the cases when $N = \emptyset$ and $|N| = 1$ as situations when sorting is trivial and recursion is not invoked. Such cases are needed to deal with degenerate digraphs (i.e. the very easy problems – often forgotten in the rush to deal with the more complex examples) and to provide an escape clause from the recursion. We have not been so particular with the central part of the specification, namely the splitting of D into D_1 and D_2. Notice that taking $N_1 = \emptyset$ and $N_2 = N$ (etc.) is always valid but gets us nowhere because $D = D_2$ and the 'size' of the problem never decreases indicating non-termination of the process.

Since we know that $|N| \geqslant 2$ we ought to be able to ensure that both recursive sub-problems do become smaller and hence a successful conclusion is eventually reached. Taking the $|N| = 1$ case **into** one of the recursive calls, reduces the number of such calls to one, and we have:

$$\text{post-}TSORT4(,D,,\langle sortable,L \rangle) \triangleq$$

$$D = \langle N,A \rangle$$

$$\wedge \text{ if } \quad |N| = 0$$

$$\text{then } \quad \langle sortable,L \rangle = \langle \text{True},\langle \rangle \rangle$$

$$\text{else } \quad Lset = \{ \ell : \ell = \langle x \rangle \| L_2$$

$$\wedge x \in N$$

$$\wedge \neg(\exists y \in N)(\langle y,x \rangle \in A)$$

$$\wedge \langle \text{True},L_2 \rangle = TSORT4(D_2)$$

$$\wedge D_2 = \langle N_2,A_2 \rangle$$

$$\wedge N_2 = N \backslash \{x\}$$

$$\wedge A_2 = A \backslash \{\langle x,z \rangle : z \in N_2\}\}$$

$$\wedge \text{ if } \quad Lset = \emptyset$$

$$\text{then} \quad \langle sortable,L\rangle = \langle \text{False},\langle\,\rangle\rangle$$
$$\text{else} \quad L\in Lset$$
$$\wedge\, sortable$$

Notice here that we have taken the liberty of changing the quantifier. We have used the identity

$$\neg(\exists y\in N)(\langle y,x\rangle\in A)\Leftrightarrow(\forall y\in N)(\langle y,x\rangle\notin A)$$

to emphasise the negation. (Logically these expressions are, of course, equivalent.)

The data-flow diagram for the business part of the specification is now as in Figure 12.5. At this stage it would seem sensible to rename *SPLIT* as *REDUCE* since, by virtue of removing x, we do reduce the size of the problem to be solved by the next recursive call of *TSORT4*.

Fig. 12.5

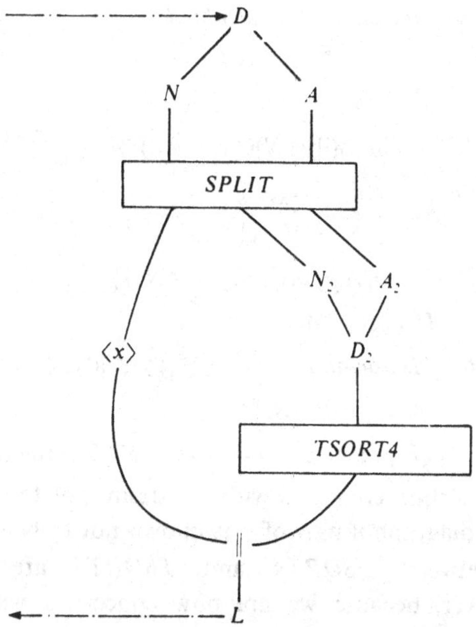

We now set about attempting to construct an iterative procedural realisation which performs the sort.

12.3 Towards PDL

Since the list concatenation operator, $\|$, is associative we could attempt to use the *associative recursion* technique (detailed as transformation T5 in appendix D) to deliver an iterative form. However, T5 uses parallel assignments and a simpler solution to the current problem is possible.

First we alter the functionality of *TSORTn* to act on states. This enables us to merge recursion into the concatenation.

TSORT5

States: $Digraph \times \mathbb{B} \times Node^*$

type: $\rightarrow$

pre--$TSORT5(\langle D,sortable,L \rangle,) \triangleq sortable = True$

$\qquad\qquad\qquad\qquad\qquad \wedge$ 'D is well-formed'

post-$TSORT5(\langle D,sortable,L \rangle,,\langle D',sortable',L' \rangle,) \triangleq$

$\quad D = \langle N,A \rangle$

$\wedge$ if $\quad N = \varnothing$ (i.e. $|N| = 0$)

$\quad$ then $\quad \langle D',sortable',L' \rangle = \langle D,sortable,L \rangle$

$\quad$ else $\quad D\_Lset = \{(d,\ell): \ell = L \| \langle x \rangle$

$\qquad\qquad\qquad\qquad \wedge x \in N$

$\qquad\qquad\qquad\qquad \wedge \neg(\exists y \in N)(\langle y,x \rangle \in A)$

$\qquad\qquad\qquad\qquad \wedge d = \langle N_x,A_x \rangle$

$\qquad\qquad\qquad\qquad \wedge N_x = N \backslash \{x\}$

$\qquad\qquad\qquad\qquad \wedge A_x = A \backslash \{\langle x,z \rangle : z \in N_x\}\}$

$\quad \wedge$ if $\quad D\_Lset = \varnothing$

$\qquad$ then $\quad \langle D',sortable',L' \rangle = \langle \langle \varnothing,\varnothing \rangle,False,\langle \rangle \rangle$

$\qquad$ else $\quad \langle D_1,L_1 \rangle \in D\_Lset$

$\qquad\qquad\qquad \wedge \langle D',sortable',L' \rangle = TSORT5(\langle D_1,True,L_1 \rangle)$

Notice that the pre-condition coincides with the desire not to continue attempting to sort the diagraph if part of it is known not to be sortable.

The differences between *TSORT4* and *TSORT5* are mostly straightforward, however, because we are now concerned with state changes, we must take note of the previous state. In practical terms this means that the $\ell = \langle x \rangle \| L_2$ clause of post-*TSORT4* relates the resultant list, ℓ, to the list still to be produced, L_2; whereas in post-*TSORT5*, $\ell = L \| \langle x \rangle$ says that the list so far, L, is updated to ℓ which is then passed on to the next call of *TSORT5*. All this is allowed because of the associativity of concatenation (and, equivalently, because of the acyclic nature of D when it is sortable). One way to visualise the processing achieved by *TSORT5* is as the transference of nodes from N to L if allowed by A. (See Figure 12.6.)

Notice now that, in post-*TSORT5*, the state obtained from the recursive call is exactly the final state of the post-condition and hence we have tail recursion. This can be seen more easily from the control diagram in Figure 12.7 where *REDUCE* creates L_l and D_l from L and D. (Remember that clauses such as $D = \langle N, A \rangle$ do not indicate any computation and therefore do not occur in the flowchart.)

The flowchart in Figure 12.7 unwinds to

> while *can_make_progress* do *REDUCE* od;

> if *abnormal_termination* then *indicate_failure* fi

but how does it relate to the original requirement for a routine of functionality $Digraph \rightarrow \mathbb{B} \times Node^*$? The answer is easy, we merely add an

Fig. 12.6

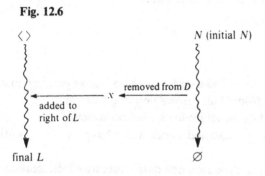

Fig. 12.7

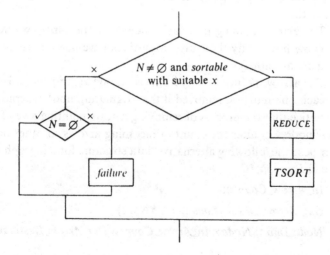

extra level to the specification, to include the appropriate initialisation.

 TSORT

 States:

 type: *Digraph* → $\mathbb{B}$ × *Node**

 pre--*TSORT*(,D) ≜ True

 post-*TSORT*(,D,,⟨*sortable*,L⟩) ≜

$$⟨D',sortable,L⟩ = TSORT5(⟨D,\text{True},⟨\,⟩⟩)$$

12.4 Data structure considerations

 Having made headway with the control structure of the sort we must consider how data is to be held so as to facilitate the required manipulation.

 The key clauses in the specification are

$$\neg(\exists y \in N)(⟨y,x⟩ \in A)$$

and

$$A \setminus \{⟨x,z⟩ : z \in N_x\}$$

In graphical terms we must find a node x with no arrows pointing to it, and we must then delete from A all arrows pointing from x.

 We would like a data structure for a digraph which

  (a) makes it easy for us to find a node which has no arrows pointing to it and

  (b) makes it easy to produce a new data structure which represents the same digraph as before but with the chosen node (and any arrows pointing away from it) removed.

We deduce that:

  (a) The arrows coming into each node are important – we need to know how many there are (in particular we need to know when there are none).

  (b) The arrows pointing away from each node are important because each one must be removed if the originating node is removed.

We also notice that the process of removing arrows pointing away from a particular node will alter the count of incoming arrows to other nodes.

 We propose the following alternative data structure for a digraph which we will call *Digraph_IO*.

   In_Arrow_Count :: $\mathbb{P}$

   Out_Arrow_Destinations :: $\mathscr{P}(Node)$

   Node_Info :: *Node* × *In_Arrow_Count* × *Out_Arrow_Destinations*

Digraph_IO ::   𝒫(Node_Info)

Using this data structure we can represent the digraph in Figure 12.8 by

$$\{\langle A,0,\{B,C\}\rangle,$$
$$\langle B,1,\{C,D\}\rangle,$$
$$\langle C,2,\{D\}\rangle,$$
$$\langle D,2,\varnothing\rangle\}$$

Fig. 12.8

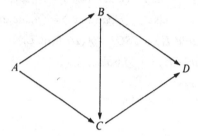

Rewriting *TSORT5* with the new data structure we obtain *TSORT6* as follows

In_Arrow_Count ::   ℙ

Out_Arrow_Destinations ::   𝒫(Node)

Node_Info :: Node × In_Arrow_Count × Out_Arrow_Destinations

Digraph_IO :: 𝒫(Node_Info)

TSORT6

states: Digraph_IO × 𝔹 × Node*

type:

pre--TSORT6(⟨D,sortable,L⟩,) ≜

                    sortable = True ∧ 'D is well-formed'

post-TSORT6(⟨D,sortable,L⟩,,⟨D',sortable',L'⟩,) ≜

      if   D = ∅

      then   ⟨D',sortable',L'⟩ = ⟨D,sortable,L⟩

else $Start\_Nodes = \{n: \langle n,iac,oad \rangle \in D \land iac = 0\}$

$\land$ if $Start\_Nodes \neq \varnothing$

then $n \in Start\_Nodes$

$\land \langle n,0,oad \rangle \in D$

$\land L_1 = L \| \langle n \rangle$

$\land D_1 = \{\langle n',iac',oad' \rangle : \langle n_1,iac_1,oad_1 \rangle \in D$

$\land n_1 \neq n$

$\land$ if $n_1 \in oad$

then $\langle n',iac',oad' \rangle = \langle n_1,iac_1 - 1,oad_1 \rangle$

else $\langle n',iac',oad' \rangle = \langle n_1,iac_1,oad_1 \rangle\}$

$\land \langle D',sortable',L' \rangle = TSORT6(\langle D_1,\text{True},L_1 \rangle)$

else $\langle D',sortable',L' \rangle = \langle \varnothing,\text{False},\langle \rangle \rangle$

This may be interpreted as follows:
If the sort is to proceed, there will be an element of D

$\langle n,iac,oad \rangle$

with the *iac* field equal to zero.

$iac = 0$

The node involved, n, is added to the end of the list of sorted nodes

$L \| \langle n \rangle$

and the reduced digraph (D_1) is composed of all the members of the existing digraph (D) *except the one containing* n

$n_1 \neq n$

and the *iac*'s which included an arrow from n are reduced by *1*

if $... \in oad$

then $...\langle ...,... - 1,... \rangle$

else $...\langle ...,...,... \rangle$

In order to help even more with finding a node with $iac = 0$, we introduce a list of all such nodes (*Start_Nodes*) into the data structure. The information that this gives is 'redundant' in the sense that it could be deduced from the *Node_Info* set. We justify this by comparing the work of 'rediscovering' the information when required with the cost of storing it in several different forms. It any case even the *Node_Info* form of the digraph is redundant – the *in_counts* could be deduced from the *oad* sets!

The new data structure and its effect on the specification are shown as *TSORT7* below.

$In\_Arrow\_Count ::$ $\qquad \mathbb{P}$

$Out\_Arrow\_Destinations ::$ $\quad \mathscr{P}(Node)$

$Node\_Info :: Node \times In\_Arrow\_Count \times Out\_Arrow\_Destinations$

$Digraph\_IO :: \mathscr{P}(Node\_Info)$

$Start\_Nodes :: \mathscr{P}(Node)$

$Digraph\_IOSN :: Digraph\_IO \times Start\_Nodes$

TSORT7

states: $Digraph\_IOSN \times \mathbb{B} \times Node*$

type:

pre--$TSORT7(\langle DIOSN,sortable,L \rangle,) \triangleq$

$sortable \wedge$ '$DIOSN$ is well-formed'

post-$TSORT7(\langle DIOSN,sortable,L \rangle,,\langle DIOSN',sortable',L' \rangle,) \triangleq$

$\qquad DIOSN = \langle D,SN \rangle$

$\wedge$ if $\quad D = \varnothing$

then $\quad \langle DIOSN',sortable',L' \rangle = \langle DIOSN,sortable,L \rangle$

else if $\quad \neg(SN = \varnothing)$

$\qquad$ then $\quad n \in SN$

$\qquad\qquad \wedge \langle n,iac,oad \rangle \in D$

$\qquad\qquad \wedge L_1 = L \parallel \langle n \rangle$

$\qquad\qquad \wedge D_1 = \{\langle n',iac',oad' \rangle : \langle n_1,iac_1,oad_1 \rangle \in D$

$\qquad\qquad\qquad \wedge n_1 \neq n$

$\qquad\qquad\qquad \wedge$ if $\quad n_1 \in oad$

$\qquad\qquad\qquad\quad$ then $\quad \langle n',iac',oad' \rangle = \langle n_1,iac_1 - 1,oad_1 \rangle$

$\qquad\qquad\qquad\quad$ else $\quad \langle n',iac',oad' \rangle = \langle n_1,iac_1,oad_1 \rangle\}$

$\qquad\qquad \wedge SN_1 = \{n : \langle n,0,oad \rangle \in D_1\}$

$\qquad\qquad \wedge \langle DIOSN',sortable',L' \rangle$

$\qquad\qquad\qquad = TSORT7(\langle D_1,SN_1 \rangle,\text{True},L_1 \rangle)$

$\qquad$ else $\quad \langle DIOSN',sortable',L' \rangle = \langle\langle \varnothing,\varnothing \rangle,\text{False},\langle \rangle\rangle$

12.5   PDL

To show the algorithm that we have obtained at its simplest, assume that

Node = *1* .. *nmax*

Then the *in_arrow_counts* can be stored in a list, *d_in*, of length *nmax* and the count for node *n* can be found at

d_in[*n*]

Similarly the *out_arrow_destinations* sets can be stored in a list *d_out* of length *nmax* where each element of *d_out* is itself a list of nodes.

The PDL for *TSORT7* could then be written as

     d_in : ℕ*

     d_out : (*Node**)*

     sn : *Node**

     sortable : 𝔹

     ℓ : *Node**

     function *tsort7*

     type: →

     while   not *q_empty*(*sn*)

     do   *nxt* ← *serve_q*(*sn*)

           ℓ ← ℓ ‖ ⟨*nxt*⟩

           out ← *d_out*[*nxt*]

           d_out[*nxt*] ← ⟨ ⟩

           while *out* ≠ ⟨ ⟩

           do   *n* ← *head*(*out*)

                  out ← *tail*(*out*)

                  d_in[*n*] ← *d_in*[*n*] − *1*

                  if   *d_in*[*n*] = *0*

                  then   *join_q*(*sn*,*n*)

                  fi

           od

     od

     if   *length*(ℓ) = *nmax*

     then   *sortable* ← True

     else   *sortable* ← False

            $\ell \leftarrow \langle \rangle$

     fi

TSORT7 assumes that 'ℓ' has been initialised to the empty list which is part of the responsibility of the routine *TSORT* which was introduced earlier (see also Exercises 12).

Exercises 12

1 Write in PDL the function appropriate to *TSORT* (no number) given earlier in such a way that it can call the function *tsort7*.

2 Using the method of Chapter 9, write the PDL definitions for

         q_empty

         join_q

         serve_q

as used in *tsort7*.

3 Design a suitable form of input for the topological sort program and then specify and code into PDL the operation of reading the data and building the data structure representing the digraph.

4 How would you arrange output from this program? What would be the effect of making *tsort7* output the sorted nodes one-by-one as they are found?

Appendix A
Glossary of symbols

Symbols introduced in Chapter 1

+	add
−	subtract
*	multiply
÷	divide (integer)
/	divide (real)
=	equals
≅	approximately equals
<	less than
≤	less than or equal to
>	greater than
≥	greater than or equal to
□	end of proof

Symbols introduced in Chapter 2

$\{\ldots,\ldots,\ldots\}$	enumerated set
$\{x:x\ldots\}$	set defined by rule
∈	set membership
∉	non-membership of set
∪	set union
∩	set intersection
⊆	subset
⊂	strict subset
\	set difference
∅	empty set
$\langle x_1, x_2, \ldots, x_n \rangle$	n-tuple
$(x_1, x_2, \ldots, x_n)$	n-tuple of parameters
&	logical 'and'
←	assignment
→	operation or function type
$\langle x_1, x_2, \ldots, x_n, \ldots \rangle$	denotation for a list
$\langle \, \rangle$	empty list
‖	list concatenation
two_words	use of 'underline' in multi-word identifiers

Symbols introduced in Chapter 4

$\mathbb{N}$	set of natural numbers
$\mathbb{P}$	set of positive integers, $\mathbb{P} = \mathbb{N} \cup \{0\}$
$\mathbb{Z}$	set of integers
$\mathbb{R}$	set of real numbers
$\mathbb{B}$	set of Boolean values $= \{True, False\}$
$\triangleq$	IS_DEFINED_TO_BE
$\neq$	not equal
$A_1 \times A_2 \times \ldots \times A_n$	Cartesian product
$\wedge$	logical 'and'
$\vee$	logical 'or'
$\neg$	logical 'not'
$X*$	set of all lists with elements from X, i.e. X-List
$\mathscr{P}(X)$	set of all sets with elements from X, i.e. X-Set

Symbols introduced in Chapter 5

$m \,.\,.\, n$	$\{i : i \in \mathbb{Z} \wedge i \geqslant m \wedge i \leqslant n\}$

Symbols introduced in Chapter 7

$\Rightarrow \rightarrow$	implies
$\nRightarrow \nrightarrow$	does not imply
$\equiv \Leftrightarrow \leftrightarrow$	equivalence
$\prec$	'in some sense less than'
$\mapsto$	function definition
$f \circ g$	function composition
$\exists$	'there-exists', the Existential Quantifier
$\forall$	'for-all', the Universal Quantifier
$\sum x_i$	$x_1 + x_2 + \ldots$
$\bigwedge b_i$	$b_1 \wedge b_2 \wedge \ldots$
$\bigvee b_i$	$b_1 \vee b_2 \vee \ldots$
$\mathbb{E}$	$\mathbb{B} \cup \{Undefined\}$ – Three Valued Logic

Symbols introduced in Chapter 10

$\dot{-}$	truncated subtraction

Symbols introduced in Chapter 11

$\prec$	subtree ordering
$\{\ldots\}$	Pascal comment/assertion

Appendix B
Syntax of standard specifications

A specification is a collection of

  data-type specifications

and

  operation specifications.

Data type specifications
Primitive data types
The primitive data types from which all constructed data types are built are

$\mathbb{R}$	or	Real
$\mathbb{Z}$	or	Integer
$\mathbb{B}$	or	Boolean
Char		

The following types are strictly subranges of $\mathbb{Z}$ but are often regarded as primitive:

$\mathbb{N}$	or	NaturalNo
$\mathbb{P}$	or	PosInt

Constructed data types
A new data type T' may be defined in terms of an existing data type T in any of the following ways.

(i) Renaming

$T' :: T$

The data type T' is a renaming of data type T. The values in type T' are the same as those of T.

(ii) Set

$T' :: \mathscr{P}(T)$ or $T' :: T\text{-Set}$

A value in type T' is any set of values taken from T.

(*iii*) *List*

$T' :: T^*$ or $T' :: T\text{-List}$

A value in type T' is any list of values taken from T.

(*iv*) *Cartesian Product*

$T' :: T_1 \times T_2 \times \ldots \times T_n$ or $T :: T_1 - T_2 - \ldots - T_n\text{-Tuple}$

A value in type T' is any n-tuple of values in which the first is taken from T_1, the second is from $T_2, \ldots$ and the nth is taken from T_n.

(*v*) *Union*

$T' :: T_1 \cup T_2 \cup \ldots \cup T_n$

A value in type T' is any value taken from T_1 or T_2 or $\ldots$ or T_n.

(*vi*) *Enumeration*

$T' :: \{v_1, v_2, \ldots, v_n\}$

A value in type T' is any of the **enumerated** values $v_1, v_2, \ldots, v_n$.

(*vii*) *Subrange*

$T' :: v_\ell \ldots v_h$

If $v_\ell \in T$ and $v_h \in T$ and $v_\ell \leqslant v_h$ then $T' = \{v : v \in T \wedge v_\ell \leqslant v \wedge v \leqslant v_h\}$.

A value in type T' is any value from T which lies in the **subrange** from v_ℓ to v_h. This implies that T must be ordered.

Operation specifications

An operation is specified by its name, its state, its type, its pre-condition and its post-condition as follows.

OP

states: S

type: $D \to R$

pre--$OP(s,d) \triangleq$

   $\ldots$ a Boolean expression involving $s,d \ldots$

post-$OP(s,d,s',r) \triangleq$

   $\ldots$ a Boolean expression relating s' and r to s and $d \ldots$

OP is the name of the operation. S, D and R are types.

If the state is empty the operation behaves like a function and the argument s of the pre-condition and the arguments s and s' of the post-condition are omitted as shown below.

OP

states:

type: $D \to R$

pre--$OP(,d) \triangleq$

   $\ldots$ a Boolean expression involving $d \ldots$

post-$OP(,d,,r) \triangleq$

... a Boolean expression relating r to d ...

If the specification of an operation OP depends on another operation $OP2$ then the post-condition of OP will include something like

post-$OP(s,d,s',r) \triangleq$

...

pre--$OP2(s2,d2)$ &

post-$OP2(s2,d2,s2',r2)$ &

...

where $s2$, $d2$ depend on s, d.

Notationally this is very inconvenient and is usually abbreviated to

post-$OP(s,d,s',r) \triangleq$

...

$(s2', r2) = OP2(s2, d2)$ &

...

which is taken to mean that $s2, d2$ satisfy pre-$OP2(s2, d2)$ and that $s2, d2, s2'$, $r2$ satisfy post-$OP2(s2, d2, s2', r2)$. In general s', r will depend on $s, d, s2', r2$.

If in addition $OP2$ is really a function, then $s2$ and $s2'$ are omitted and an obvious additional abbreviation is

post-$OP(s,d,s',r) \triangleq$

...

$r2 = OP2(d2)$

...

The pre-condition and post-condition are Boolean expressions built up from the forms below.

In the forms below, $b1$, $b2$, $b3$ stand for Boolean expressions and $e1$, $e2$ stand for expressions of any matching type.

True	Constant True
False	Constant False
$\neg b1$	NOT $b1$
$b1 \wedge b2$	$b1$ AND $b2$
$b1 \vee b2$	$b1$ OR $b2$
$b1$ & $b2$	& is written in place of $\wedge$ only at the end of a line

if	*b1*	*b1* ∧ *b2*
then	*b2*	∨
else	*b3*	¬*b1* ∧ *b3*

(∀*x*:…)(*p(x)*)	FOR_ALL *x* such that…, *p(x)* is True
(∃*x*)(*p(x)*)	THERE_EXISTS an *x* such that *p(x)* is True
(*b1*)	parentheses to override operator priorities
e1 = *e2*	*e1* IS_EQUAL_TO *e2*
e1 ≠ *e2*	*e1* IS_NOT_EQUAL_TO *e2*
e1 ⇔ *e2*	*e1* IS_EQUIVALENT_TO *e2*
e1 ⇒ *e2*	*e1* IMPLIES *e2*
e1 < *e2*	*e1* IS_LESS_THAN *e2*
e1 ≤ *e2*	*e1* IS_LESS_THAN_OR_EQUAL_TO *e2*
e1 > *e2*	*e1* IS_GREATER_THAN *e2*
e1 ≥ *e2*	*e1* IS_GREATER_THAN_OR_EQUAL_TO *e2*

The expressions *e1*, *e2* above may be **arithmetic** expressions involving

$$+ \quad - \quad * \quad \div \quad /$$

or **character** expressions involving character constants, for example

'a' '.' '0'

or **list** expressions involving

$head(\ldots)$ $tail(\ldots)$ ‖   ⟨⟩   ⟨…,…,…⟩

or **set** expressions involving

∈ ∪ ∩ ⊂ ⊆ \ ∅ {…,…,…} {*x*:*x*…}

The expressions may be in parentheses to override operator priorities.

Appendix C

The description of a PDL

A PDL program consists of a function definition with subsidiary function definitions as required.

Function definition

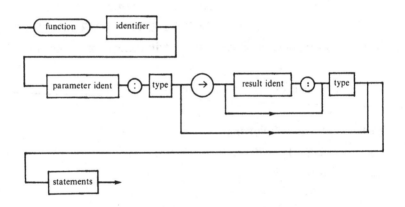

Notes
1. This definition apparently restricts all functions to one parameter. Strictly this is true. However several parameters can be assembled into a record and the record passed as a single parameter. However the access to each parameter is then a little clumsy leading to a shorthand – see example involving *dist_from_origin* in Chapter 5.
2. If 'result ident' is omitted it is assumed to be the same as the function identifier.
3. If there is no result, the function is more conveniently called a procedure.
4. Function, parameter and result identifiers are written in lower case.

Statement

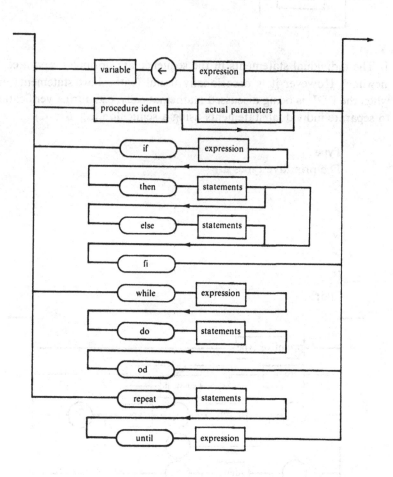

Notes

1. The assignment statement uses ←.
2. A counting loop 'for ... do' is not considered necessary.
3. The syntax rules are drawn to suggest a style of layout.
4. The keywords 'fi' and 'od' are used to delimit the end of 'statements' in an unambiguous way that does not depend on layout. Some other languages use 'begin ... end' or {...} to achieve this.

Statements

Notes
1. The individual statements in the sequence are normally separated by 'newline'. However it is occasionally useful (with short statements and when the PDL is being discussed mathematically, e.g. during verification) to separate individual statements using a semicolon (e.g. *S1*; *S2*).

Type
The primitive types are

$\mathbb{R}$

$\mathbb{Z}$

$\mathbb{N}$

$\mathbb{P}$

$\mathbb{B}$

Char

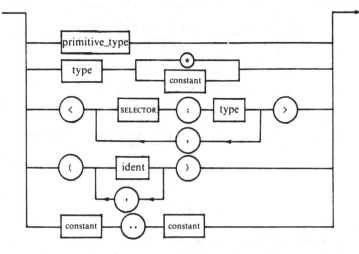

Type

Notes
1. *T** declares a list of type *T* of unrestricted length. *Tⁿ* declares a list of fixed length *n*.

2. $\langle S1:T1, S2:T2, \ldots, Sn:Tn \rangle$ declares a record of mixed types $T1$, $T2, \ldots, Tn$ with field names $S1, S2, \ldots, Sn$. The field names are always in upper case and are used as selector functions when accessing and updating the record.

3. The last two type options are called **enumerated** type and **subrange** type respectively.

Variable

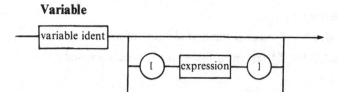

Notes

1. If a variable is not of primitive type then at the outermost level it will be either a list type or a record type.

  (i) List type (T^* or T'')

    If the number of elements of a list v is known to be n then $v[1]$, $v[2], \ldots, v[n]$ can be used otherwise use $head(v)$, $tail(v)$.

  (ii) Record type

    $\langle S1:T1, S2:T2, \ldots, Sn:Tn \rangle$

    This type defines selector functions $S1(\;), S2(\;), \ldots, Sn(\;)$ with result types $T1, T2, \ldots, Tn$ and these functions are used to select the components of the record both for access and update, e.g.

$$v: \langle I:\mathbb{Z}, R:\mathbb{R}, B:\mathbb{B} \rangle$$

$$I(v) \leftarrow I(v) + 1$$

if $B(v)$

then $R(v) \leftarrow 1.0$

fi

2. Variable identifiers are written in lower case.

Expressions

  An expression is formed from constants, variables, function calls separated by operators in the usual way.

Constants

    $\langle\;\rangle$ the empty list

$\langle C1, C2, \ldots, Cn \rangle$ a list if all the Ci are of the same type, a record otherwise

$1, +12, -123$

$1.1, +1.2, -1.23$

True, False

'a', '1'

Built-in functions

$head: T^* \rightarrow T$ returns the first element of a list

$tail: T^* \rightarrow T^*$ returns a list with the head removed

Operators

The normal arithmetic operators

$+ \quad - \quad * \quad /$

The relational operators

$= \quad \neq \quad < \quad > \quad \leqslant \quad \geqslant$

The append or concatenate operator

$\|$

this produces a list containing all the elements of the first list followed by all the elements of the second list , e.g.

$\langle 1,2 \rangle \| \langle 3,4 \rangle = \langle 1,2,3,4 \rangle$

Appendix D
Transformations that remove recursion

The specification of functions and processes by means of pre-conditions and post-conditions requires that any repetitive or accumulative aspects of the computation must be indicated by recursion. Now, although many modern procedural programming languages support recursion and hence allow programming in a functional style, the run-time overhead of large amounts of stack manipulation imposed by the related control mechanism is unacceptable in certain applications.

Throughout this book, our central premise has been that to make best use of programmer efforts we should concentrate on correctness and ignore run-time efficiency considerations. Of course, to spend much time and effort developing a correct program only to have its correctness violated by the introduction of some slick trick which substantially reduces execution time – but does not quite always work – is to invalidate the whole exercise. Consequently all such transformations and optimisations must also be proven correct and, if appropriate, programmed into the system so as to protect them from human error.

As noted in Chapter 9 we already trust hardware extensions to the minimal set of arithmetic functions which, for instance, compute integer sums and products without recursive recourse to the increment and decrement instructions. On the software side, we showed in Chapter 7 how certain dataflow charts can be unwound into iterative control flowcharts.

The recursion-to-iteration transformation given in Chapter 7 is particularly useful in that it is widely applicable. In fact, provided suitable iterative mechanisms are also available, the type of recursion encountered there is **technically** all that we need. However, specifications and programs written in the appropriate form may be overly convoluted and obscure, therefore other forms that occur naturally must be examined.

The purpose of this appendix is to present, in a fairly concise way, some transformations from the technical literature (to which the reader is referred for more detailed justification). The transformations are given in chronological order and where appropriate will be informally justifed by giving a partial trace of a typical execution sequence. However some of these justifications will be omitted because the general form is too complex to be adequately described in the space available.

We begin by giving a stylised presentation of the transformation already met in Chapter 7.

T1 Tail recursion [24]

A function f with specification:

pre--$f(x) \triangleq (\exists n \in \mathbb{P})(p(h^n(x)))$

post-$f(x,y) \triangleq y = $ if $p(x)$

                  then $g(x)$

                  else $f(h(x))$

can be implemented by the PDL scheme:

    $y \leftarrow x$

    while $\neg p(y)$

    do $y \leftarrow h(y)$

    od

    $y \leftarrow g(y)$

This scheme, and the others in this appendix, are applicable to functions of any type. The only essential type component is $p: ? \rightarrow \mathbb{B}$ which ensures validity of the *if then else* construct in the specification and the *while do od* statement in the PDL.

In order to restrict discussion to the major, transformational, considerations we shall presume that all the functions within the specifications are type-wise compatible. Transformation T1 is called tail recursion because the sequence of actions within the *else* branch concludes with a recursive reference to f and hence iteration is achieved by looping back to the beginning of this alternative and use p to control the loop exit. An informal trace of the resultant PDL code is as follows:

(control)	(y)
	x_0
$\neg p(x_0)$	$h(x_0)$
$\neg p(h(x_0))$	$h^2(x_0)$
$\neg p(h^2(x_0))$	$h^3(x_0)$
$\vdots$	$\vdots$

$$\frac{\urcorner\, p(h^{n0-1}(x_0)) \qquad h^{n0}(x_0)}{p(h^{n0}(x_0)) \qquad\quad g(h^{n0}(x_0))}$$
$$= f(x_0)$$

where $n0$ is the integer, dependent on x_0, occurring in the pre-condition.

We now turn to a transformation which utilizes a special property of the function which logically precedes a single recursive call of f within the *else* branch of the specification.

T2 Invertible recursion [10]

$$\text{pre-}f(x) \triangleq (\exists n \in \mathbb{P})(\ell^n(a) = x)$$

$$
\begin{aligned}
\text{post-}f(x,y) \triangleq y = \text{if} \quad & x = a \\
\text{then} \quad & g(a) \\
\text{else} \quad & h(f(k(x)),x)
\end{aligned}
$$

where

$$\ell : k(\ell(z)) = z \text{ (i.e. } \ell \text{ is a function such that} \ldots)$$

So k is invertible, its inverse being ℓ, and we shall compute k **backwards** by using the sequence

$$a, \ell(a), \ell^2(a), \ldots$$

The iterative PDL segment used to realise this function will utilise parallel assignments. These will allow the essential structure of the realisation to be more clearly seen. A parallel assignment is of the form:

$$(v_1, \ldots, v_n) \leftarrow (e_1, \ldots, e_n)$$

where $v_1, \ldots, v_n$ are variable identifiers and $e_1, \ldots, e_n$ are expressions (possibly involving $v_1, \ldots, v_n$).

The parallel assignment can be expanded into the ordered sequence of simple assignments:

$$t_1 \leftarrow e_1$$
$$\vdots$$
$$t_n \leftarrow e_n$$
$$v_1 \leftarrow t_1$$
$$\vdots$$
$$v_n \leftarrow t_n,$$

where $t_1, \ldots, t_n$ are new intermediate variables introduced so as to force the evaluation of the expressions $e_1, \ldots, e_n$ before any of the values associated with $v_1, \ldots, v_n$ are altered.

Now for the appropriate PDL segment:

$$(y, v) \leftarrow (g(a), a)$$

while $\neg(x = v)$

do $(y, v) \leftarrow (h(y, \ell(v)), \ell(v))$

od

On execution, this unfolds as follows:

(control)	(y	, v)
	($g(a)$	, a)
$\neg(x_0 = a)$	$(h(g(a), \ell(a))$	, $\ell(a)$)
$\neg(x_0 = \ell(a))$	$(h(h(g(a), \ell(a)), \ell^2(a))$	, $\ell^2(a)$)
$\neg(x_0 = \ell^2(a))$	$(h(h(h(g(a), \ell(a)), \ell^2(a)), \ell^3(a))$	, $\ell^3(a)$)
$\vdots$	$\vdots$	$\vdots$
$\neg(x_0 = \ell^{n0-1}(a))$	$(h(h(\ldots h(h(g(a), \ell(a)), \ell^2(a)), \ldots, \ell^{n0-1}(a)), \ell^{n0}(a))$	, $\ell^{n0}(a)$)

$|\!\!-n0-\!\!|$

$(x_0 = \ell^{n0}(a))$ (result)

But now $k(\ell(z)) = z$ for suitable z

so

$$k^{n0}(x_0) = a$$

and

$$y = h(h(\ldots h(h(g(k^{n0}(x_0)), k^{n0-1}(x_0)), k^{n0-2}(x_0)), \ldots, k(x_0)), x_0)$$

as required.

We next turn to a sequence of transformations which use special characteristic properties of the functions applied last in the recursive *else* branch.

T3 Right-permutative recursion (based on [10] as presented in [13])

pre--$f(x) \triangleq (\exists n \in \mathbb{P})(p(h^n(x)))$

post-$f(x, y) \triangleq y = $ if $p(x)$

then a

else $g(f(h(x)), k(x))$

where

$$(\exists \ell)((\forall x, y, z)(g(\ell(x, y), z) = \ell(g(x, z), y)))$$

and

$$g(a, x) = \ell(a, x)$$

so that the related functions g and ℓ allow the right-most parameters (y and z) to be permuted.

This form of recursion can be realised iteratively by the scheme:

$$(y, z) \leftarrow (a, x)$$
$$\text{while } \neg p(v)$$
$$\text{do} \quad (y, v) \leftarrow (\ell(y, k(v)), h(v))$$
$$\text{od}$$

which executes as:

(control)	(y	, v)
	(a	, x_0)
$\neg p(x_0)$	($\ell(a, k(x_0))$	, $h(x_0)$)
$\neg p(h(x_0))$	($\ell(\ell(a, k(x_0)), k(h(x_0)))$	, $h^2(x_0)$)
$\vdots$	$\vdots$	$\vdots$
$\neg p(h^{n0-1}(x_0))$	($\ell(\ell \ldots \ell(\ell(a, k(x_0)), k(h(x_0))), \ldots, k(h^{n0-1}(x_0)))$	, $h^{n0}(x_0)$)
	$\mid\!\!-\!\!n0\!\!-\!\!\mid$	
$p(h^{n0}(x_0))$		

whence

$$y = \ell(\ell \ldots \ell(\ell(a, k(x_0)), k(h(x_0))), \ldots, k(h^{n0-1}(x_0)))$$
$$\mid\!\!-\!\!n0\!\!-\!\!\mid$$
$$= \ell(\ell \ldots \ell(g(a, k(x_0)), k(h(x_0))), \ldots, k(h^{n0-1}(x_0)))$$
$$\mid n0-1 \mid$$
$$= \ell(\ell \ldots \ell(g(\ell(a, k(h(x_0))), k(x_0)), \ldots) \ldots, k(h^{n0-1}(x_0)))$$
$$\mid n0-2 \mid$$
$$\vdots$$
$$\vdots$$
$$= g(\ell(\ell \ldots \ell(a, k(h(x_0))), \ldots, k(h^{n0-1}(x_0))), k(x_0))$$
$$\mid n0-1 \mid$$
$$\vdots$$
$$\vdots$$
$$= g(g(g \ldots g(a, k(h^{n0-1}(x_0))), \ldots, k(h(x_0))), k(x_0)) \quad \text{as required.}$$
$$\mid\!\!-\!\!n0\!\!-\!\!\mid$$

Of course there is nothing special about permuting parameters on the right, a similar left-permutative scheme can easily be derived. The next two transformations require the final function on the recursive branch to be associative.

T4 Double recursion [22]

Here there are two recursive calls, combined by an associative function. Additionally notice that the realisation uses variables of type list as a stack.

$$\text{pre-}f(x) \triangleq (\exists n \in \mathbb{P})(j^n(\{x\}) = \emptyset)$$

where

$$j(S) = \{k(x) : x \in S \land \neg p(x)\}$$
$$\cup \{\ell(x) : x \in S \land \neg p(x)\}$$

(i.e. after recursion to depth n all combinations of k and ℓ guarantee that p is satisfied.)

$$\text{post-}f(x, y) \triangleq y = \text{if} \quad p(x)$$
$$\text{then} \quad g(x)$$
$$\text{else} \quad h(f(k(x)), f(\ell(x)))$$

where

$$(\forall x, y, z)(h(x, h(y, z)) = h(h(x, y), z))$$

and

$$(\exists a)(h(a, x) = x)$$

This can be realised by:

$$(y, s) \leftarrow (a, \langle x \rangle)$$
$$\text{while } s \neq \langle \rangle$$
$$\text{do} \quad (v, s) \leftarrow (head(s), tail(s))$$
$$\qquad \text{if} \quad p(v)$$
$$\qquad \text{then} \quad y \leftarrow h(y, g(v))$$
$$\qquad \text{else} \quad s \leftarrow \langle k(v) \rangle \| \langle \ell(v) \rangle \| s$$
$$\qquad \text{fi}$$
$$\text{od}$$

Here there are two recursive calls, possibly to different levels, which make a general execution trace rather messy. Nevertheless we can describe how the realisation works. The input value, x_0, is put on the stack. The functions k and ℓ are then applied to the top of the stack until the predicate p is satisfied, values which do not satisfy p being processed by k and ℓ (separately) and restacked. If $n0$ is the lowest value of $n : j^n(\{x_0\}) = \varnothing$ then the partial computations required to feed h can be depicted by a tree such as the one given in Figure D1.

Fig. D.1

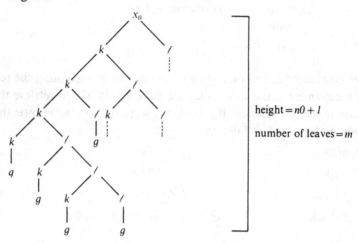

height $= n0 + 1$

number of leaves $= m$

In this example the first term which causes execution of h is $k^4(x_0)$ followed by $k(\ell(k^3(x_0)))$, etc. We therefore achieve:

$$y = h(h \ldots h(h(a, g(k^4(x_0))), g(k(\ell(k^3(x_0))))), \ldots)$$

$$\vdash\!\!-m-\!\!\dashv$$

which is equivalent to the required result since the h functions associate across to the right to compute $h(g(k(w)), g(\ell(w)))$ for some appropriate w. In the course of these manipulations the constant a moves to the right and is finally removed.

Our next transformation uses the associative property of h in a similar way to T4, but only has a single recursion and hence does not require a stack.

T5 Associative recursion [12]

pre-$f(x) \triangleq (\exists n \in \mathbb{P})(p(k^n(x)))$

post-$f(x, y) \triangleq y = $ if $\quad p(x)$

$\qquad\qquad\qquad$ then $\quad g(x)$

$\qquad\qquad\qquad$ else $\quad h(f(k(x)), \ell(x))$

where

$$(\forall x, y, z)(h(x, h(y, z)) = h(h(x, y), z))$$

Such a specification can be realised by:

> if $p(x)$
> then $y \leftarrow g(x)$
> else $(y, v) \leftarrow (\ell(x), k(x))$
>   while $\neg p(v)$
>   do $(y, v) \leftarrow (h(\ell(\ell(v), y), k(v))$
>   od
> $y \leftarrow h(g(v), y)$
> fi

Informal justification of T5 is a simple matter of expanding the resultant expression for y and then using the associativity of h to retrieve the form given in the specification. If $p(x_0)$ then $y = g(x_0)$ otherwise we enter the while loop and proceed as follows:

(control)	$(y$	$, v)$
$\neg p(x_0)$	$(\ell(x_0)$	$, k(x_0))$
$\neg p(k(x_0))$	$(h(\ell(k(x_0)), \ell(x_0))$	$, k^2(x_0))$
$\neg p(k^2(x_0))$	$(h(\ell(k^2(x_0)), h(\ell(k(x_0)), \ell(x_0)))$	$, k^3(x_0))$

$\vdots$

$\neg p(k^{n0-1}(x_0))$ $(h(\ell(k^{n0-1}(x_0)), h(\ell(k^{n0-2}(x_0)), \ldots, h(\ell(k(x_0)), \ell(x_0)) \ldots))$ $, k^{n0}(x_0))$

$p(k^{n0}(x_0))$ $h(g(k^{n0}(x_0)), h(\ell(k^{n0-1}(x_0)), \ldots, h(\ell(k(x_0)), \ell(x_0)) \ldots))$

so

> $y = h(g(k^{n0}(x_0)), \ldots, h(\ell(k^2(x_0)), h(\ell(k(x_0)), \ell(x_0))) \ldots)$
> $y = h(g \ldots h(h(\ell(k^2(x_0)), \ell(k(x_0))), \ell(x_0)) \ldots)$

$\vdots$

> $y = h(h \ldots h(g(k^{n0}(x_0)), \ell(k^{n0-1}(x_0))), \ldots, \ell(x_0) \ldots)$ as required.
> $|-n0-|$

The next transformation requires no special properties of the functions used within the specification. It takes any single recursion and uses a stack to keep track of intermediate states of the computation.

T6 Linear recursion [34]

pre-$f(x) \triangleq (\exists n \in \mathbb{P})(p(k^n(x)))$

post-$f(x, y) \triangleq y = $ if $p(x)$

then $g(x)$

else $h(f(k(x)), x)$

The realisation is:

$$(y, s) \leftarrow (x, \langle \rangle)$$

while $\neg p(y)$

do $\qquad (y, s) \leftarrow (k(y), \langle y \rangle \| s)$

od

$y \leftarrow g(y)$

while $s \neq \langle \rangle$

do $\qquad (y, s) \leftarrow (h(y, head(s)), tail(s))$

od

The first loop of the realisation merely creates the stack

$$\langle k^{n0-1}(x_0), k^{n0-2}(x_0), \ldots, x_0 \rangle$$

where $n0$ is the smallest value of n to give $p(k^n(x_0))$. The function g is applied to $k^{n0}(x_0)$ and the second loop then dismantles the stack one element at a time to give the progression

$$g(k^{n0}(x_0)),$$
$$h(g(k^{n0}(x_0)), k^{n0-1}(x_0)),$$
$$h(h(g(k^{n0}(x_0)), k^{n0-1}(x_0)), k^{n0-2}(x_0))$$
$$\vdots$$
$$h(h(h \ldots h(g(k^{n0}(x_0)), \ldots, k(x_0)), \ldots, k(x_0)), x_0)$$
$$\vert\!\!-\!\!-n0-\!\!-\!\!\vert$$

which yields the required answer.

T7 Embedded single recursion

This is tail recursion (T1) applied in a more general context. Here there is a function of one variable whose application follows that of the recursive function. The inward recursion is performed as in tail recursion and is restricted by the same pre-condition. The unwinding of the recursion is modelled by iteration. This is controlled by a count accumulated by a corresponding increment included in the first phase. Hence, a function f with specification:

$$\text{pre-}f(x,) \triangleq (\exists n \in \mathbb{P})(p(h^n(x)))$$

$$\text{post-}f(x, y) \triangleq y = \text{if} \qquad p(x)$$
$$\text{then} \quad g(x)$$
$$\text{else} \quad k(f(h(x)))$$

can be implemented by the PDL scheme:

$$(y, n) \leftarrow (x, 0)$$

while $\neg p(y)$

do $(y, n) \leftarrow (h(y), n+1)$

od

$y \leftarrow g(y)$

while $\neg(n=0)$

do $(y, n) \leftarrow (k(y), n-1)$

od

Justification of T7 follows simply by noticing that the realisation generates the following sequence of states,

$$x, h(x), h^2(x), \ldots, h^n(x),$$

$$g(h^n(x)),$$

$$k(g(h^n(x))), k^2(g(h^n(x))), \ldots, k^n(g(h^n(x)))$$

as required.

T8 Multiple or extended recursion

This is an extension of the 'double recursion removal' (T4) considered earlier. For clarity of expression we will write the associative function h as the binary operator '@'. Then

$$h(x, y) = x @ y$$

$$h(a, x) = a @ x = x$$

and

$$h(h(x, y), z) = h(x, h(y, z)) = (x @ y) @ z = x @ (y @ z) = x @ y @ z$$

Using this notation we can show the form of function covered in the 'double recursion removal' case as

$$f(x, y) \triangleq y = \text{if}\quad p(x)$$

$$\text{then}\quad g(x)$$

$$\text{else}\quad f(k_1(x)) @ f(k_2(x))$$

We wish to extend the double recursion solution to the case where f is defined by

$$f(x, y) \triangleq y = \text{if}\quad p(x)$$

$$\text{then}\quad g(x)$$

$$\text{else}\quad f(k_1(x)) @ k_2(x) @ f(k_3(x))$$

and eventually to an even more general situation where f is defined by

$$f(x, y) \triangleq y = \text{if} \qquad p(x)$$
$$\text{then} \quad g(x)$$
$$\text{else} \quad K_1(x) @ K_2(x) @ \ldots @ K_n(x)$$

where for each K_i, $i \in 1 \ldots n$

$$\text{either} \quad K_i = f \circ | k_i$$
$$\text{or} \qquad K_i = k_i$$

where k_i does not involve recursion on f.

In the realisation of the double recursion two **values** were pushed onto the stack to simulate the double recursive call. In the extended case it will be necessary to push **n records** onto the stack. The records have a *mark* field and a *value* field as shown below.

$$Stack = Rec*$$

$$Rec = \langle MARK : \mathbb{B}, VALUE : Value \rangle$$

The *mark* field is True if the K_i with which it is associated involves recursion on f, False otherwise. The *value* field will be produced by a call to k_i.

The realisation is then

$$(y, s) \leftarrow (a, \langle \langle \text{True}, x \rangle \rangle)$$
$$\text{while} \quad s \neq \langle \rangle$$
$$\text{do}$$
$$\qquad (v, s) \leftarrow (head(s), tail(s))$$
$$\qquad m \leftarrow MARK(v)$$
$$\qquad w \leftarrow VALUE(v)$$
$$\qquad \text{if} \qquad p(w)$$
$$\qquad \text{then} \quad y \leftarrow y @ g(w)$$
$$\qquad \text{else}$$
$$\qquad\qquad \text{if} \qquad \neg m$$
$$\qquad\qquad \text{then} \quad y \leftarrow y @ w$$
$$\qquad\qquad \text{else} \quad s \leftarrow K_1'(w) \|$$
$$\qquad\qquad\qquad\qquad\qquad K_2'(w) \|$$
$$\qquad\qquad\qquad\qquad\qquad \vdots$$
$$\qquad\qquad\qquad\qquad\qquad K_n'(w) \| s$$
$$\qquad\qquad \text{fi}$$
$$\qquad \text{fi}$$
$$\text{od}$$

where for each $i \in 1 .. n$,

$$K'_i(x) = \langle \text{True}, k_i(x) \rangle \qquad \text{if } K_i = f \circ k_i$$
$$\quad\quad\; = \langle \text{False}, k_i(x) \rangle \qquad \text{otherwise}$$

Conclusion

These transformations, particularly T2 to T5 and T8, require careful checking of appropriate properties of functions and subsequent manipulation of specifications into PDL (or extended PDL) realisations. As will be apparent this does not lend itself immediately to human manipulation but would be an ideal application of a symbolic manipulation system.

References

1 ANSI, *USA Standard FORTRAN*, ANSI X3.9 – 1966, American National Standards Institute (1966).
2 ANSI, *American National Standard Programming Language FORTRAN*, ANSI X3.9 – 1978, American National Standards Instiute (1978).
3 Ashcroft, E. & Manna, Z., 'The translation of 'goto' programs into 'while' programs,' *Proc. IFIP Congress*, **71**, Ljubljana (1971).
4 deBakker, J. W., *Mathematical Theory of Program Correctness*, Prentice-Hall (1980).
5 Bird, R., *Programs and Machines*, J. Wiley (1976).
6 Burstall, R. M. & Darlington, J., 'A transformation system for developing recursive programs,' *J. ACM.*, **24**(1), pp. 44–67 (1977).
7 Cooke, D. J. & Abdollahzadeh, F., 'Insecurities in FORTRAN DO-loops,' *Software – Practice and Experience*, **16**(3), pp. 201–15 (1986).
8 Cooke, D. J. & Bez, H. E., *Computer Mathematics*, Cambridge Computer Science Texts No. 18, CUP (1984).
9 Cooke, D. J., 'Arithmetic congruence and semantic composition,' *Int. J. Comp. Maths.*, **6**(4), pp. 257–64 (1978).
10 Cooper, D. C., 'The equivalence of certain computations,' *Comp. J.*, **9**, pp. 45–52 (1966).
11 Currie, I. F., *In Praise of Procedures*, RSRE Memo 3499 (1982).
12 Darlington, J. & Burstall, R. M., 'A system which automatically improves programs,' *Acta Informatica*, **6**(1), pp. 41–60 (1976).
13 Dershowitz, N., *The Evolution of Programs*, Birkhäuser, Boston USA (1983).
14 Floyd, R. W., 'Assigning meanings to programs,' *Proc. Symp. Appl. Maths.*, **19**, pp. 19–32 (1967).
15 Foster, J. M., Currie, I. F. & Edwards, P. W., *Flex: A Working Computer with an Architecture Based on Procedure Values*, RSRE Memo 3500 (July 1982).
16 Goguen, J. A. & Tardo, J. J., 'An introduction to OBJ,' *Proc. IEEE Conf. on Specifications of Reliable Software*, Cambridge Mass., pp. 170–89 (April 1979).
17 Hayes, I. J., 'Applying formal specification to software development in industry,' *IEEE Trans-SE*, **11**(2), pp. 169–78 (1985).
18 Hoare, C. A. R., 'An axiomatic base for computer programming,' *Comm. ACM*, **12**(10), pp. 576–80 (1969).
19 Jackson, M. A., *Principles of Program Design*, Academic Press (1975).
20 Jones, C. B., *Software Development: A Rigorous Approach*, Prentice-Hall (1980).
21 Kernighan, B. W. & Plauger, P. J., *Software Tools*, Addison Wesley (1976).
22 Knuth, D. E., 'Structured programming with 'goto' statements,' *Computing Surveys*, **6**(4), pp. 261–301 (1974).
23 Manna, Z., *Mathematical Theory of Computation*, McGraw-Hill (1974).
24 McCarthy, J., 'Towards a mathematical science of computation,' *Proc. IFIP Congress*, **62**, Munich (1962).

25 Mills, H. D., *Mathematical Foundations of Structured Programming*, IBM Document FSC-6012, Federal Systems Division, IBM Corp., Gaithersburg, MD (1972).

26 Nassi, I. & Schneiderman, B., 'Flowchart technique for structured programming,' *ACM Sigplan Notices*, **8**(8), pp. 12–26 (1973).

27 Naur, P. (ed) *et al.*, 'Revised report on the algorithmic language ALGOL,' *Comm. ACM*, **6**(1), pp. 1–17 (1963).

28 Rothon, N. M., 'Design structure diagrams: a new standard in flow diagrams,' *Comp. Bull.*, Series 2, No. 19, pp. 4–6 (1979).

29 Stone, R. G. & Cooke, D. J., 'Design language and coding templates,' *Comp. Bull.*, Series 2, No. 41, pp. 13–17 (1984).

30 Tausworthe, R. C., *Standardized Development of Computer Software, Part I – Methods*, Prentice-Hall (1977).

31 Welsh, J. & Elder, J., *Introduction to Pascal*, 2nd edition, Prentice-Hall (1982).

32 Wirth, N., *Systematic Programming: An Introduction*, Prentice-Hall (1973).

33 Woodward, P. M. & Bond, S. G., *Guide to ALGOL68*, Edward Arnold (1983).

34 Wossner, H., Pepper, P., Partsch, H. & Bauer, F. L., *Special Transformation Techniques*, Proc. Int. Summer School on Program Construction, Marktoberdorf (1978).

35 Young, S. J., *An Introduction to ADA*, 2nd edition, Ellis Horwood (1984).

36 Consortium of Sheffield City Polytechnic & Loughborough University of Technology & The Hatfield Polytechnic, *Essential Mathematics for Software Engineers*, sponsored by the Alvey Directorate (1986).

Index

abstract data type, 227–88
acyclic digraph, 328
ADA, user-defined ADTs, 258
ADT
  abstract data type, 227–88
  binary tree, 237
  queue, 228, 233
  stack, 228
  tree, 228, 237
algebra, of diagrams, 46
algorithm language, 77
alternation, proof, 178–83
and
  equational specification, 264–9
  logical operator, 12, 157
arc, of graph, 55
assembly language, templates, 126–43,
  143–54
assertion, in program, 312
assignment, 90, 100, 115, 129, 144
assignment statement, 73
  parallel, 355
  PDL, 79
  semantics, 217
associative recursion, 359

base step, of inductive proof, 198
binary tree, 56
  ADT, 237
Boolean, type, 18
Boolean algebra, 157
BOOLEAN type, equational specification,
  262
built-in function, of PDL, 82

call-by-name, 225
call-by-reference, 225
call-by-value, 224
Cartesian product, 62
case constructs, semantics, 222
Char, type, 18
CLEAR, specification language, 6
COBOL, templates for, 115–26

code
  final, 72
  target, 77
code generation, 88–154
coding template, 88
complete tree, 56
completeness, of ADT specification, 266
compound data structure, 95, 107, 139, 151
concatenation
  equational specification, 270–1
  of lists, 26
consistency, of ADT specification, 266
constant, in equational specification, 262
constructed data type, 18
control-flow diagram, 166
control structures
  assembly language templates, 129–38,
    144–51
  COBOL templates, 151–21
  FORTRAN templates, 100–6
  Pascal templates, 90–4
correctness, of program, 322
correctness theorem, 174
cutpoint, in program analysis, 319
cycle, in a digraph, 55, 327

data, 11
data structure
  external, 98
  file, 98
  internal, 95
  List, 24
  Pair, 18
  Set, 28
  Triple, 21
  Tuple, 22
data structure diagram, 39
data structures
  assembly language templates, 139–43,
    151–4
  COBOL templates, 121–6
  FORTRAN templates, 106–15
  Pascal templates, 95–9

data type
  constructed, 18
  encapsulation, 258
  in specification, 344
data-flow diagram, 166, 331
decision node, 302
declarative programming language, 70, 72
design structure diagram, 50
diagram, 39
  control-flow, 166
  data structure, 39
  data-flow, 166, 331
  design structure, 50
  fall-back notation, 50
  Nassi–Schneiderman, 54
  program structure, 39
  repetition on, 39
  selection on, 39
  sequencing on, 39
  syntax, 39
digraph
  acyclic, 328
  cycle, 55, 327
  directed graph, 55, 328
  restricted to network, 55
direct proof, 160
directed graph, digraph, 55, 328
DO-loop, semantics, 222
documentation, 88
does not imply, logical operator, 162
domain, of an operation, 174
domain rule, 174
double recursion, 358
dynamic storage allocation, 88

edge, of graph, 55
effect, of an operation, 287
element
  of a list, 24
  of a set, 28
embedded single recursion, 361
empty list, 25
empty set, 29
encapsulation, of data type, 258
enrichment, of an equational specification, 273
enumerated type, 107, 121, 139, 151
  in PDL, 80
eqns, components of equational specification, 264
equals-for-equals, substitution, 264
equational specification, 262–88
err eqns, error equations, in an equational specification, 271
existential quantifier, 195

expression
  syntax in PDL, 81
  syntax in specification, 346
extended recursion, 362
external data structures, templates for, 98, 110, 124, 143, 154

fall-back, shown on diagrams, 50
False, logical value, 15
false acceptance, 177
file
  data structure, 98
  random access, 98
  sequential, 98
flag
  restructuring, 304
  set by machine instruction, 127–9
Flex/Algol68, user-defined ADTs, 260
flowchart, 39
flowgraph, 291
folding, transformation step, 65
for-all, logical operator, 195
for-loop, semantics, 221
FORTRAN
  multiple-entry subroutines, 257
  templates for, 99–114
  user-defined ADTs, 256
function, syntax in PDL, 78
function definition, 93, 105, 120, 134, 149
functional programming language, 72
functional specification, 32

ghost variable, 313, 321
graph, 55
  arc of, 55
  directed, 55, 328
  edge of, 55
  node of, 55

head
  of list, 25
  of list, equational specification, 270–1

identity process, 46
if statement, 91, 101, 117, 131, 146
if ... then ... else
  formal definition, 164
  proof, 179
imperative programming language, 70, 72
implication, logical operator, 156, 158
induction, proof method, 195–9
induction hypothesis, 198
induction step, of a proof, 198
initialisation of state, 336
input, 12, 37
input list, in specification, 98

Integer
  equational specification, 274–80
  type, 18
internal data structures, templates for, 95,
    107, 122, 140, 151
intersect
  equational specification, 282–5
  set operation, 28
invar, *see*: iterative proof, 206, 212
invertible recursion, 355
iteration, proof of iterative construct, 201–15

label node, 302
layout, of PDL, 79
leaf, of tree, 56
linear ordering, 326
linear recursion, 360
linked tree, 290
list
  concatenation, 26
  data structure, 24
  element, 24
  empty, 25
  head, 25
  head, equational specification, 270–1
  member, 24
  of fixed length, 95, 107, 122, 140, 151
  of variable length, 96, 108, 122, 140
  restricted tree, 57
  tail, 25
  tail, equational specification, 270–1
LIST type, equational specification, 270
load, operation parameters, 167–8
logic programming language, 72
logical operator
  and, 12, 157
  does not imply, 162
  for-all, 195
  implication, 156, 158
  not, 157
  or, 157
  there-exists, 195
loop invariant, *see also*: invar, 319

member
  of list, 24
  of set, 28
method of inductive assertions, 313
modus ponens, 160
multiple recursion, 362
multiple-entry subroutines, FORTRAN, 257

Nassi–Schneiderman diagram, 54
natural number, 18
network
  restricted diagraph, 55
  restricted to tree, 56

new, procedure for space allocation, 96, 109
node, of graph, 55
non-recursive implementation, in PDL, 242
non-result, in an equational specification,
    268
non-terminal node, of tree, 56
not
  equational specification, 264–9
  logical operator, 157

OBJ specification language, 6
object form, of program, 289
operation, 13
  domain of, 174
  post-condition, 13
  pre-condition, 13
  range of, 174
  sequencing of, 16
  set intersect, 28
  set membership, 28
  set union, 28
  set without, 29
  state associated with, 33
  subset of set, 28
  type of, 13
operation specification, 345
operators, in PDL, 82
ops, component of equational specification,
    264
or
  equational specification, 264–9
  logical operator, 157
output, 12, 37
output list, in specification, 98

package, in ADA, 258
Pair, data structure, 18
parallel assignment, definition, 355
parameter passing, 224–6
partial correctness, of program, 207, 322
Pascal, templates for, 88–99
PDL, 72–87
  built-in function, 82
  description of, 78–82, 348–52
  enumerated type, 80
  expression syntax, 81
  layout, 79
  list data type, 82
  non-recursive implementation in, 242
  operators in, 82
  primitive type, 80
  record data type, 80, 82
  recursion removal, 242
  recursive implementation in, 240
  selector function, 80
  statement syntax, 79
  subrange type, 80

syntax, 80
type syntax, 80
union data type, 84
variable syntax, 81
peep
    equational specification, 285–6
    stack ADT operation, 229
pop
    equational specification, 285–6
    stack ADT operation, 229
positive integer, 18
post-check loop
    diagram, 41
    see also: repeat ... until
post-condition, of operation, 13
postfix, operator notation, 228
powerset, 63
pre-check loop
    diagram, 41
    proof, 201
pre-condition, of operation, 13
pred, predecessor function, 273
predicate, 11, 156
prefix, operator notation, 228
primitive data type, 95, 121, 139, 151
primitive type, in PDL, 80
procedural specification, 32
procedure call, 90, 100, 116, 130, 145
process node, 302
Program Design Language, PDL, 72
Program Development Language, PDL, 72
program structure diagram, 39
programming language
    declarative, 70, 72
    functional, 72
    imperative, 70, 72
    logic, 72
    semantics, 217
proof
    of alternation, 178
    of *if ... then ... else*, 179
    of pre-check loop, 201
    of sequencing, 171
    of transformation, 61
proof method
    direct, 160
    induction, 195
push
    equational specification, 285–6
    stack ADT operation, 229

quantifier
    existential, 195
    universal, 195
queue, ADT, 228, 233

random access file, 98
range of an operation, 174
range rule, 174
Real, type, 18
record, data type, in PDL, 80
record, 108, 122, 142, 153
recursion, 27
    associative, 359
    double, 358
    embedded, single, 361
    extended, 362
    invertible, 355
    linear, 360
    multiple, 362
    right-permutative, 356
    tail, 352
recursion removal, 353–64
    from PDL, 242
recursive implementation in PDL, 240
refinement, of specifications, 32
repeat statement, 92, 103, 119, 133
repeat ... until
    semantics, 220
    transformation, 301, 307
repetition, shown on diagrams, 39
restructuring, of programs, 302–11
results, 11
right-permutative recursion, 356
root
    of tree ADT, 238
    of tree, 56

selection, shown on diagrams, 39
selector function, in PDL, 80
semantics
    DO-loop, 222
    of assignment statement, 217
    of *case* construct, 222
    of *for*-loop, 221
    of programming language, 217
    of *repeat ... until*, 220
sequencing
    of operations, 16
    proof, 171–8
    shown on diagrams, 39
sequential file, 98
set
    data structure, 28
    empty, 29
    intersect operation, 28
    membership test, 28
    subset operation, 28
    union operation, 28
    without operation, 29
set membership, equational specification,
    282–5
set type, equational specification, 282–5

side-effect, of an operation, 287
simplification, of expression, 65
simply linked tree, 290
size, of a set member, 196
sorts, component of equational specification, 264
source form, of program, 289
spaghetti code, 289
specification, 14
  data type, 344
  equational, 262–88
  functional, 32
  input list, 98
  of operation, 345
  output list, 98
  procedural, 32
  refinement, 32
  syntax, 344
  transformation, 32, 61, 331
  two level scheme for recursion, 202
specification language
  CLEAR, 6
  OBJ, 6
  VDM, 6
  Z, 6
stack
  ADT, 228
  peep operation, 229
  pop operation, 229
  push operation, 229
state
  associated with an operation, 33
  initialisation of, 336
statement, syntax in PDL, 79
statement sequence, 90, 101, 116, 131
subrange type, 107, 121, 139
  in PDL, 80
subset
  equational specification, 283–4
  operation, 28
substitution
  equals-for-equals, 264
  transformation step, 65
subtree, of tree ADT, 238
succ, successor function, 272
syntax, of PDL, 78, 80
syntax diagram, 39

tail
  of list, 25
  of list, equational specification, 270–1
tail recursion, 195, 335, 354
target code, 77, 217–26
template code, 88
templates, 217–26
  for assembly language, 126–43, 143–54
  for COBOL, 115–26

  for FORTRAN, 99–114
  for Pascal, 88–99
term, *see*: iteration proof, 207, 212
terminal node, of tree, 56
there-exists, logical operator, 195
three-valued logic, 165
to-end, *see*: iteration proof, 207, 212
topological sort, 326
total correctness, of program, 322
transformation
  folding step, 65
  of specification, 32, 61, 331
  proof of, 61
  substitution step, 65
  unfold–fold, 65
  unfolding step, 65
  while loop, 191
transitive property, 159
  equational specification, 276
tree
  ADT, 228, 237
  binary, 56
  complete, 56
  leaf, 56
  linked, 290
  non-terminal node, 56
  restricted network, 56
  restricted to list, 57
  root, 56, 238
  simply linked, 290
  subtree of, 238
  terminal node, 56
Triple, data structure, 21
True, logical value, 15
truth value, =logical value, 15
Tuple
  data structure, 22
  notation for, 62
two level scheme, for recursive specification, 202
type
  abstract data type, 227
  Boolean, 18
  BOOLEAN, equational specification, 262
  Char, 18
  constructed data type, 18
  equational specification, 264
  Integer, 18
  INTEGER, equational specification, 274–80
  LIST, equational specification, 270
  of an operation, 13
  PDL list data type, 80, 82
  PDL record data type, 80, 84
  PDL union data type, 84
  primitive in PDL, 80

Real, 18
set, equational specification, 282–5
syntax in PDL, 80

undefined, logical value, 165
unfold-fold transformation, 65
unfolding, transformation step, 65
union
    data type in PDL, 84
    equational specification, 282–5
    set operation, 28
universal quantifier, 195
until...do, transformation, 300
update, of state, 167–8

variable, syntax in PDL, 81
VDM, specification language, 6
verification, 155–216

well-ordered set, 200
well-ordering, 322
    see also: size, 200
    while loop, transformation, 191
    while statement, 91, 103, 118, 133
    while...do, transformation, 307
without
    equational specification, 283–5
    set operation, 29

Z, specification language, 6